D1242695

RECOVERY
ZONE Volume 2

Other books by Patrick Carnes, Ph.D.

Out of the Shadows: Understanding Sexual Addiction

A Gentle Path through the Twelve Steps: The Classic Guide for All People in the Process of Recovery

A Gentle Path through the Twelve Principles: Living the Values Behind the Steps

Contrary to Love: Helping the Sexual Addict

Don't Call It Love: Recovery From Sexual Addiction

Sexual Anorexia: Overcoming Sexual Self-Hatred

The Betrayal Bond: Breaking Free of Exploitive Relationships

Open Hearts: Renewing Relationships with Recovery, Romance and Reality

Facing the Shadow: Starting Sexual and Relationship Recovery: A Gentle Path Workbook for Beginning Recovery from Sex Addiction

In the Shadows of the Net: Breaking Free of Compulsive Online Sexual Behavior

Clinical Management of Sex Addiction

Recovery Start Kit: The First 130 Days

Facing Addiction: Starting Recovery from Alcohol and Drugs

Recovery Zone: Volume 1: Making Changes that Last: The Internal Tasks

Shadows of the Cross: A Christian Companion to Facing the Shadow

Facing Internet Technology and Gaming Addiction: A Gentle Path to Beginning Recovery from Internet and Video Game Addiction

RECOVERY ZONE Volume 2

Making Changes That Last: The External Tasks

Patrick J. Carnes, Ph.D.

Gentle Path
PRESS

Carefree, Arizona

Gentle Path
P R E S S

Gentle Path Press
PO Box 2112
Carefree, Arizona 85377

www.gentlepath.com

Copyright © 2021 by Patrick Carnes

ISBN: 978-0-9832713-2-1

All rights reserved. No part of this publication may be a retrieval used or reproduced, stored, or entered into system, transmitted, photocopied, recorded, or otherwise reproduced in any form by any mechanical or electronic means without the prior written permission of the author and Gentle Path Press, except for brief quotations used in articles and reviews.

For more information contact Gentle Path Press at 1-866-575-6853 (toll-free U.S. Only)

Table of Contents

Introduction

"We made a decision to turn our life over…"

Alcoholics Anonymous

The decision is made. We realize we can no longer live like this. The costs are too high. For some of us, the decision must be remade at times, but inch by inch we resolve to make it different. The phrase that makes sense is that there is a "dark passenger" in our head who argues about our choice to be better.

Yet, consider a child in danger. Even the most hard-bitten or self-absorbed of us instinctively will protect children in danger. Without hesitation, we will place ourselves between the threat and the child. If a child wanders in front of an oncoming car, we will grab that child. We will do all that we can to ensure the protection of that child even if it is life-threatening to us. Most everyone, upon reflection, will remember a previous effort to help a child. There was no deliberation. No stopping to reflect on whether that child was worthy of life. Nor was there consideration of whether the child was a friend, a family member, or unknown to us. We just did it. Collective consciousness, genetic coding, or cultural imprint, it did not matter. The decision was made to save the life of the child.

In the world of addiction, the willingness to go to any length to make life different is elusive to both addicts and loved ones. We have compared the addictions and the accompanying attachments and feelings to a "black hole." The analogy is that negative dark energy in a star becomes so powerful, the star system collapses in on itself. Nothing—not even light—can escape. The systems of our life, including our very biology, recycle the toxic, the unreal, and the destructive through the electrochemical rivers of our brains. Obsession keeps us in a series of closed loops as families, as persons, and as organisms. The original decision to be who we are is lost in the turmoil and gravity of our own darkness. What we would commit to for a child, we could not do for the child within us.

Yet that original sense of self has been in us from the very beginning. That part of ourselves that says a profoundly personal "yes" to a dream, talent, or way of being is visible from the outset of life. In traditional peoples, it was common to find the elders of the tribe observing and reinforcing the early affirmations and tendencies of the young. Reflections on those tendencies went into a process called a "naming" ceremony around the ages of five or six. The name that was given reflected the gifts and propensities of the child that the elders perceived would be assets to that child as an adult and to the community. The process allowed nurturing of the talent and self-knowing of what trauma therapist Marilyn Murray and others call the "original feeling child."

Busy parents and events in life can obscure these early desires. Furthermore, as Alice Miller describes in the *Drama of the Gifted Child*, the theft, brutalization, or denial of these original inclinations gives power to wounded feelings and may lead to addiction. As we now know, trauma and shame are not just toxic thoughts; over time, they become encoded as biological realities. They are etched into the synapses of the brain. Massive scientific evidence shows that these dark events are encoded at a cellular level. Even when cells reproduce, the message is carried forward in the new cells. Like circles in the core of a tree that encode the impact of the year, the tree will always know. The human body is the same; it does keep score. Voices of the past are more than voices of the past; they become us.

I now have had some firsthand experiences with the power and value of those early inclinations. After *Recovery Zone I* was finished, my wife of twenty years, Suzanne, died. When we met as single parents, we had seven children between us and ultimately ten grandchildren. One of those was a granddaughter named Kiran, who at the time was six going on seven. She was a very gifted first-grader. She had an older sister who had blazed a trail in high school of many accomplishments. Yet Kiran's talents were very different. She admired her sister but was already determined not to walk in her sister's shadow.

After the funeral, Kiran and her family stayed with me at our cabin in northern Minnesota. It was Christmastime, and the snow, the smell of pine trees, and the presence of family was a great comfort to me. Kiran's parents came to me concerned for Kiran because she was having difficulty sleeping. The issue was that Kiran knew how proud Suzanne was of her sister, Brianna, and of all of her achievements. Kiran wanted her grandmother to see who she was and all she was about, but now her grandmother would not be able to see it. She felt cheated by her grandmother's early death and being denied that affirmation.

I understood that but was at a loss about how to help her through that. I had the task of sorting through Suzanne's clothes and personal items as part of post-funeral realities, and I asked Kiran to help me through this painful task. As we sat there touching the things that Suzanne had touched, her energy was around us. I asked Kiran about her sorrow and her sleep. She told me about profoundly wanting her grandmother to know her the way she had gotten to know Brianna. I shared the history of the naming ceremonies of Native American tribes and how elders were more than just old people. They had many responsibilities, but one special task was to watch their young ones with great care. Then, at about age six, the character traits, abilities, interests, and behaviors were discussed at length by the elders. At that time, a new name was given in a ceremony that reflected the true nature of the person.

I shared with Kiran that Suzanne and I were the elders of her clan. We watched our young carefully. I told her of the many conversations her grandmother and I had about her. I was very specific about how Suzanne would remark about how creative and witty Kiran was. I told Kiran that Suzanne was impressed at how disciplined and determined she was, and how Suzanne often speculated about her artistic abilities. Kiran and I spent a couple of days together sorting and talking. I am not sure who helped who more. I do know that Kiran started to sleep soundly and that I got through Christmas.

The bottom line is how important early acknowledgment of the inclinations and strengths of a young person is. Already the DNA pulls energy like little tuning forks that tell the body how to develop and call for the strengths and abilities that person is to have. By age six, Kiran's natural inclinations had started to emerge, and she knew them already. When I brought those specific examples up, she knew that Suzanne saw them as well. Sometimes we laughed and sometimes we cried, but knew that her grandmother "saw" her and "knew" in the way she wanted to be seen and known. Kiran knew enough about life to know she needed that validation, and as an elder of the tribe, I was a witness to her reality, and through me, Suzanne was also a witness. Being a witness is sometimes all that we can do, all that is necessary, and enough.

Randy Pausch wrote a very moving account of this phenomenon in his book *The Last Lecture*. The book describes his struggle in learning that he was dying of cancer. He realized that it was important for him to leave a legacy of the most important realizations of his life in the form of one last lecture at MIT. His family resisted this effort at first because they knew they had little time left with him. But his passion won the day, and in his lecture he speaks to how he was able to reconcile his passion with his love of family and leave an important legacy to all. I encourage you to read the book and actually watch the lecture on YouTube. Core to his message was that to be fulfilled, you have to be in your passion, but to do that, you have to be true to yourself and do whatever you have to do to make your passion part of your life. And the parallel truth was making his intimate relationships more meaningful as a result.

Pausch states that at an early age he knew his dream was to be an engineer who designed adventures for kids, and he knew that he wanted to work for Walt Disney. His career as an engineering professor at MIT was integrated with assisting in the design of Disney theme parks. He got to fulfill both of his childhood dreams, and that brought him happiness. And a happy person is a great person with whom to be in a relationship. This formula was so important that he felt a significant catalyst for his legacy was to tell people that. (Note the importance of legacy is passing it on—a form of being a witness.) He urged his listeners to use the formula that once you know your dream, you follow a vision with a priority. The guiding phrase he suggests is, "If nothing else, I will...." (This phrase parallels Alcoholics Anonymous' call to "go to any lengths" and Yoda's famous phrase from *Star Wars*, "Do or do not. There is no try."

Randy Pausch was clearly living in his best energy even in his dying process. Not always is everyone so fortunate to have that clarity from the beginning. I knew that by the fourth grade that I wanted to be a writer. I loved words. I loved reading. I had no idea I would be a psychologist or a specialist in addictions. That call came much later. All I knew is that I loved reading stories and science. My father and I had a constant struggle over "book learning." He felt that I needed to be in the real world and that I was escaping with books. He saw it as laziness and a way to avoid my schoolwork and chores. He put a limit on how many books I could read in a week for most of my elementary years. When I completed my Ph.D., one of his cutting phrases was "even a Ph.D. should know that."

My uncle, who was a physician, felt compassion for me and told me that both my mother and father flunked out of college in their freshman years, a secret kept well hidden from me, and that alcohol was a part of that. I know that my father struggled in school and life. He and my mother both were brilliant people who struggled through the Depression and World War II. Together, they had a number of successful careers. For example, at age fifty my dad taught himself electrical engineering and went on to make a fortune. This self-made man formula was something he took pride in. But his shame about school was real, and his fear was that what he had done would not count.

We shared that actually. I had trouble in school because I had trouble focusing. Trauma and anxiety affect brain function, and I dealt with both. My ability to focus and capacity to calm myself was impacted. Plus, given the uproar of alcoholism in our family, I had no real support about school. I actually have lesions on my frontal lobes from when I was battered as a child. I had to learn how to focus and compensate, and that was not easy. With the turmoil and lack of support, my dreams of being an author were obscured and, for many years, lost to me.

For a long time, I did not know how badly I had been hurt, so I had shame about academics. When my brain was scanned, I was stunned at how many things I had misperceived about myself. I was not defective. When I eventually graduated with honors or succeeded in other tasks, I would always feel surprised or unworthy or that a mistake was made. Now, much later in life, I see all that.

Paulo Coelho spoke eloquently on this matter in his book, *The Alchemist*. His introduction is one of the most worthy, succinct statements about following your dream to appear in literature or science. He states that achievement and happiness have to do with hearing your call, and the elements of that call are known to you in your earliest years. But they can be shrouded in darkness. And that is the first obstacle Coelho says we must meet:

We are told from childhood onward that everything we want is impossible. We grow up with this idea, and as the years accumulate, so too do the layers of prejudice, fear, and guilt. There comes a time when our personal calling is so deeply buried in our soul as to be invisible. But it is still there ... if we have the courage to disinter the dream.

Once that courage is accessed, another obstacle awaits: the approval of others. We fear that others will be hurt or leave us if we are true to who we are. Coelho, however, observed that "those who genuinely wish us well want us to be happy and are prepared to accompany us on that journey." The truth of that is realized in Randy Pausch's message in his last lecture, which deepened his family's bonds.

Coelho also names the third obstacle we must face: the fear of defeat, where courage falters. There will always be setbacks, losses, and "rabbit holes" in which we lose ourselves. It is part of the ordeal of excellence. In the history of warfare, it is axiomatic that losing battles can win a war. For example, Nathaniel Greene, a deeply believing Quaker, saw that he had to set aside his peaceful ways because the rebellion in 1776 was for deeper values. He joined the American Revolution and ultimately was the general leading the Southern Army. He lost every battle but did it so strategically that he won the war in the south and gave Washington the momentum to win American independence. Also consider the Canadian tank battalions on D-Day who found themselves facing Rommel's more experienced, better equipped, and much larger Panzer division. The Canadians were ordinary men—fishermen, carpenters, and farmers—who found a creative way to destroy a Panzer tank but at the cost of their own lives. They lost the battle but, in their sacrifice and creativity, saved hundreds of thousands of lives on D-day and ultimately made winning the war possible. To this day, every tank commander in Canada walks through the tracks of those brave men and relives the defeat that won the war.

Coelho says it simply, "The secret of life, though, is to fall seven times and get up eight times." (Like Randy Pausch's "if nothing else, I will… or the *Big Book's* "half measures availed us nothing" or Yoda's "do or do not.")

The final test of our call is when we succeed. Coelho sees it as the most difficult hurdle: sabotaging our own excellence. He cites Oscar Wilde, who remarks about how we will destroy that which we love the most. So strong are the forces of darkness and the voices of the past that we still can lose faith with the call. The covenant that started to be drafted in our earliest years is lost. That initial decision of yes becomes "I guess I did not want it anyway." Coelho says such self-denial can have a saintly aura, making us like others of our race who resign themselves to unhappiness. He observes that there is always suffering, but failure to use it to rise to the challenge creates a different pain that eats away our very soul to our end days. I could have…. I should have.

Marianne Williamson, reflecting on a *Course in Miracles,* writes:

Our deepest fear is not that we are inadequate. Our deepest fear is that we are powerful beyond measure. It is our light, not our darkness that most frightens us. We ask ourselves, "Who am I to be brilliant, gorgeous, talented, fabulous?" Actually, who are you not to be? You are a child of God. Your playing small does not serve the world. There is nothing enlightened about shrinking so that other people won't feel insecure around you. We are all meant to shine, as children do. We were born to make manifest the glory of God that is within us. It's not just in some of us; it's in everyone. And as we let our own light shine, we unconsciously give other people permission to do the same. As we are liberated from our own fear, our presence automatically liberates others.

Think of people of extraordinary talent that you know of who went to treatment. They had extraordinary success but addiction and mental illness thrived in the trauma and stress of fame and performance. Sometimes whole bands or whole high-profile families would seek help. Sometimes they would have to go more than once—maybe even multiple times. Because of their success, this was noteworthy to our media, which caters to an audience of people who enjoy the failures of people who followed their talent.

Shakespeare knew that audience and talked about jealousy and envy as a "green-eyed monster which mocks the very meat it feeds upon." Media commentators roll their eyes and make fun when someone ends up in treatment again. Pundits discuss whether recovery or treatment works when someone in the news repeatedly goes to treatment and then dies of an overdose or destroys their life with bad behavior.

What really happens is core to understanding this book and the whole Recovery Zone process. Residential treatment of thirty to ninety days is seen as the end goal. They should be fixed by the end of treatment. The reality is that in most cases, the patient has progressed to where they are starting to get traction in their recovery and are now available for the deep work that needs to continue.

I am one hundred percent confident that those "treatment failures" were told that they needed to take some time to solidify their recovery. Definitely the discharge summary would recommend not returning to high-stakes performances or stressful lifestyles. They were instructed that there was deeper work that was necessary and they failed to follow through on the long-term work of creating a lifelong recovery.

Often, they return to handlers and advisors whose own welfare is dependent on them returning to high-pressure situations. To tell them that the band cannot tour that summer or the movie contracts have to wait curtails not only their own income and lifestyle but the income and lifestyle of others. Or they are advised that the window of opportunity in the political world or the sports world will close and what they always wanted will go away. So they say they will make it different this time, but then business realities collide with the lack of understanding of the medical therapeutic community. The internal and external restructuring of life that is needed to maintain recovery does not happen.

The irony is that those who pause long enough to do this foundational work often go on to extraordinary achievements that had eluded them before because of their addiction and mental health issues. I have seen both outcomes happen in my career, and there never seems to be an in-between.

I remember an interview with a correspondent world-renowned for her investigative reporting. She asked for the interview by saying she wanted to understand the nature of addiction and treatment. She, her producer, and her crew flew to Arizona to do the interview. She was personable, talented, and today is still a household name. The interview started cordially, then it took a sharp turn and I learned the true purpose of the interview. A very public situation had occurred where a patient had tragically relapsed. She laid out on camera the details and posed the question, "Doesn't this event prove that addiction treatment does not work?"

I asked if she had a copy of the discharge summary and the requirements and recommendations for the next level of care (knowing full well that by law she could not have them). She admitted she did not. Then I asked her if the patient had met the critical recommendations of the care necessary for the person to become healthy. Again, she had no records, releases, or information on the patient's progress. I said that without having that information, there is no way to speculate. I explained to her that the key parts of treatment and recovery occur over the course of years.

The real problem was the assumption that her interview question was based on: that going to residential care is the cure, when in fact addiction recovery is a three to five-year process—the most important segments starting about six months into sobriety, when there are significant changes in brain patterns and affect management. That intense period is transformational and involves about a year to eighteen months of diligent, conscientious work toward implementing a radically different life. Then, as a result of all of this change, the family relationships shift, and this takes at least another year to play out. To the interviewer's credit, we had a very courteous and lively discussion, and then the segment was canceled.

Our media is punctuated with scandal and revelations, especially around those who seek help. The admission of a problem becomes a criterion for disqualification for politicians, clergy, business leaders, and anyone artistic. News story after news story is a chronicle about the addictive nature of our culture. In reality, addiction is our number one health problem. Alcoholism and drugs continue to be a problem. Two-thirds of adults in North America have used prescription drugs such as hydrocodone for non-medical purposes. Over a third of our adults (and children) fit the diagnostic criteria for obesity. Studies show over two-thirds of our preteen and early teenagers are sexually active digitally while doing homework. Estimates are that over a third of those children will struggle with sex addiction. An example is that the age of onset of throat cancer has begun decades earlier than previous generations because of the sexual promiscuity in our high schools. North America is the primary producer of pornography on the internet.

We are the least healthy of developed nations and have the most expensive medical care. Our number one public health problem is addiction, and it is eroding our economy and our abilities to be viable and competitive. We are in a financial crisis proportionately because of our mistaken beliefs about mental health and addiction. Anyone in this culture who enters recovery is swimming against the current of opinion.

Yet another view is emerging. An example is the work of Dr. Nassir Ghaemi. In his book, *A First-Rate Madness*, he describes how our greatest leaders struggled with addiction and mental health issues. Abraham Lincoln struggled with bipolar issues. Winston Churchill led a nation while having trouble with alcoholism. John Kennedy, Martin Luther King, and Generals Grant and Sherman lead a long list of people who were decisive in our history but had mental health issues. His point was that working through the problems makes for greater perseverance, insight, and ingenuity. As people, individuals who've struggled are much more likely to think "outside of the box." That insight is well reflected in the psychology and psychiatric literature, which tells us that the struggle and learning connected with these issues have led to breakthroughs in science, economics, literature, spirituality, and business. Apple as a company is, in part, a success because of Steven Jobs' obsessive-compulsive disorder. He is joined by the likes of Thomas Jefferson, Estee Lauder, Charles Lindberg, and Ted Williams.

In essence, having a mental health or addiction problem is really a sign of extraordinary ability and promise. That is the point our media misses, as well as our culture. Not everyone who goes to treatment is famous, but it is rare for patients not to discover their unrealized talents and abilities that have been thwarted by trauma and addiction. Addiction then becomes a solution for unrealized abilities. The media and public perception simply add more barriers to getting help.

This brings us to the very premise of *Recovery Zone II*. In *Recovery Zone I*, we built on the work of University of Chicago psychologist Mihaly Csikszentmihalyi. Csikszentmihalyi conducted and collected studies worldwide challenge, the stress of which matters to you. Discovering where your passions reside is critical to being able to raise your life to a new level. Obsession becomes productive focus. To disinter the dream means reclaiming those original inclinations and building on them. The focus and time necessary for this do not happen in a thirty-day or even ninety-day program.

A Simple Way To Look At What Has To Change ....

There is a classic model of looking at how to make changes that, at this point, may be useful to you. There are four phases to it, and to explain it we will use the example of road building. Phase One is to use what you already know works. In building roads, the Romans used concrete for their main roads and bridges. Today, some of those are still in use. It was an effective technology. But we changed. Today, concrete methodologies have improved; we build six- and eight-lane highways to handle more traffic, and our bridge building has improved in both design and layout. But we use the same basic material. That is Phase Two. With Phase Two, you do much more with the same material.

Phase Three is to add technology and strategies you have never used before. Today, we have improved cars by making them more efficient. We have created hybrids that use a combination of electric and fossil fuels, and even totally electric vehicles. The technology for cars driving themselves more safely than humans can is now available. Soon, no transport trucks will have human drivers. We are quickly adding safety features including backup cameras and warning technologies to keep cars safe. Some of those safety features are only on the most expensive cars, but soon they will be on all cars. In this phase, we are adding technology that already exists but we have not used before.

Finally, in Phase Four, there are things we need to invent to make routine travel safer and more comfortable. Air lanes and flying autos that are safe and self-directed are very possible to create. Lots of private companies are working on creating space-capable air/ spacecraft that will shorten air travel time. All kinds of things are possible.

Using this model of change, the first question you have to ask is: what have you been doing that works? Journaling, seeing a therapist, or going to a twelve-step meeting. To change, you increase the quality, consistency, or amount of time spent using this tool. Does that mean a daily journal? If twelve-step meetings were sporadic, they could become routine. If twelve-step meetings were routine, you could get more involved by reading literature, being of service, or providing sponsorship. If therapy has helped, it may be time to get into group psychotherapy. Think of workshops, intensives, or longer times with your therapist beyond the fifty-minute hour. Also, intensive outpatient long-term programs are readily available—and often recommended. When we first started to track people over time, the optimum for recovery was 175 hours of treatment and recovery work. Maybe there is a fellowship you need to add, some therapy or a therapist you do not have, or a program that has helped others you know.

There are hosts of options here. Eye Movement Desensitization and Reprocessing (EMDR) has demonstrated real effectiveness for many. If you have not immersed yourself in a proven method of meditation, doing so could lead to great gains in your brain growth. Throughout this book, you will find constant exposure to new or different resources you can explore. Neurofeedback specialists can teach you much about your brain function. Or you can go to a clinic that specializes in brain scans, which have been extremely helpful for many people in recovery. The point is to start thinking about things you have not done. *Recovery Zone II* will help you develop clarity about what would be most helpful to you, but it may mean investing in technology that is not familiar to you.

Finally, there may be some things you have to invent for yourself or something experimental to try. Maybe it is as simple as some unique changes in lifestyle or your business that could transform how you live. Or maybe the innovation is the creativity of letting go of some things you felt you had to do but no longer need in your life. The purpose, at this point, is to start thinking about the levels of change necessary, as well as your willingness.

The next two pages are divided in half so that you can record in your mind what you already know would be helpful. Then, as you explore the dimensions of your life (money, work, talents, relationships, your own awareness/consciousness) in the following chapters, you can loosen up the "hard categories" as you start to implement your inner work. The four questions to answer as you complete this initial work are:

1. What already is working?
2. What works but you need to improve and increase?
3. What could you add that would help this huge adaptation of your life?
4. What needs to be invented or created that would make for successful change in your life?

The Four Phases of Change

Record here reflections on what you know works:

Record here reflections on what you need to improve or increase:

Exercise 0.1

Record here reflections on what new technologies or methods you could use with the changes you need to make:

Record here reflections on what you need to create or invent to enable you to implement change:

Exercise 0.1

A group of researchers and I spent seven years following a thousand families and synthesizing what worked best for them. We described these findings in a variety of places including the first *Recovery Zone* volume. It is important to remind you of them now because we will use them to make sense of how to change and improve your brain function (next chapter). Briefly, as you will remember, there were six stages people went through:

The Course of Recovery Over Time

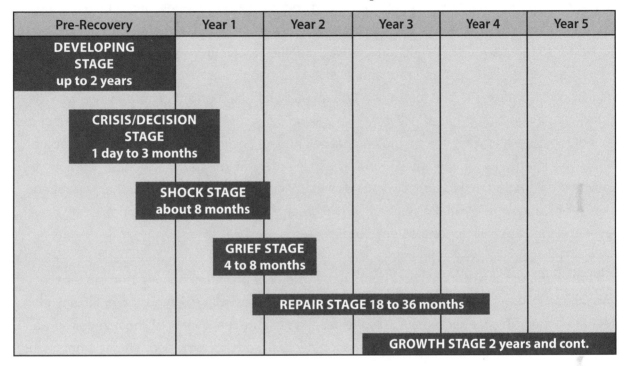

Pre-Recovery	Year 1	Year 2	Year 3	Year 4	Year 5
DEVELOPING STAGE up to 2 years					
CRISIS/DECISION STAGE 1 day to 3 months					
SHOCK STAGE about 8 months					
	GRIEF STAGE 4 to 8 months				
	REPAIR STAGE 18 to 36 months				
			GROWTH STAGE 2 years and cont.		

Figure 1

Developing — The awareness grew that addiction, family dysfunction, and powerlessness were destroying the life of the addict and those living with the addict.

Crisis — Almost always there is a crisis in which something stark, problematic, or destructive has happened. Addicts and family members make a "decision" that they cannot go on like this, though not always at the same time. And some have failures of courage or support. But crisis is the moment where a person decides "I will go to any lengths to make this different." They also accept that "by myself I cannot do it."

Shock — At this point, recovering people change their behaviors, but it is very uncomfortable. Plus, it is difficult to know how all this change will turn out. They are in what we call "free fall." Simultaneously, whatever trouble or consequences caused by the behaviors play themselves out to resolution. What sustains recovery during this time is the deep desire to never go back. What also helps is that the structure and support of treatment and therapy initiate changes in the brain. Basic tools are acquired on a number of levels. A "first step" (and the corollary second and third steps) consolidates the brain changes and provides context and meaning to the use of the tools. Intermittently strong feelings—fear, shame, anger, and sorrow—start to bubble up, adding to the discomfort. They announce the next stage and the introduction of a profound grieving process. This process is a leap in what we call emotional intelligence.

Grief — As the chaos settles and more consciousness emerges, the brain as a functioning organism starts to improve dramatically. As part of increasing coherency, the brain starts to integrate. So there are new realizations and realities. Memories long buried add depth and pain to the new awareness. Clinicians use the terms "intolerance of affect" to describe how, prior to recovery, addicts and families would set aside the unbearable aspects of their lives by avoiding deep feelings. Long ago, twelve step people learned about this phase starting with Bill W's "grudge list." The fourth and fifth steps taught us that listing our feelings was the gateway to immersion in our affective world. Making sense of them helps the brain connect the dots of memories, ancient voices, the original self and its "inclinations," and the terrors of the night. This integration brings about a further expansion of emotional intelligence. It is how you know the next right thing to do, how you become willing to make yourself do what is right and meaningful and what will make you happy. The dreams are disinterred. The moral compass is reset and the capability for character returns.

This is not an easy task. In fact, it is an ordeal of the first order. Moreover, this work is done in one of those critical spots in recovery when relapse often occurs. Sometimes the unbearable is just that: unbearable. To return to my interview with the reporter, did this work become unbearable for her famous relapse case? I am sure the level of stillness required was never achieved, and the structure and direction needed were not provided. The attempt might have been made, but the old loops and synapses which helped the individual cope before prevailed, as did the inevitable consequences. In our research, we learned that if relapse was to occur after a period of real success, this was the most likely moment.

Repair and Rebuilding — Once the emotional reset button has been triggered, the recovering person realizes that substantial changes must happen. The reordering of one's life takes about a year or sometimes two. It requires focus, daily attention, a plan, and a clear picture of what it would mean to be congruent with the original feeling child and the original inclinations of happiness. Repair work needs to be done. Some things simply have to go. New directions are implemented. People consistently reported the shifts towards challenge and reward. Stories of returning to school, completing degrees, and finishing major projects, old jobs dropped and fruitless relationships abandoned. Businesses, books, travel, family priorities reflected a new congruency with life's bucket list. There was much less drama, more simplicity, and a commitment to much less time in things which did not matter. A new spirituality is found in the pursuit of the ordinary.

This stage is roughly akin to restoration of a house—the remodeling metaphor we used in the opening of the book. As a lens to look at the change, it is worth expanding. One uses the same foundation even if somewhat altered. The ill-conceived, the worn-out, and the outmoded features are abandoned. The functional structures are kept with the goal of making the house more usable, fitting the life of its dwellers. More beautiful to lift the hearts and spirits of the inhabitants. Expanded and altered so more can be done with less. A private space given over to peacefulness, focus, and ways to access the self. In short, it is restoration that creates an environment which, in itself, restores by how it now is. Such restorations take real time, resources, outside help, and daily attention. Done well, however, they can be a platform for living for a lifetime. Recovery requires this foundational work to provide the platform to bring life to a new level.

The unplanned-for achievement of this restorative work is learning how to focus instead of living in obsession. In no other way does this happen. Did our famous relapsing patient get this year of stillness? Probably not. An educated guess is that the turbulent waters of this person's life continued without the tools or resolve to navigate out of them.

Growth — All the change reshuffles the deck of cards of relationships. The irony exists that as people in recovery become more available to themselves, they become more accessible to others. Their friends and family have become their witnesses, and new allies have come to help. In turn, the process and openness to change deepens and grows. The features of this growth stage actually overlap with the rebuilding stage and continue for up to a year or longer. The reshuffling comes not without its own perils. There can be cross-purposes and existential realities to relationships, as the darkness clears, that are breathtaking in complexity and beyond daunting. Great care has to be taken here, for choices ill-made can last a lifetime. As we shall see, sometimes the most significant and the most difficult work happens at the end. Shrinking from those tasks can cause people to flee into the oblivion of relapse or even new addictive modes.

The Heroic Journey and the Six Stages of Recovery

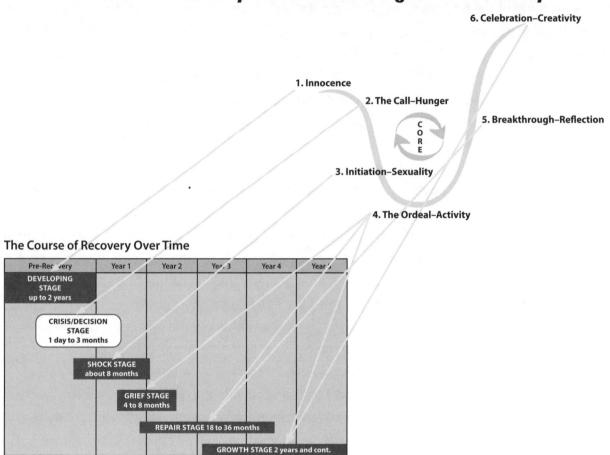

Figure 2

In *Recovery Zone I,* we compared the six stages of growth to the heroic journey, pioneered by Joseph Campbell and others. The concept is that all the heroines and heroes of our great stories have the same basic experiences, and these experiences teach them basic lessons about life that we all must learn. Medieval storytellers, for example, referred to good stories as teaching Jedermann or Everyman. In the beginning, heroes do not see what is coming. There is an innocence to that lack of foresight. Luke Skywalker is naive in his loyalty to his adoptive family. He is also restless because he has more skills, desires, and abilities than being a farmer on Tatooine. Hermione Granger in *Harry Potter* worked tirelessly on her book knowledge but she could not see that her arrogance left her friendless and without purpose. Harry Potter had not a clue about his heritage and knew only his unhappiness as the boy who lived under the stairs. Transformation started when he learned that he was the "boy who lived." Aragorn in *The Lord of the Rings* lived in his father's shadow, immobilized by his belief that his destiny was lost. Frodo Baggins in that story heard the whisper of the "adventure" of his uncle Bilbo, but clung even more fiercely to the order and safety of his Hobbit life in the Shire.

All these great stories are familiar to our culture. I listed so many parallels because together they show how resistance can undermine the work. They share commonalities of marginalized childhood, trauma, and attachment issues. These great stories portrayed in our recent decades all teach the same lessons. Something unforeseen happens, which propels the hero into a world the hero did not know. The initial challenge always teaches them that they are more than they knew. Their "inclinations" had value. And with this, they now know a new purpose. Always there is the unfolding of a story—often about the family—about which they had no idea. They had to risk themselves without guarantees of success. An example is Frodo entering free fall when he said, "I will take the Ring, though I do not know the way." After the initial challenge, they had to acquire new skills and allies. They faced unending ordeals but were transformed. Harry Potter stayed with his courage and never lost sight of what was important. Hermione learned that her talents were refined by the ordeal and that loyalty and friendship tempered judgement. All, upon reflection, became aware of both assets and limitations. Their new emotional intelligence poured their energy into creative challenge. Frodo wrote the book, Aragorn put his country back together, and Luke Skywalker founded an academy of enlightened peacekeepers to support democracy.

The parallels between the hero's journey and the recovery story are unmistakable. For starters, neuroscience tells us that storytelling is critical to brain change. Mastering our own story helps significantly to restore brain integration and function. It is one of the most complex activities the brain can do—and fundamental to the recovery process. So recovering people retell their stories over and over, though often with the observation: this is the way I told my story then, but now I know more of the story.

Recovery in many ways is heroic. That recovery will test you is a good thing to know. Because until enough of us get into recovery that it becomes the story of everyman, our country will not be restored. Our medical system reels under the impact that we are a nation mired in addiction and mental health issues. No disease ever got what it needed—funding, research, treatment, or respect—until people who had the problem spoke up. Recovery is filled with heroes and they should not be mocked or disparaged. Their voices will ultimately be key to saving us from where we are. Sometimes our media and journalists have the sense to see that, but it will not sell newspapers or television time. It really is up to the recovering community.

Recovery Zone I starts when a person has changed their behavior and faced the initial challenge. This is what intervention and treatment does. Trauma therapists use the phrase 'narrative integration.' The story they tell themselves is changing, and with that change so does the energy in the brain called the self. Most heroes have a map of sorts that leads them to and perhaps through their challenge. With recovery, we realized the outlines of that map did not exist. So, we have built a map on the basis of what people have done that worked. We distilled the process so everyone could access it. The process starts by asking people new to recovery to look at how to make decisions and to think about where they were at their best. These two steps began to define their purposes. Also, readers were asked to look at how addiction manifested and interacted in their lives. This helps them to further frame the real challenge of recovery. In other words, the task is not to just change, but to make the changes so completely that there is a fundamental new way of life that prepares the addict for the further challenges.

Then the ordeal starts: sorting through the elements of one's history and facing the truths obscured by conflicted feelings. Deep therapy and the fourth and fifth step processes bring a person to new sets of explicit terms in a contract with the self. This new relationship with the self we called a covenant. The ordeal results in a new compass, an emotional intelligence about the self.

Recovery Zone I is a structure to help bring people from the shock stage into the grief stage. With that, however, the incongruities between who they are and how they have lived are glaring. There is an essential series of tasks for implementing the self into a way of living. This rebuilding process is the phase of healing that *Recovery Zone II* provides. *Recovery Zone II* structures how to make life reflect who you are. It takes about a year to eighteen months, and it starts with the perfect storm.

Chapter 1 **Beyond Sobriety in the Eye of the Storm**

*When the solid ground is falling out from underneath my feet,
between the black skies and my red eyes I can barely see, when
I realize I've been sold out by my friends and my family, I can
feel the rain reminding me, in the eye of the storm ....*

Lyrics from *Eye of the Storm*
Ryan Stevenson

A common observation in treatment groups by both addicts and family members is, "I wish my therapist before I got into recovery had known more about addiction." This complaint usually is about lost time, money spent, and deteriorating circumstances. When the losses are great, such as a divorce that was now seen as unnecessary, or positive HIV status that could have been avoided, or the tragic opiate death, the therapist's lack of knowledge is perceived as part of the problem. But experienced addiction therapists usually respond by pointing out the web of lies and secrets that addicts weave around their compartmentalized lives. To vilify your past therapist when you did not tell them the whole story may be a convenient piece of denial, but the truth is therapy does not work well without the whole picture.

In consulting with referring therapists from the perspective of a much more complete story in an inpatient setting, "Nobody told us anything about that!" is often reported. Most experienced therapists have experienced the deliberate self-deceptions of their clients. Oftentimes, when the truth topples the house of cards, the current therapist does not even know the patient has been to an inpatient or intensive outpatient setting. The "truth" has a way of accelerating things and therapists experience the "gaps" in the story they were working with.

A further fact we know empirically is that addicts can take up to two years or longer to commit to a treatment process, even though they know in the recesses of their hearts that they have to face it inevitably. One of the hallmarks of that period of "precontemplation" is to see a therapist and be a non-committed client. Most often, something has to happen that is so disastrous, so painful, and so costly that addicts and their family members accept the inevitable. In other words, commitment starts with the perfect storm. Plus, honesty.

The addict's house of cards was, in reality, fragile. When you believe the deceptions, however, as addicts usually do, many things go wrong at once. In weather, at the center of all the whirling turmoil an eye in the middle of the storm emerges, and it remains relatively calm even though all the winds and rain are at the worst around the edges.

When it is a house of cards, there is no calm. You have to create one. Within your mind an observer exists that can be called upon. This Inner Observer has sources of wisdom that have not been accessed. It watches the brain as inner conversations, debates, and terrifying scenarios rage back and forth. Buddha referred to this observing as watching the "monkey business" of the mind. For most in early recovery, this is the beginning of transformation. They discover they have a wise mind, a new ally for the tests to come. It is in the creation of the eye—or an inner calm—that the storm starts to unravel.

As the storm loses its power, the eye extends and breaks through the turmoil at some point along the edge. Meteorologists know this is a sign that the disturbance is losing its energy. Therapists also watch for the "wise mind" in the patient and help the patient realize they already have good ideas within them that come from a piece of the brain that is above the fray. There needs to be enough psychological distance to provide perspective on creating sense out of their chaos. In fact, many strategies of therapy stem from the knowledge that the therapeutic process is helping patients discover what they already know. These are helpful analogies in understanding the two survival tasks necessary in creating a recovery zone that works for you.

In the post Vietnam War era, Admiral James Stockdale (the highest ranking American naval officer imprisoned) was interviewed about his seven years in a prisoner of war camp. He was asked how his people survived. He said those who lived did two things. First, they had to totally and at all times see how bad things really were. Even noticing the nuances of a guard's face could save a prisoner's life. This commitment to total reality echoes Scott Peck's famous phrase in his classic book *The Road Less Traveled* that mental health is a "commitment to reality at all costs."

Stockdale then said the second was is to have a vision of what you wanted your life to be. You had to carry a picture of what was most important to you. The admiral referred to hard times teaching us what is important and who we really are. His statements echo the experience of Viktor Frankl in the Nazi concentration camps. Frankl wrote, "He who has a why to live for can bear almost any how." Frankl describes how every night certain inmates would stop and talk to each person. They would probe and ask each person what would be worth committing to survival. Both Stockdale and Frankl literally mean that one has to take worst moments and transform them into meaning. The transformation of suffering into meaning is the bedrock of facing adversity. At times this means finding the "why behind the why," a process we will repeatedly revisit as we explore your choices to survive and to be in a zone of power, resilience, and happiness.

After being sober or in your recovery process six months to a year, when the storms start to dissipate, the temptation is to normalize and return to earlier patterns. However, you have resolved to make changes and not to use or return to old behaviors. The next steps of recovery require a great deal of time and effort to change. But people think they know enough and are able to handle it. Therapy takes a back seat to the stresses of career and life. Working on steps and therapy slows to nothing, and meeting attendance and therapy sessions become spotty. The resolve starts to melt. Like the high-profile people we described in the introduction, we all have handlers. We are surrounded by people invested in keeping things the same. Actually, the original *Big Book of Alcoholics Anonymous* describes in Chapter 2 a member who starts to handle things alone, and how this soon leads to relapse. All fellowships' literature recognizes this vulnerable moment of choice.

In *Recovery Zone I,* we introduced you to Mihaly Csikszentmihalyi and his work about changing the very premises of your life to a zone of happiness and challenge. Without this translation of resolve into actual daily life, which brings commitment to an implementation of change, those old "bargains with chaos" will return. Csikszentmihalyi observed that getting sober was easy compared to the deeper work of staying sober. Staying sober is the heart of the transformation, translating all your hard work into workable, sustainable change. If not, the deceptions return, chaos starts to gather, and this time relapse creates a much deeper hole of betrayal and distrust. It takes at least eighteen months of intense work to redesign how you live and practice that plan every day. There are risks in recovery. You will discover the deeper issues and the why behind the why. Those closest to you may misperceive your progress and react to that. You will develop new skills and test how they work. You will see yourself differently, and you may have intense grieving about what it was like to be with you in your other life. This is where the "ordeal" of the hero's journey really occurs. Joseph Campbell says that having ordeals is the experience of all humans. All the great stories follow this path. All heroes inevitably are transformed by the perfect storm (or even a series of storms). Learning the skills to overcome adversity is the essence of courage and resilience. And if courage and resilience prevail, so does achievement, purpose, and a spiritual consciousness.

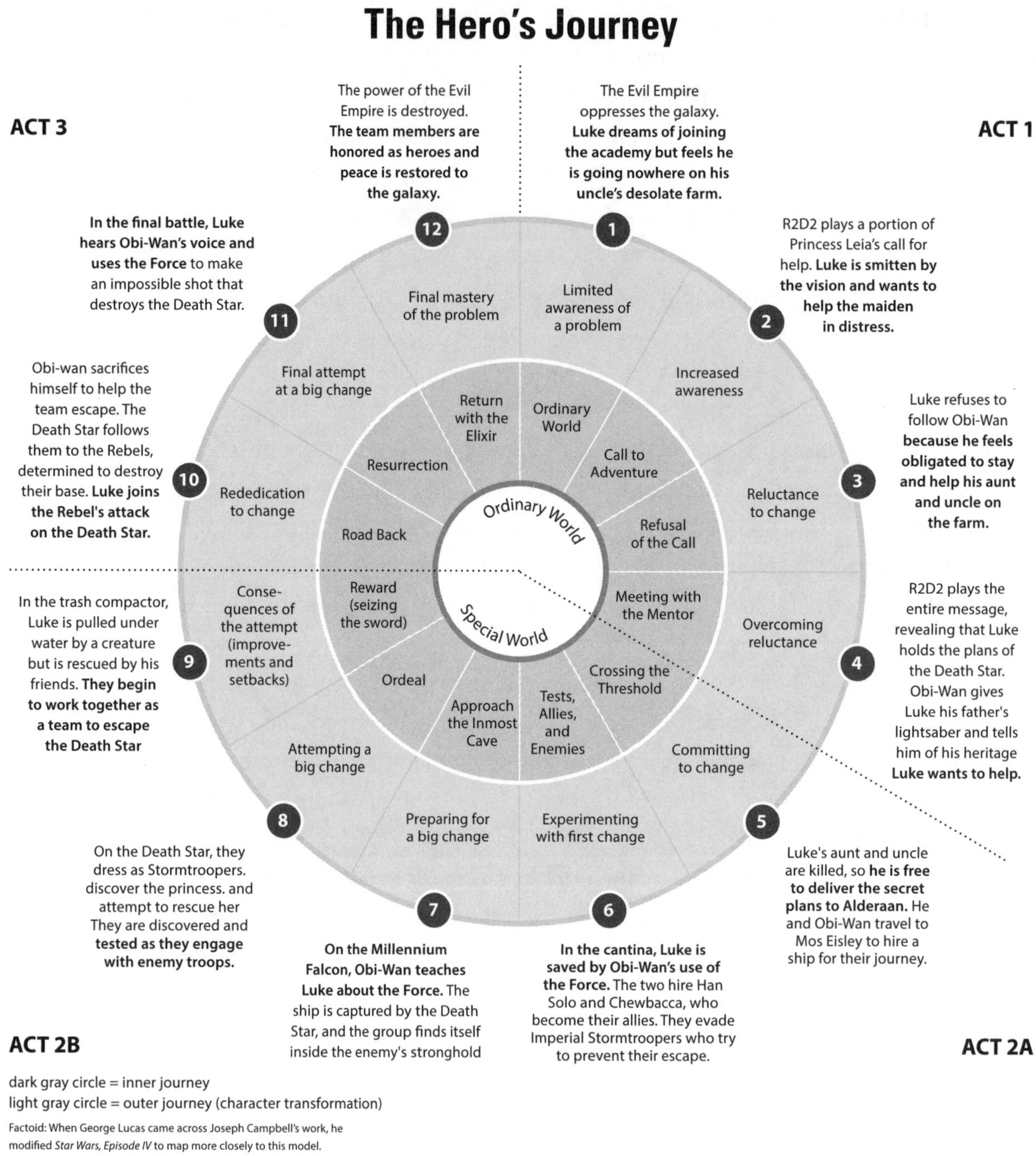
The Hero's Journey
ACT 3
ACT 1
ACT 2B
ACT 2A
The power of the Evil Empire is destroyed. **The team members are honored as heroes and peace is restored to the galaxy.**
The Evil Empire oppresses the galaxy. **Luke dreams of joining the academy but feels he is going nowhere on his uncle's desolate farm.**
R2D2 plays a portion of Princess Leia's call for help. **Luke is smitten by the vision and wants to help the maiden in distress.**
Luke refuses to follow Obi-Wan **because he feels obligated to stay and help his aunt and uncle on the farm.**
R2D2 plays the entire message, revealing that Luke holds the plans of the Death Star. Obi-Wan gives Luke his father's lightsaber and tells him of his heritage **Luke wants to help.**
Luke's aunt and uncle are killed, so **he is free to deliver the secret plans to Alderaan.** He and Obi-Wan travel to Mos Eisley to hire a ship for their journey.
In the cantina, Luke is saved by Obi-Wan's use of the Force. The two hire Han Solo and Chewbacca, who become their allies. They evade Imperial Stormtroopers who try to prevent their escape.
On the Millennium Falcon, Obi-Wan teaches Luke about the Force. The ship is captured by the Death Star, and the group finds itself inside the enemy's stronghold
On the Death Star, they dress as Stormtroopers. discover the princess. and attempt to rescue her They are discovered and **tested as they engage with enemy troops.**
In the trash compactor, Luke is pulled under water by a creature but is rescued by his friends. **They begin to work together as a team to escape the Death Star**
Obi-wan sacrifices himself to help the team escape. The Death Star follows them to the Rebels, determined to destroy their base. **Luke joins the Rebel's attack on the Death Star.**
In the final battle, Luke hears Obi-Wan's voice and uses the Force to make an impossible shot that destroys the Death Star.
1 Limited awareness of a problem
2 Increased awareness
3 Reluctance to change
4 Overcoming reluctance
5 Committing to change
6 Experimenting with first change
7 Preparing for a big change
8 Attempting a big change
9 Conse-quences of the attempt (improve-ments and setbacks)
10 Rededication to change
11 Final attempt at a big change
12 Final mastery of the problem
Ordinary World
Call to Adventure
Refusal of the Call
Meeting with the Mentor
Crossing the Threshold
Tests, Allies, and Enemies
Approach the Inmost Cave
Ordeal
Reward (seizing the sword)
Road Back
Resurrection
Return with the Elixir
Ordinary World
Special World
dark gray circle = inner journey
light gray circle = outer journey (character transformation)
Factoid: When George Lucas came across Joseph Campbell's work, he modified *Star Wars, Episode IV* to map more closely to this model.

Figure 1.1

Used with permission of Nancy Duarte, and the author wishes to acknowledge the generosity of Nancy Duarte and her support of people in recovery.

Nancy Duarte describes this universal journey in her book *Resonate*, which is probably one of the best books on public presentations in the digital age. The focus of the book is how to build incentive and motivation in people, which requires understanding the change process.

Figure 1.1 is a model Duarte uses to explain how the ordeal really works and where it fits into the common scenario of the hero. She takes Luke Skywalker from *Star Wars* as a well-known, universal example of how the journey goes. Luke first appears as a farm boy loyal to his family but who knows there is something wrong. He needs something more than farm work and tech repair of the family's farm droids. He seeks meaning and challenge. He buries his unhappiness until he sees the message from Princess Leia. He is introduced to Obi-Wan Kenobi, who asks him to join in the rebellion. But Luke rejects the message and the urgency, and more importantly, refuses to join with Obi-Wan. When he returns home after his encounter with Obi-Wan, he finds his home destroyed and his aunt and uncle murdered by soldiers of the emperor. No longer can he ignore the message. It is thrust upon him in a heart-wrenching way.

When Luke joins Obi-Wan he enters an extraordinary "special world" he did not know existed. He starts to learn new skills, comes to a new level of awareness of who he is, confronts his deepest fears, and attempts to utilize what he is learning, although he often fails. All this transforms him to be ready to enter the ordinary world, which is in chaos.

Recovery is also an extraordinary world in which the key to survival is a whole new dimension of self-understanding. Skills are acquired and tested. Very unsettling realizations occur. Purpose and intentionality brought Luke to doing what mattered. At this point, with your experience so far, you would most likely admit that the world of recovery and therapy brought you to facing things you had no concept of. In fact, many patients joke that in therapy they have learned to speak a different language—a language that is foreign to those not in recovery. Like so many jokes, at its core there is much truth.

Luke's process parallels the wrenching changes necessary to create a life-long recovery. As we have noted, it takes a while to come to the painful realizations that provide the motivations necessary to making life change.

As stated above, Duarte's book is one of the finest books on public speaking and motivation that we have. The problem she highlights is the one we face in helping people enter into recovery and do the longer-term work beyond sobriety. Most addicts know there is a problem but they push it off until the truth hits them so hard that they need help. They resist those who try to assist them, and they have to learn a new language of the self. At first it is awkward, but the brain helps with phrases and words. New skills and perspectives emerge. They work at it until they can think in it, speak in it, and act on it without having to stop. We call it an unconscious competence or expert system. This language of the self involves changing the brain. **Figure 1.2** uses Duarte's model (with her kind permission), but adapting it to the experience of recovery. The special world of recovery means new skill sets, confronting the demons, and preparing for the test of re-entry to real life. It also means stepping back while doing this work and starting to use and trust the Inner Observer or Wise Mind.

The Recovery Journey

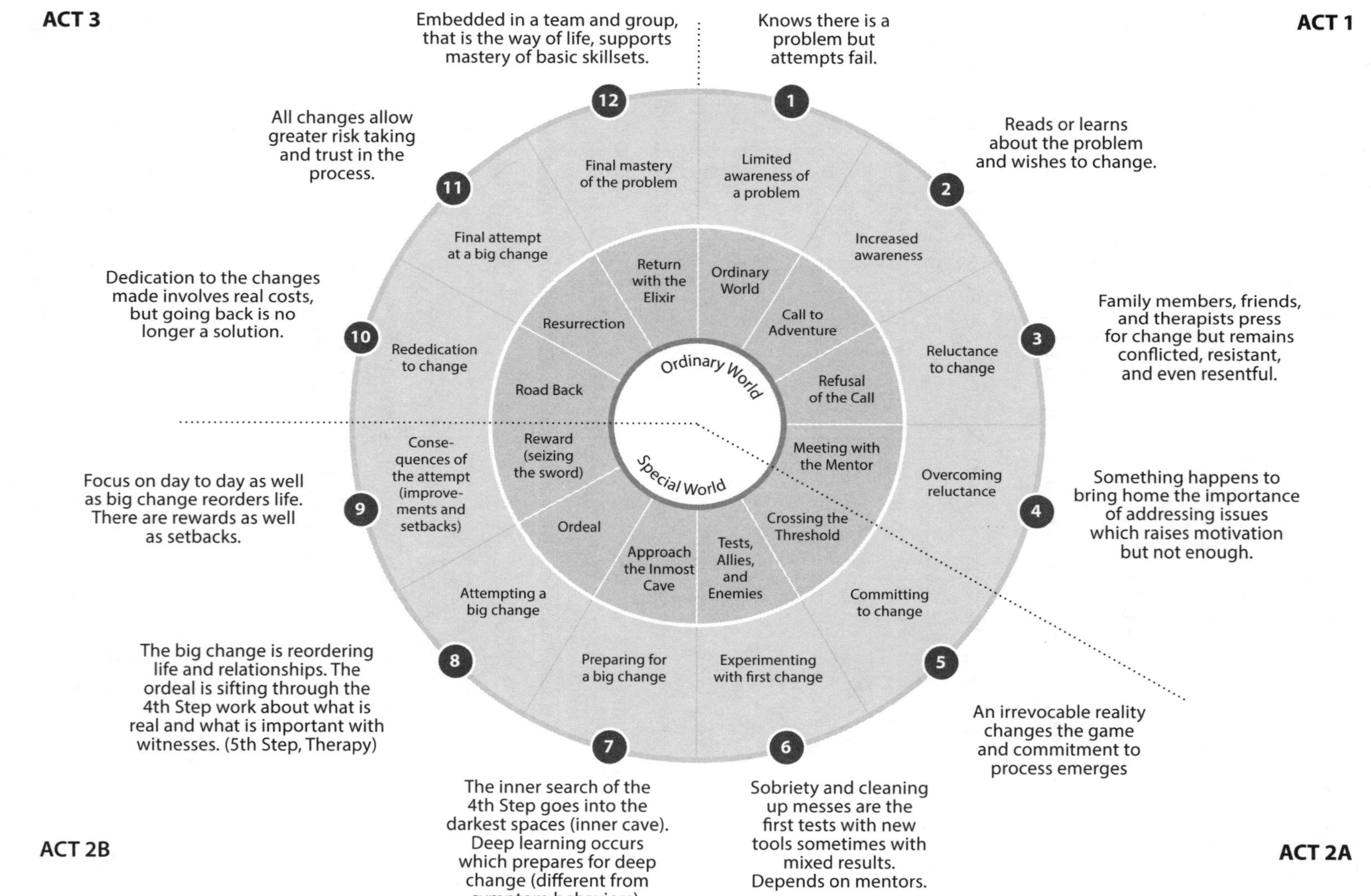

ACT 1

ACT 2A

ACT 3

ACT 2B

Reads or learns about the problem and wishes to change.

Knows there is a problem but attempts fail.

Family members, friends, and therapists press for change but remains conflicted, resistant, and even resentful.

Something happens to bring home the importance of addressing issues which raises motivation but not enough.

An irrevocable reality changes the game and commitment to process emerges

Sobriety and cleaning up messes are the first tests with new tools sometimes with mixed results. Depends on mentors.

The inner search of the 4th Step goes into the darkest spaces (inner cave). Deep learning occurs which prepares for deep change (different from symptom behaviors).

The big change is reordering life and relationships. The ordeal is sifting through the 4th Step work about what is real and what is important with witnesses. (5th Step, Therapy)

Focus on day to day as well as big change reorders life. There are rewards as well as setbacks.

Dedication to the changes made involves real costs, but going back is no longer a solution.

All changes allow greater risk taking and trust in the process.

Embedded in a team and group, that is the way of life, supports mastery of basic skillsets.

1 Limited awareness of a problem

2 Increased awareness

3 Reluctance to change

4 Overcoming reluctance

5 Committing to change

6 Experimenting with first change

7 Preparing for a big change

8 Attempting a big change

9 Consequences of the attempt (improvements and setbacks)

10 Rededication to change

11 Final attempt at a big change

12 Final mastery of the problem

Ordinary World
Call to Adventure
Refusal of the Call
Meeting with the Mentor
Crossing the Threshold
Tests, Allies, and Enemies
Approach the Inmost Cave
Ordeal
Reward (seizing the sword)
Road Back
Resurrection
Return with the Elixir

Ordinary World

Special World

Figure 1.2

dark gray circle = inner journey
light gray circle = outer journey (character transformation)

Factoid: When George Lucas came across Joseph Campbell's work, he modified *Star Wars, Episode IV* to map more closely to this model.

Exercise 1.1 takes the six stages of recovery we have documented and matches them with the components of the hero's journey. Think of earlier transformations in your life. You can maybe see when change was thrust upon you during some of your worst moments. Did you have trouble with trusting people to help you? You can use **Exercise 1.1** to map how your recovery has progressed so far.

It is important as part of your process to look at this from the basic elements of change so that you understand the next phases you face—and the ones you may repeat. That would be an act of honesty that passes the Stockdale test of facing reality. Simultaneously, a new picture of what matters takes form and may surprise you. But this will be about much more than just changing perceptions.

Your Own Journey

Below, find the same stages with blank spaces. Think of your own history and the perfect storm propelling you into an extraordinary world. Reflect on your resistance to new or strange ways of coping. Did you resist people who were teaching you these new strategies? Were there dark parts of yourself that you had to confront? Did you try new skills with mixed success, and have you now mastered some? Fill in the blank spaces with examples that parallel the hero's journey.

The Recovery Journey

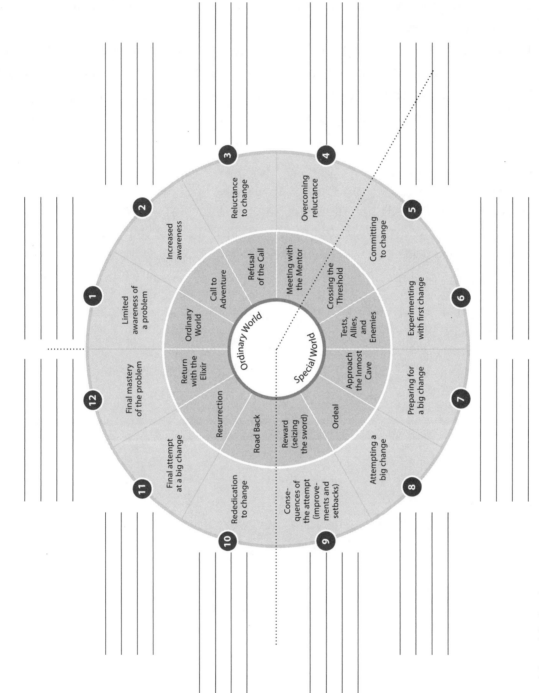

Exercise 1.1

dark gray circle = inner journey
light gray circle = outer journey (character transformation)

Entering The "Ordinary" World

Making re-entry into the ordinary world is the real test of lasting sobriety. The purpose of this book is to help with that transition so you can meet your greatest challenges and be successful. The focus and skill set necessary require persistence and work. It helps greatly to understand how the brain functions and makes changes permanent. This process also introduces the skills of resilience, which are necessary because obstacles are inevitable. And more than likely they will not be just "speed bumps" to slow you down.

How does the brain change? First, there has to be safety. That is why the eye of the storm is important. Somewhere there has to be internal calm. Secondly, reading, hearing, and telling a story is the most complex thing a brain does. With new understanding and honesty, the story shifts. In the early months of recovery, much effort goes into getting the story straight. The very telling of the story in a safe environment gives the brain cohesion and self-understanding. In therapy, we describe the essential change of the "narrative." All of us operate out of this script/story. Dr. Bob and Bill W. had their first moment of connection when they admitted to each other that they had hidden bottles in the dog house. Such moments of connection create the safety of knowing you are understood. In the treatment of torture victims, few would enter therapy until they were placed in a room filled with other torture victims. Similar stories meant safety. Safety meant the stories could be told. Then the truth of the narratives could be challenged, expanded, and better understood.

Norman Doidge in his book *The Brain's Way of Healing* describes how hard this is. For many in early therapy there is neural wiring that is not used or active. For various reasons, parts of brain function become dormant. For example, once the reward center of addictions is engaged, the brain actually shuts down parts of itself, actions perceived by the brain as necessary for survival. Even simple mechanisms like memory or compassion are short-circuited or bypassed.

There is also the problem of the noisy brain. In the perfect storm there is so much chaos and stimulation that the brain has trouble focusing or keeping promises or even hearing what people say. For example, it is very common in an inpatient setting to have a patient complain that a certain task or rules were not told to him or her. Then a nurse or staff-person sits with the patient and shows them a sheet describing that they were told of these requirements the day before and signed off on understanding them. The patient is often surprised and confused. When this happens, I ask if at home the patient has been told by family members or work associates that events or rules they didn't know about had been told to them a number of times. The dawn of recognition comes with the realization that chaos impacts basic brain function. For some, this is the start of reclaiming the calm of the eye of the storm.

One of the hallmarks of a noisy brain is specific intentions cannot be maintained because of high arousal, fear, or stimulation. The result is that the neurons cannot track or fire regularly, so promises made go unfulfilled. The best of intentions do not happen, which adds to the chaos. Work stress, family problems, legal complications, and super anxiety or stimulation overwhelm the brain. This is the advantage of inpatient treatment or intensive outpatient, which, for a moment in time, gives the brain a chance to calm down. On an outpatient basis, therapists and sponsors work hard to encourage reducing scheduled commitments, finding time for oneself, and dropping unnecessary activities.

Finally, there are "coded networks" or patterns of thinking that float on neural networks we call belief systems or paradigms. They may be true or not. Either way, they often carry error codes that cause us to make the same mistakes over and over. For example, "women cannot be trusted" and "all men are alike" are beliefs that can be carried by some almost as articles of faith. Perceptions persist even when they're not true. Rather than being the present truth, they are echoes of voices from the past that have been incorporated into self-perceptions, which are difficult to bear and even more difficult to confront.

Doidge describes five clear phases involved in the brain's change. Every two years all the cells of the brain are replaced, just like every six months your blood supply is replaced. Your brain changes all the time, allowing the opportunity for phenomenal growth. It is possible to regain focus and brain function and improve your brain. This makes getting traction in recovery and therapy more than worth the time.

Phase One is the correction of cellular function. Toxins, foods, sugars, chemicals, excess stimulation—all can interfere with brain capacities. All of these are challenges. One cannot be using drugs and at the same time one attempts to stop dangerous sexual behaviors. Being in the chaos of the storm keeps the brain surging in its efforts to keep various spinning pie plates in the air. Oftentimes in early recovery, it means withdrawal from the unnecessary demands on your energy such as committees, boards, charity work, excessive work responsibilities, hobbies, excessive exercise routines—*anything* that you do not have to do. This list can be extensive and is best reviewed with your therapists and trusted recovery peers.

Phase Two is neurostimulation. There are many strategies that help here. Exercise helps the brain immensely. Whatever you do for your heart helps your brain as well. Processes that confront the error codes of the brain are also helpful. Consider what a good first step in a recovery program does. It exposes how often your brain would take a very bad idea and make it look logical or even compelling to you. Information about addiction and mental health further break down the error codes that keep you locked into dysfunctional patterns. Learning focus skills helps you to live out your intentions for the day. Early therapy is filled with exercises to expose contradictions between what you do and what you say or even between what you believe is real and what all those around you see.

Phase Three is neuromodulation. There are two tasks here. First is learning the skill set of self-regulation—how to control your overreactions and high arousal. Second is cultivating the ability to be present and calm. A major part of that is learning how to show up and stay engaged with others in a functional way that fosters brain growth. Terms like mindfulness, being present, meditation, and "showing up" are used for this collection of indispensable human capabilities. A term often used for both sets of skills is "emotional intelligence" after Daniel Goleman's book by that title. Emotional intelligence is an indispensable part of brain growth, and one of the master skills of resilience, and it requires focus and time. This is why there needs to be at least a year in which these skill sets become so much a part of who you are that you do not have to think about them.

Phase Four is neurorelaxation. The brain needs to rest and catch up. It needs time to put the pieces together that have been put on the shelf or compartmentalized or "unprocessed" as events. These often result in "aha" moments, which concentration can inhibit. The brain actually processes "behind your back" in ways you can be unaware of but that allows you to emerge with sudden clarity. Ironically, the "aha" moments usually happen when you are doing something totally unrelated. Nature's rhythm requires rest in order to renew. And your brain is very much part of those natural processes.

Phase Five is neurodifferentiation and learning. The brain uses this process to integrate all your new awareness and create more effective responses and coded networks that enhance overall function. Some use the term "connecting the dots," but really this phase means that a story is emerging that provides meaning and happiness. The brain thinks in patterns and stories. It is critical in your story how it continues, not to mention how it ends. Once you understand this fact of the brain, you become more conscious, and working on your story becomes a lifetime task.

The *Recovery Zone* series asks for a year to learn the process and then up to a year to practice. Returning to the phases of recovery, one starts to see how the brain starts to regain and enhance its focus. **Figure 1.3** shows graphically how these brain changes flow back and forth with recovery progress. Most recoveries start with irrevocable realities that were life-changing. After the whitewater of getting a workable sobriety, the temptation is to see yourself as finished. Sobriety simply opens the door to improving your brain and your ability to focus. The door shuts if sobriety is seen as the end goal. Slips and relapses will be problematic.

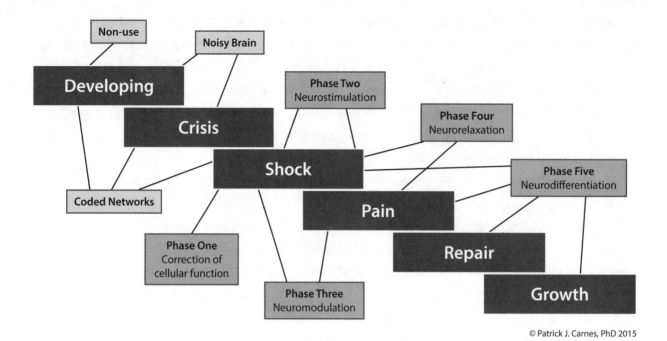

© Patrick J. Carnes, PhD 2015

Figure 1.3 (the tasks and Doidge's stages)

I have faced death twice in the last decade. I did witness my wife's death after twenty years of marriage. All three events left me with the realization that you have to focus on what is important. Nothing else. I remember sitting with my wife Susanne on a fall afternoon a few months before she succumbed to cancer. She looked at me and said the biggest mistake we all make is that we always think we have more time. And the truth is we both had realized we really did not have much time. There is an ancient story about a famous yoga teacher who spoke of living like there was a sword dangling about his head held up by a fragile spider web. His point was that awareness of how quickly things can end changes what matters to you. Every moment starts to matter. There is perhaps no greater truth in this whole book: life happens with a basic illusion that you have more time. In the end, you will be most grateful about the parts when you were present and focused on what really matters to you.

So it is with therapy. Elizabeth Lesser in her book *Marrow* tells the story of how out of all of her siblings she was the only match to be able to give her sister bone marrow to fight off her cancer. Yet this was her sister who was most different and estranged from her. Before they were to share her bone marrow, they decided to do therapy and work through their differences so they could also share their "soul marrow." The book is a moving account of the whole process. Most importantly, Lesser observed—and I am convinced of the truth of this observation—how fast she and her sister were able to move through huge issues in therapy when they had so little time. Recovery and the substantial changes that occur can happen when you give it the urgency it needs. Otherwise, therapy will take all the time you give it—and sadly you may never get to what you want. *Recovery Zone* is built with time parameters for precisely this reason. From the introduction to the last chapter, this book brings the message you do not have the time to wait.

Recovery is like dodging a persistent illness. You know there is more stuff to do and you promise yourself you will get to it. Right now, digging into how you ended up like you did is what is next. It is hard and takes some time. Use your momentum and decide to change the story. In many ways it is like waking up from a dream. Yet it only happens when there is a concentrated effort of the eye of the storm to break through the chaos. It is what heroes do.

Chapter 2 **Cultivating the Inner "Eye"**

"A bit of advice
Given to a young Native American
At the time of his initiation.
As you go the way of life,
You will see a great chasm. Jump.
It is not as wide as you think."

Joseph Campbell

Throughout *Recovery Zone,* we have used the term "Inner Observer" to describe that part of your mind that detaches from all the inner dialogues, debates, and reactions that are active in your brain's consciousness. This "wise" mind notes what makes sense, or is useful, or what really matters. Many of our best thinkers, like Gary Zukav, call this the "seat of the soul," meaning this is the part of the mind that is the real "self." In the seat of the soul, one knows what matters. This is important to recovery because this sense of self is what keeps things calm in the mind. This is vital when unexpected or threatening events occur. Most importantly, this part of the reflective self uses intention to change the habits of the brain.

The part of the brain that is most conscious and orderly is located in your head. Goal-setting, planning, information-gathering, and your good intentions occur there. It is that part of your brain that knows to have a plan or someone will have one for you. Because it keeps perspective, it is also the seeker of solutions and the problem solver. Dan Goleman in his book *Focus,* calls this the "top-down brain."

Yet a good part of your brain is located in collections of neurons (brain cells) from the base of your skull to around your heart. These brain cells are connected to every organ and part of your body. This is the part of the brain that does things automatically, without thinking. This part of your consciousness knows immediately whether something fits or does not, whether you like something or do not, or if something is the right decision for you or not. Your emotions also reside in this mosaic synaptic connection, making it your emotional compass and your conscience.

Since this part of your brain is wired to every organ in your body, it is the part that keeps everything working together without much thought. It is the automatic transmission of the nervous system. It reacts immediately without much (or any) consideration on your part.

Thus, your body truly and immediately knows your reactions and gives credence to the phrase "speaking from the heart."

Dan Goleman explains in his book *Focus* that at the heart of things is what is termed an "expert system." A quarterback makes a play starting with a plan, but when things unfold instantly looks at the field of options and knows in a millisecond what the best option at that moment is. The surgeon focusing on surgery does not have to stop and think about what is next. They know how to do these things without thinking because of years of focus, and they might even be hard pressed to explain how they knew what the next right thing to do was. But they spent time practicing the "language" of the game or medicine until it was part of them. Think of the movie Karate Kid, when Mr. Miyagi started to teach Karate to Daniel with "wax on, wax off." It does not make sense as Daniel starts until Mr. Miyagi helps him put the pieces together. So the intentional brain (top-down brain) purposely focuses on each skill, and in time this evolves into an "expert system." This is how skills become automatic.

Therapists help teach expert systems. They use the term "mechanisms of attention." In early recovery, you are asked to read a morning meditation that provides an inspiring or motivational thought for the day. It is ironic how often those initial reflections are exactly what you need to hear. That realization alone can easily be of assistance in the minutes or even hours of a stressful day. Astute practitioners also encourage you to "bookend" the day with another meditation at night. Without a doubt, one of the most common strategies is to make your reflections concrete through various forms of journaling and exercises or step assignments to broaden the "attention" of your Inner Observer.

Recovery Zone as a process is designed to help you focus on getting this "higher self" on board. Plus, reading and studying is indispensable. We mention books which would be important for you to spend time with. Some are important to read. Some are so painfully relevant that you may want to just do a few pages a day. And some stretch us to be our better selves. Your therapists will no doubt assign some of these. Some will call out to you depending on your need.

It is important, however, to recognize there are also systems or processes you need to incorporate. Meditation is one that almost all therapists recommend, but not always are these recommendations specific about what is meant by meditation. Learning a good meditation process is fundamental to building a solid Inner Observer. There are many ways to do this. Search out the ones that are well researched.

HeartMath is one of the best documented methodologies for learning the basics of meditation and self-integration. Doc Childre, founder of HeartMath Institute, and his staff have described in the books *HeartMath* and *Heart Intelligence* the science and importance of a meditation process. They ask you to download an app and within minutes you can be learning. The book *HeartMath* is eye opening with what you may not have known about how you could improve your mental and emotional functioning. Consider also Jon Kabat Zinn's *Mindfulness for Beginners*. He calls it the easy "glide" into the meditative process. His program is fundamental to over 800 hospital-based pain programs, which speaks to the success of his design. Yoga has many varieties of contemplation, some with centuries of proven value. Your therapists may also utilize programs to introduce you to the basics of the process. The point is you need to pick at least one and do your best to learn from it as we go along.

Living in a twelve step world is a course in inner observation. Many of the steps require making a list and others require that you share those lists. In the safety of common issues and the combined intelligence of a committed community, a whole revision of your life occurs. The epic words that give testimony to an emerging Inner Observer wise-mind self are those which most twelve step programs call the promises. Each fellowship, whether it is for addicts, mental health issues, adult children, or family members has its nuances, but the promises are always similar. Reflect on the first statement of the promises, which appeared in the late 1930s in a group called Alcoholics Anonymous:

The AA Promises

1. If we are painstaking about this phase of our development, we will be amazed before we are halfway through.
2. We are going to know a new freedom and a new happiness.
3. We will not regret the past nor wish to shut the door on it.
4. We will comprehend the word serenity and we will know peace.
5. No matter how far down the scale we have gone, we will see how our experience can benefit others.
6. That feeling of uselessness and self-pity will disappear.
7. We will lose interest in selfish things and gain interest in our fellows.
8. Self-seeking will slip away.
9. Our whole attitude and outlook upon life will change.
10. Fear of people and of economic insecurity will leave us.
11. We will intuitively know how to handle situations which used to baffle us.
12. We will suddenly realize that God is doing for us what we could not do for ourselves.

Trauma experts often talk about "self-regulation," which is essential to recovery and to successful living. Dan Siegel refers to this top-down and bottom-up process in the book *Mindsight* as essential to flow or living in the Zone. You already have made progress. By this point you have started to assimilate basic processes essential to the "practice" of recovery. You may have started to explore how meditation is much more than counting your breaths. Recovery includes exploring, practicing, and mastering different methodologies of developing a functional Inner Observer. Future chapters will help you prioritize, develop more focus, and connect the dots. In our resilience bibliography we have collected further resources for you to add to your skills, and in Resilience: Living One Year in Focus and Meaning journals we have provided a framework for you to continue working on these skills after *Recovery Zone*.

Notice what you do not have! Time. This seems like so much at once. Can we spread this out and live our lives a little? Not if we have a disease and we need to manage it to have a quality of life different from the hell we were in. Most of us were selfish or selfless, and many, many of us did both. Most of us are surrounded by those who are invested in returning to the old patterns. They do not expect or believe that we are serious. Whether it is a spouse who is ready to give up or a parasitic employee who lives off of your income, and the many others who have some investment in your failure, they are betting you will not make this happen. One guideline really helps to clear up the dilemmas: Only do that which matters. Make your mental health a priority. Watching football does not matter. Helping out the neighbor who really does not like you much does not matter. Spending time with people you do not like does not count. Doing work for others because you fear their disapproval degrades the self. Hafiz wrote, "Fear is the cheapest room in the house. I would like to see you in better living conditions."

The promises have been echoed many times and in many cultures. Deepak Chopra observes, "And if you really get in touch with it, if you become familiar with this center of your awareness that you really are, you will see it is your ticket to freedom." Iyanla Vanzant adds, "The truth will make you free, but you have to endure the pains of birthing it." Do what is necessary. Let go of what you do not need. Focus on this work. Have others in your life who are doing the same. Notice your resistance and name it.

Developing your Inner Observer starts with four challenges. First, you must reorient all perceptions from the point of view of a platform of gratitude. Gratitude is the most powerful change strategy humans have. Second, the real you has to start sorting out your window of tolerance. This space starts first with what you can tolerate in order to live in recovery but eventually leads to a profound sense of your own zone and what matters. Third, your Inner Observer with its wise mind has to referee the swirl of currents in your brain. Then it has to reach confluence and transparency of who you are to others. Translated: the real you will have to stand up. Finally, the Inner Observer searches out the paradoxical in making choices. Life puts you constantly where you have to decide between competing realities and simultaneous truths (paradoxes). Because this is hard, we learn who we are. Here is each challenge broken down.

Building a Platform of Gratitude

Gratitude is one of the most important game-changers of personal perspective that we know. There are a variety of researchers of happiness who suggest that everyone has a "set point" to their emotions that limits how happy one can be. This perspective says that even major happy events will raise your joy juice for a short time but then the brain will regress back to its usual settings.

However, there is a body of literature on the impact of gratitude that says the set point not only can be moved significantly higher but can change brain architecture and function. You can find references to this in our bibliography.

One of the best examples comes out of psychology. Psychologists spend a lot of their careers measuring various aspects of being human. For some time, there has been concern about focusing just on the negative aspects of human behavior. One effort to change this orientation is an instrument called the MMPI (Minnesota Multiphasic Personality Inventory), which measures more than just problematic behaviors by looking at additional measures of wellbeing based on things like no depression or little conflict with authority. These key measures are called the PSY-5. (You can find the details in Google.) If someone is high in an ongoing sense of gratitude, studies show that it trumps the PSY-5 all the time.

One of the founding grandfathers of the modern science of mental health, William James, put it this way: "The greatest revolution in our generation is the discovery that human beings, by changing the inner attitudes of their minds, can change the outer aspects of their lives." Out of this perspective came the whole concept of positive psychology. Based on this, Abraham Maslow articulated a whole new way of looking at human achievement. One of the other early pioneers of positive psychology, Martin Seligman, coined the term "learned helplessness" as a way of creating a bridge to make achievement and success possible for everyone. Mihaly Csikszentmihalyi defined achievement and happiness as a matter of "flow"— the essence of which is key to this series of *Recovery Zone* books.

Today, we live in an abundance of meditation, mindfulness, and consciousness raising. The core skill that keeps bubbling to the top is the ability to keep close to one's core self a sense of gratitude. Thus, the Inner Observer—no matter how bad things seem—approaches all things by finding, even in the worst of occasions, that there is still much that matters, always scouting for the meaningful and finding value in the smallest events, realities, or qualities of the moment.

When teaching about gratitude, people nod their heads and are ready to go on to the next topic. But I stop and tell them about Rhonda Byrne's little book, *The Magic*. In it, she challenges her readers to a thirty-day process of gratitude. The bedrock exercise is to record a list of ten items you are grateful for on each of the thirty days. If you miss a day, you have to go back and start the book over. I personally thought it would be easy because I thought my daily disciplines were good. However, it took two weeks for me to begin a sustained thirty-day drive to get it done. I had to start over three times. After sharing my story, I challenge the audience to try the exercise and the book and see if they can do it in thirty days. I have done this with therapists with advanced degrees and patients with very mixed backgrounds. My challenge to every person participating was that at the end of the course, those who could honestly say they started and did the thirty days in a row would receive a personal gift from me.

Whether highly trained professionals or people new to recovery, it has worked out to be about the same. No matter the size of the group, the ratio is about three out of fifty. Eventually, though, all do it. And they all have similar responses at the end. Thinking about gratitude each day creates a habit to perspective. The commonalities most people notice are:

- Gratitude for what is right in your world is an important framework for thinking about what is not going well.
- Problem-solving is easier because you have in mind other times of distress, which turn out to have contained real gifts, and that will be true of this moment too.
- Gratitude teaches you to focus on what matters, which changes your priorities, decisions, and focus on your own state of flow.
- Gratitude assists with feeling deeply necessary grief, letting go of what you cannot control and unnecessary drama over that which changes.
- Being grateful helps you to notice traits in others you need to affirm to deepen your relationships, promote successful teamwork, and sustain positive family function.
- The positive attitudes of gratitude improve body functions, including heart, brain, and organs, which in turn add significantly to immune response and longevity.
- In times of challenge, gratitude helps with courage because you are aware of assets you must protect, of risks worth taking, and of your clarity of purpose.
- Gratitude is key to intimacy because you do not lose track of why you must show up for those in your circles of intimacy.
- Great achievements are possible when gratitude sustains the persistence necessary to say, "I get to do this."
- All spiritual traditions recognize that gratitude is the doorway to the here and now or what some term "stillness."

In short, the Inner Observer has little perspective without gratitude. Little peace exists in the war-torn inner world of the soul without it.

I attended a small conference of spiritual teachers from all over the world. Shamans, Medicine men and women, leaders of major religions and denominations, and medical professionals were present. The first to speak was the youngest. Trained in western medicine, he had been immersed also in traditional Chinese medicine. Before speaking, he came to each of us and presented a gift. His presentation on the healing process was amazing and thought-provoking. In the discussion that followed, he was asked about the gift-giving because usually students give gifts to their teachers. His response changed me profoundly. He said that in

Chinese medicine, the tradition was for the teacher to always give a meaningful gift to each of their students at the start. The belief was that the teacher always learned more from their students than what the students received from the teacher. I immediately knew what he meant. I often feel both in therapy and teaching that I learn more than students or patients do. To this day, when I can and it is appropriate, I start with a gift that is personal, or that I made, or that I found—and that I paid for.

What my Chinese colleague was telling us is that gifting your students indicates your realization that you are as much a learner as they are. Another way of looking at it is the old observation that he who teaches best is teaching about what he needs to learn the most. My career has had moments of great discomfort, times of loss, and extreme challenges. But it was a career in which my efforts to help others called me to be a better self, and for that I have no words to form my gratitude. What I need to notice always is that they come to "sit" with me, for which I am grateful.

Rhonda Byrne asks the reader to do additional tasks each day and some of them seem odd at first. One of them is find a rock and then each night acknowledge, with the rock in your hand, the "best" thing today. In other words, out of your whole day select out of all that happened that day what you valued the most or made you happiest. I shared this with my wife Pennie, and we have made it a regular ritual for us. Each of us shares the day's "best" thing. We have added the best "couples" thing, which basically is what occurred to both of you that each partner valued. Most often, we perceive the same thing as important in our coupleship. However, there are times when the differences in our best moments are quite different. We learn much about each other's values and needs that way.

There are many ways gratitude can emerge. I have a colleague who has the discipline of writing one thank you note to someone each day. I have another friend who writes these wonderful letters during a time when texts predominate. There is a famous story about Einstein expressing the opinion that gratitude should be noted a hundred times each day. My belief is that recording the ten best things each day is a good way to start. For sure it is fundamental to an Inner Observer view of the happenings of your life.

Determining the Window of Tolerance

Another lens for the Inner Observer to use in being a wise mind is what we call the window of tolerance. Dan Siegel in his book, *Mindsight*, used the term Window of Meaning to describe what you could tolerate. Phillips and I designed an exercise around that concept for a book called *Betrayal Bond*. The central concept is that recovering people have things (negative stressors) that can trigger them into over-reacting and old behaviors. These triggers often include things like:

- Critical judgments made by spouses and other family members (real or unreal)

- Feeling unheard
- Feeling overwhelmed by many things to do
- High stress at work
- False accusations
- Being talked about behind your back in a negative way
- Lack of appreciation after lots of effort
- Emotional distance and lack of communication
- Constant criticism
- Attacks on your children or family members
- Topics that are volatile or sensitive
- Shameful history that is exposed or referenced
- Making mistakes with inordinate reactions by others
- Certain types of people
- Threatening behavior including violence or sexual assault

The list can actually be quite extensive. The problem is these things can trigger despair, rage, acting out, drug or alcohol relapse, or any other dysfunctional behavior that disrupts your calm center. The Window of Tolerance exercise is way to map out your responses. You list the possible triggers, and then you list the tools and strategies you need when these triggers come up. This helps keep the eye of the storm calm and, as time goes on, you can integrate these new skills into your flow. Integration is really another word for the "wax on, wax off" experience being knitted together as an expert system.

Let us explore this in another way. If you did encounter something that would knock you off the rails, you would have things in place that automatically can keep you on the tracks. Your Inner Observer has plans and strategies in place. After practice, these become automatic or an expert system. So consider the example of the quarterback we used earlier. The initial plan for the play may not work, but the quarterback's success is built on being savvy and quick (without thinking) to make another play that does work. Similarly, the surgeon knows when something goes awry, another procedure can immediately be put in place

The Inner Observer recognizes trouble and has a playbook of proven tool and plans. In many ways, cultivating this part of yourself is preserving the "zone" in which you function best. Recovery practices, then, are essential to defining that larger zone of being at your best, living in a way that matters, and making you happy. You have created part of yourself with the psychological distance not to take the bait of your triggers. That inner wise mind is an essential building block to living in the zone with an integrated flow of those parts of you at your best.

Window of Tolerance Exercise

HYPERAROUSAL
Fight Or Flight

- Anxiety
- Impulsivity
- Emotional reactivity
- Anger/rage
- Insomnia
- Feeling unsafe
- Nightmares
- Hypervigilance
- Overwhelmed
- Rigidity
- Difficulty concentrating
- Addictions
- Obsessive/compulsive thoughts and behaviors
- Over-eating/restricting
- Disabled cognitive processing
- Panic
- Easily startled
- Jumpy

TOOLS FOR REGULATION: What are behaviors that you can engage in to help regulate and return to the window of tolerance?

1. _____
2. _____
3. _____
4. _____
5. _____
6. _____
7. _____
8. _____
9. _____
10. _____

Window of Tolerance

When we are in the window of tolerance we:

1. Are able to self-soothe
2. Stay emotionally regulated
3. Remain flexible
4. Are connected to ourselves (mind, body, emotions)
5. Are able to connect to others

Warning signs of flooding:

Warning signs of flooding:

TRIGGERS: These are the memories, core beliefs, feelings, and body sensations which are connected to the past trauma and have the potential to move us out of the window of tolerance.

1. _____
2. _____
3. _____
4. _____
5. _____
6. _____
7. _____
8. _____
9. _____
10. _____

HYPOAROUSAL
Freeze

- Fatigue
- Depression
- Dissociation
- Not present
- Auto pilot
- Disconnection
- Memory Loss
- Shut down
- Numb
- Disconnected from emotions and body
- Reduced physical movement
- Aches and pains
- Disabled cognitive processing

Exercise 2.1

Trauma and toxic stress lead to over- and under-reaction. Bessel van der Kolk describes this reactivity as "going from stimulus to response without thinking." The Window of Tolerance uses the Inner Observer to keep the calm so there is a way to think about whatever the challenge is. This non-reaction is very important in recovery. Viktor Frankl, in writing about what Holocaust victims had to learn from their experience, states, "Between stimulus and response there is a space. In that space is our power to choose our response. In our response lies our growth and our freedom." The Inner Observer has the power of "pause." In turn, how we react becomes key. Dan Siegel in the book *Mindsight* writes, "Response flexibility harnesses the power of the middle prefrontal region [the "thinking" part of the brain] to put a temporal space between input and action. This ability to pause before responding is an important part of emotional and social intelligence." That temporal space that Siegel describes is the ability to "pause" before reacting.

Earlier, we talked about developing meditation and mindfulness practices. One common element to them all is the ability to experience stillness. An experienced practitioner of mindfulness has learned to go into his or her inner stillness if necessary, even if only for a few moments. This provides a sense of total presence in breath, heartbeat, and whatever else is there. This is also called internal coherence. It is standing in the shower and feeling the hot water, feeling your body, and knowing where you are with yourself. It is not standing in the shower, oblivious to your body, and planning what you want to say at your nine o'clock meeting. As your recovery consciousness evolves, a sign of progress is creating moments of stillness throughout the day.

When you know how to go into your own stillness, how to pause because your window of tolerance is threatened, you will make your best choices. As the promises say, you will know what to do in situations that used to baffle you. So many times, I have heard people speak to their surprise in recovery about not having to even think about relapse now because they respond differently. There occurs a moment where something reminds them of the pre-recovery storm. So they know that they still have challenges, but they realize that the old self-destructive urges are not present. That is a pivotal moment in recovery.

There is an old aphorism repeated often in recovery circles: No matter how long any of us have been on the road of recovery, we all remain the same distance to the ditch. Partly that is true. Partly it is not true. What is accurate is that addiction and mental health issues have changed part of our brain structure. We have no way of erasing or deleting this change once it occurs. It is like a piece of software that can always be plugged in, upgraded, and empowered. Most of us have that software etched into the paradigms and organic structures of our brains, and with that we have the capacity to return to our bargains with chaos.

That said, those who develop skills in resilience, emotional and social self-regulation, and self-awareness will change their brains by installing new software. With this, they have a consciousness of what matters to them, and they dramatically reduce the odds of regression to a set point of dysfunction. So, whether you use the term functional adult, wise mind, or Inner Observer, you need to grow your brain and develop the skills to access this internal ally to help you limit the possibility of relapse. To make growth happen, your Inner Observer must sort out who you really are.

Finding the Transparent Self

Michael Singer writes, "Real spiritual growth happens when there is only one of you inside." His book *The Untethered Soul: The Journey Beyond Yourself* is already a classic description of the cultivation of an Inner Observer. Unobserved brains are never still. They are a tempest of rehearsing conversation, persistent fantasies, obsessing over decisions, conflicting arguments with the self about what is true, or easy, or escapist. In the movie, *The Secret Life of Walter Mitty*, the character loses himself in his fantasy life and gets to the point where he loses contact with reality and lives entirely in his fantasies. We all have experienced some of the Walter Mitty scenario of having a fantasy story that finishes our real story differently. In essence, the fantasies are a way to disassociate from the disappointment and pain of life. Or there is "the grass is greener on the other side," whether it be in a different marriage, job, country, family, school, or economic status. Or we can anesthetize by addictions, or put ourselves in high-risk situations, or lose faith in living further. Or we obsess about betrayals and traumas of our life.

Usually, there is a lot of traffic going through the brain. The point is you are not in the here and now. When not in the present, you ignore the feelings you have and the dark thinking that can trail behind them. When people are present and healthy, profound feelings are owned and felt personally and publicly. They are the real you. Singer describes it as allowing the feelings to wash through you, affect you, and then letting go of them. When they are unexamined, ignored, or suppressed they become encapsulated—and sometimes they become powerful and unseen forces within the self. Singer uses the ancient Sanskrit word *Samskara*, which means the experience and the feelings become an internal cycle of feelings and meaning. These cycles can merge and reinforce others. The result is the self becomes fragmented. The famous family therapist Richard Schwarz wrote about this phenomenon and called it an internal family constellation. A collection of selves that would appear depending on the situation. To make it more complex, family members can bring out different parts of each other, which can lead to a lot of chaos.

The self that is presented to the world is often called the "separated" self. It is based on what the person thinks others want to see or hear. Being agreeable, appearing as more capable than you are, papering over that which is shameful or embarrassing about your family or past, or pretending you are successful when you are not. Or you can understate your accomplishments, avoid conflict, and hide from responsibility or the possibility of making mistakes. The facade that appears can be anything, but at best it is deceptive. If you hold out to the world that something is not really true about yourself, you are certain to experience anxiety.

Pia Mellody created controversy in the early 1980s when she took the position that trauma treatment and accessing those encapsulated feelings had to occur early in addiction treatment. Without that process, patients would not achieve sobriety let alone maturity or congruency. Part of her innovative paradigm was that this was true of all addicts (including alcohol, drugs, gambling, and sex), trauma victims, partners, and adult children. Still, even today, many treatment programs focus on relapse prevention rather than addressing the forces behind the addiction.

Siegel describes uncovering of the "Samskaras" as vertical integration of the brain. The top-down brain (the intentional Inner Observer) explores the bottom-up brain to explore and to process the affect or feelings that have been buried. In the introduction of this book, Paulo Coelho used the words "to disinter the dream," by which he means understanding the layers of messages underlying the misrepresentation of self. This work by the Inner Observer leads to the brain changes described earlier by Doidge: correction of cellular function, neurostimulation, neuromodulation, neurorelaxation, and neurodifferentiation. In short, exposing the secrets, assumptions, and beliefs, and learning how to manage a calm center, allowing your brain the time to process all you unearth and to parse out these unacknowledged cycles with a positive outlook will make a different brain.

The goal is a self that is present and transparent to others. This is a person who tells the truth, keeps promises, and "shows up." When "no" is said, no is what is meant. This person does not keep up appearances; they are willing to be misperceived rather than be deceptive. This person lives on the basis of purpose and intention. This person is clear about what they want or feel called to do. They spend time on things that matter to them. Their bonds with others are transformed because they attract people who share a purpose-driven life. The love and trust they experience helps to make up for earlier deficits. But real relationships and real transparency bring up the problems of paradox.

Searching for the Paradoxes

Key to maintaining calm is recognizing the paradoxes in hard decisions. A paradox occurs when simultaneous truths exist that make it hard to resolve conflicted situations. Recovery at its core is living in paradoxes. For example, the Serenity Prayer is basically a paradox. Sometimes, we simply have to let go because any action on our part will not help and may make it worse. At other times, we can and must take action. Knowing which action is the correct action can be very difficult in real-life situations. Recognition that this is your situation lowers anxiety and taps into your spiritual skill set, which is why the Serenity Prayer is a prayer.

Let's use another example that occurs often in intimate life. In recovery, you learn that you must be true to yourself. You build your inner trust core by being faithful to the commitments you make to yourself. This relationship with self is part of your "covenant" with yourself, which provides the internal cohesion not to sell yourself out. Yet in order to be intimate you have to be true to agreements with your partner and faithful to your relationship. Such fidelity is the essence of "showing up" in intimacy. What happens when being true to yourself is in conflict with the needs of your partner? Here is the struggle of intimacy. All relationships have this struggle. Carl Jung said that this inevitable collision of fidelity to self and faithfulness to others is one of the most spiritual dimensions of being human. Both are true realities. Both are about what matters.

The world is built on these paradoxes. Quantum physics has this problem at its core. Ask for a definition of light, and you will get very different answers because it depends on your perspective. Sometimes light's energy is like waves, other times light acts like bundles of rods. Similarly, in understanding addiction, is it a brain problem? Yes. Is it an intimacy disorder and an attachment disorder? Yes. Is it all about trauma and stress? Yes. Is it primarily a problem of the family? Yes. It all matters in your perspective, as we shall see. Problems occur when there are equally valid ways of looking at things.

In *The Road Less Traveled*, Scott Peck opens with the sentence, "Life is difficult." He is saying that all of us will experience times of trouble. In *The Lord of the Rings*, Frodo Baggins complains to the Wizard Gandalf that he wished he had never got involved with the ring. In fact he regrets even starting the journey. Gandalf responds by saying, "So do we all in difficult times." Gandalf then observes that the test is not the challenges we are given, it is how we handle them. It is not about fairness or justice or our efforts, but how we deal with the hand we have been dealt.

In the book *The Nightingale*, Kristin Hannah describes the story of two sisters who survive World War II in Nazi occupied France. The book begins with a narration of how it all started, by one of the sisters, who is in present-time 94 years old. She makes the observation that "love tells us what we want, but war tells who we really are." The true self has to choose when things get difficult. There is a moment in the tale where one sister has to choose between right and wrong. Nazi officers were billeted in local houses. This sister had a Nazi officer stationed with her. Her husband was in a Nazi POW camp. The Nazi officer is an honorable man. He brings home food and money to help and shares in house responsibilities including childcare. He also is married. Both actually long for the temporary comfort of sleeping together but honor their vows to their partners.

Then he is transferred to the front in the East. She now has a Gestapo agent stationed at her home. He is brutish, violent, and opportunistic. His job is to round up Jewish families and children to send to the camps. He expects to be fed but makes no contribution to the household. As the allies invade, finding all the Jews becomes the Nazi priority. The Gestapo learns that her neighbors were Jews and that she was hiding their children as her own. He propositions her, telling her that if she sleeps with him, he will "overlook" these children. What is the "right" thing in each situation?

When you find yourself in choices where both sides (and sometimes many sides) of a dilemma are valid, recognizing the paradox helps your Inner Observer stay calm rather than letting the brain debate and argue all sides. Ultimately, it is about perspective and what matters. The Inner Observer is the core of the self and the seat of the soul. It will know what to do. In Diana Gabaldon's epic series *Outlander*, she tells the story of a woman who ends up as a physician living in both the twentieth century and then in the eighteenth. The heroine is Claire, who loves Jamie, a Scottish noble who survives the wars in Scotland, after which the two of them go together to America, where they witness the beginning of the French and Indian War. Claire, because her twentieth century medical knowledge and values, finds herself frequently very conflicted in what are very dramatic times. Gabaldon has Jamie say to her in a difficult moment, "If you ever find yourself in the midst of paradox, you can be sure you stand on the edge of truth. You may not know what it is, mind, but it's there." Nowhere have I have found this description of paradox better said.

Recovery often places us on the edge of truth. The edge is hard and sharp at times. Yet, the choices we make do define us. It is the matrices of these choices that bring and define our own spiritual lives. These edges of truth also take us from a life in which our choices are taken from us to a life where we live with intention. Intentionality is the path to living in the zone. Almost always, this helps us to know who we really are and what give our lives spiritual meaning.

In this chapter, we have explored the path of recovery and where we are in this progress. Now is a good time to return to the decision table. Only now, we will organize the table into a search for the paradoxes in your life as part of the edges of your truth and your quests for meaning. Let's divide the table into what we call the core paradoxes:

- **The discernment paradox** — One of the most difficult areas to resolve in human experience is captured in the Stockdale paradox. It is the conflict between the realities to be faced now and the realities of what I want in my life in the future. Reconciling my choices about here and now with my choices about what I want is a conflict we all battle with. This ability to decide will be critical to how well you use this book.

- **The resilience paradox** — Einstein said that the most important decision a person makes is to decide that the universe is friendly. In other words, we must come to believe that there is purpose and meaning to life. The other truth we face is captured in the title of Rabbi Kushner's famous book *Why Do Bad Things Happen to Good*

People? There is the reality of human suffering. At times it is not about fairness or justice, but chance and tragedy. This is the transformation of suffering into meaning. Only your Inner Observer can help you by using perspective on the truth of the moment to move to a higher level.

- **The presence paradox** — Recovery teachers us to be true to ourselves. However, fundamental to recovery is our faithfulness to others. Not always are these in alignment. Do I have to give part of me in order to be with you, is an inevitable reflection and question. This conflict is the one Jung said was the most difficult. To be present requires being true to yourself and true to others. But he also says this is the most spiritual of places a human will experience.

- **The creativity paradox** — We must rest ourselves and literally smell the roses in order to keep ourselves healthy. We are truly then a human being with the emphasis on "being." It is in stillness that our Inner Observer knows the best next decisions and is at its most creative. Having a "zone" in which we can be our most creative requires action, effort, and focus. The risk is becoming a human "doing," where life is all about work, responsibilities, deadlines, and obligations. How we balance these will determine recovery success and a viable window of serenity and zone living.

In the next pages, you will find your decision table divided into four areas of potential conflict. Each is labeled by one of the above paradoxes. Record problems you currently have to resolve by how they fit the paradox in each quadrant. For example, if a major problem is with a loved one in which you are faced with being true to self or to the other, record that issue in that box.

In the middle you will see a circle labeled Inner Observer. Reflect on the problems you have noted. Go into your "wise mind" and rise above the dynamics and the debates that flood your mind. What truths emerge when you do this? What perspectives emerge by looking at your decision table this way? Bring this to your therapist and support groups. Consult with them about amplifying your best solutions.

In all of this, remember what you think about, and reflect in stillness. Then journal and use your tools to protect your window of tolerance and zone. Your behaviors based on reflection will eventually become automatic and part of your expert system. Buddha wrote:

The thought manifests as the word. The word manifests as the deed. The deed develops into a habit. And the habit hardens into character. So watch the thought and its ways with care. And let it spring from love, born out of concern for all beings.

Your Inner Observer and the Core Paradoxes Worksheet

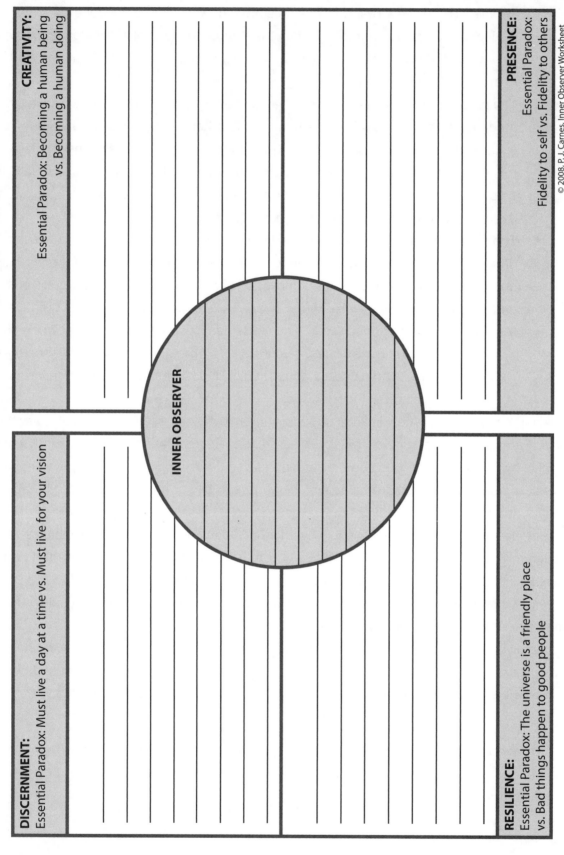

CREATIVITY:
Essential Paradox: Becoming a human being vs. Becoming a human doing

PRESENCE:
Essential Paradox: Fidelity to self vs. Fidelity to others

DISCERNMENT:
Essential Paradox: Must live a day at a time vs. Must live for your vision

RESILIENCE:
Essential Paradox: The universe is a friendly place vs. Bad things happen to good people

INNER OBSERVER

© 2008, P. J. Carnes, Inner Observer Worksheet

Exercise 2.2

Chapter 3 **Vision of a New "Ordinary" World**

The things and conditions we desire to become realities we must first create in thought.

Charles F. Haanel
The Master Key System

In *Recovery Zone I*, we introduced the concept of a Decision Table. Usually, when people start a meaningful sobriety, they have to wade through the wreckage of addiction, immediate changes that have to be made, and the realities of what recovery means. The book also asked what it would take to be in a zone of meaning and resilience. This question was asked because getting sober is not the challenge: staying sober is.

Most addicts are flooded and overwhelmed with all that has to happen. The Decision Table puts it all in one picture. In Renaissance Italy, DaVinci wrote about working with large surfaces as a critical doorway to creative work and problem-solving. He used the metaphor of putting it all on the table while staying focused on the most important elements. In chess, the primary strategy for success is to control the middle of the board. The same is true with recovery. Addicts need to make sure that what is most important is in the "middle" of their life. Priorities, purposes, and intentions are the key aspects of successful lives, as long as they are kept in the middle of the board, so to speak.

In *Recovery Zone I*, the Decision Table became a context to look at how addiction took over your life. Plus, we started the basic mechanics of your emotional intelligence to help you understand the layers of feelings driving your behavior. The purpose was to start reclaiming your relationship with yourself. You made an agreement or covenant with yourself to change how you have been living, and you learned there was much driving your addictive behavior that you were not conscious of. In other words, your recovery journey began by exploring the why behind the why.

One of the basic principles of brain change is to ask oneself if there is a "why" other than the why you tell yourself or others. And we usually find there are many whys as we drill down. This is one of the key tools of the "work" to be done. It is the exploration of what your intent really is so you can become honest with yourself and others about it. By the end of *Recovery Zone II,* you will clearly understand why intention is so important. You will also understand that intention is key to a new life.

Let's use an example of a couple (John and Karen) moving into a new house in the suburbs. What John tells family and friends is that it is time for the couple's three children to have their own bedrooms. That in fact is a true motivator of the move. But there is a why behind that. John also feels very judged by his siblings and compares himself to the siblings who stayed in the family business and as a result have reached more significant levels of affluence. He wants to send the message that his decision to not be part of the family business was right and he is doing well (even though that is not the reality). Another why is that he is the only one of the siblings who has gone through a divorce. He feels the judgment of his siblings, and he (and his wife) feel their reticence to accept her as a "real" spouse. This reluctance to embrace her fully exists despite the fact that all his children were with this woman. Further, his siblings maintain contact with his first wife even though there were no children involved in that marriage.

The final why is the most shameful for John. He is married to a beautiful woman who loves him, and he loves her. However, she spends her workdays with handsome, successful men, some of whom are single and very successful. He knows their financial issues, in terms of lifestyle, have been difficult for her although she has not complained. He desperately wants her to feel that they are living well even though they both know they will probably be living beyond their means. He feels jealous and anxious about losing her. John has never shared with wife or therapist his fears about other men. In this scenario, much therapeutic material exists. Note how key layers exist in terms of the why behind the why.

In the next sections of the book, you will be asked to work with two other tables: the Vision Table and the Legacy Table. Pursuing self-honesty about why will be critical. You have looked internally at the changes you needed to make. The task now is to translate the real you that is emerging into your everyday world. Much like the hero's journey, you have acquired new tools and perspectives. How do you make those work for you in the ordinary world? What does this mean about money and work, relationships and family, lifestyle and purpose?

- You have more to **clean up** in terms of the messes and contradictions you live with.
- To be yourself, what you intend to do needs to be **congruent** with who you are becoming.
- You have to integrate **recovery practice** into your everyday life.
- You have to access your **dreams, passions, talents, and creativity** to be in a zone of life success.
- You have to live a life which fosters **new neural networks** in your brain so you heal the damage that is the physical legacy of addiction.

Plus, like all heroes, you have to sort out what matters to you—or, to use the language of Joseph Campbell or Paulo Coelho, you have to discern what is your "call." Shefali Tsabary describes this as coming to terms with the "great forgetting." In her book, *The Awakened Family*, she describes how families take childhood dreams and talents and bend them or discard them to fit their version of "reality" or family concerns. Parents often think that what is best for the child is an extension of who they (the parents) are. How the parents see themselves or how they think others perceive them affects the standards held out to their children. If they are a doctor or successful in business, they conclude that medicine or business success is what is best for the child. Because of this, the child may lose consciousness of his or her unique gifts, deepest wishes, and most consequential choices. Piercing this veil of the "forgetting" will help you answer the why questions, which will help the real you show up.

In the above example, being in the family business was presumed to be the "right path" for John, and then he chose not to take it. He instinctively knew he would be selling out his soul if he stayed in the business. The family perceived his choice as laziness, craziness, and self-centered. They latched on to John's first wife, who shared their perceptions. His first wife felt betrayed because her "why behind the why" was that she was marrying into money. She was willing to do anything because there was so much money. Yet John intuitively knew that working daily side-by-side with and being continually responsible to his father would come at a high cost. His father was a bully whose jabbing, mean-spirited comments reminded him of childhood when his father drank and battered his mother and all the kids. Besides, the business legend told about his father was a lie. His father did not make the business. He was a trust fund kid who inherited it. He sometimes made terrible mistakes, but money papered over them. No one could ever critique or raise questions. John found family events distressing. To be in daily contact with his father was too high a cost. Still, his first wife did not want him to leave the family business, and John did not handle that well.

Thus, the toxic stress became overwhelming and addiction became a solution for John. His self-esteem was so eroded that he lived in a "Walter Mitty" kind of world—fantasizing and using sex, alcohol, and prescription drugs to escape his bitterness. One day, he realized that all his days were spent in some sort of unreality. He went to a therapist who helped him get into treatment. His mother got his father to pay for treatment. His therapist helped get a program of recovery going for him, and in time he found a new job. Then he met Karen, who provided the blessing of believing in him. He was working now but only for money and he hated that. He wanted more for Karen, the kids, and himself.

Being an addict simply confirmed, in the family's perception, that he lacked character and backbone. The reality is that he was robbed of his dreams, and internally he was gaining clarity about how he lost his purpose and meaning. The Decision Table helped clarify the internal work that had to be done. But the hero has to return and re-enter the ordinary world. The Vision Table is a set of tools to translate intent into reality. That means the external tasks of clean up, congruency, recovery practice, dreams and passions, and neural networks can be seen in a systematic way. They become the portals or windows to envisioning a different ordinary world. **Figure 3.1** represents where we are in the process. The Vision Table and its various tools become a bridging link to the Legacy Table and a map for life.

Internal to External Tasks

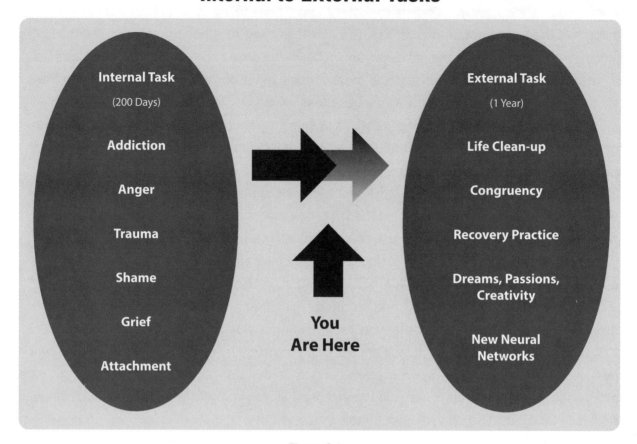

Figure 3.1

Accepting Admiral Stockdale's observation that you must have a sustaining vision is a core element of changing how you live. Your vision contains what matters to you. It is the framework by which you put each day together so that it works for you. At first, you will be practicing components in a very focused way. But ultimately your success will be measured by your resilience and your ability to stay on track. Finally, you will ask, does our vision make you happy and, if so, why?

The hallmarks of flow, living in the zone, and self-mastery are challenging activities that you are good at, and improving your abilities at those activities and other activities matter to you. In Csikszentmihalyi's classic work on flow, he said what comes out of this is happiness. In 1947, Csikszentmihalyi was a graduate student and was struck how in post-war Europe there was little happiness to be found. So, he set out in his life work to explore what makes people happy. A lifetime of his own and others' research confirmed that people are at their best when things came together in a rhythm. He also found that not finding a sense of challenge and meaning is the portal to addictive behaviors. Actress and movie producer Reese Witherspoon has said this synchrony in life seems to her to be like a productive hum. To be in the ordinary world, you need to find when, where, and how your life can "hum."

The place to start is with the end result: happiness. The idea of being happy seems antithetical to a world that seems to have so much woe. From childhood, we are educated to expect life will be hard, and we will need to be disciplined in the face of adversity. Did anyone teach you a class on how to find happiness? In your family, what was the attitude toward people who were active and happy? What did your religious background say about happiness? Even in recovery groups, we read that we have to "trudge" along, which seems different than the joys of fellowship and our progress.

In the following pages, you will explore what we call the Happiness Funnel. The overall design is to generate a list of what makes you happy and what drains your happiness away. The funnel is not intended to be exhaustive or your final vision. Rather, it creates awareness about the sources of your current or potential happiness and prepares you for what we call the Vision Table. Like the Decision Table, the Vision Table will help you determine and parse out what would make a difference in your life. The funnel exercise starts to open you up to what is currently working and not working before you take a seat at the Vision Table.

Plus, you will notice what your Inner Observer sees as the sources of resistance that will have to be faced, along with clues to your true calling.

As you follow the instructions, monitor your reactions and let your true self recognize where the contradictions and paradoxes reside. Remember that addictions thrive where contradictions exist. Contradictions disrupt the flow and are portals to potential relapse. So, you need to know the why behind those parts of your life that conflict with one another. Then you can start to parse out the elements of the deeper things you seek.

To complete the Happiness Funnel, ask yourself what makes you happy. Think of your best moments in the past year. Refine this reflection by listing what makes for happiness each week and each day. Note how much of this is actually connected to your work. Is it too much or too little? The key question remains as to what in your life prevents you from finding happiness or blocks that which makes you happy. Probably you will start to see things you wish to change. In the list provided at the bottom of the funnel, record those thoughts about you must change. A further question is to list what makes you unhappy both in your professional life and your personal life.

Happiness Funnel

List moments, times, and events in the last year that brought you happiness.

List moments, times, and events in each week that bring you happiness.

List moments, times, and events that regularly occur in each day that bring you happiness.

_____   _____   _____

_____   _____   _____

_____   _____   _____

_____   _____   _____

_____   _____   _____

Circle any of the above that are connected with your work or profession.

List those aspects of your life that interfere with the above or block you from that which makes you happy.

_____

_____

_____

_____

Greatest sources of unhappiness in work or professional life

_____

_____

_____

_____

Greatest sources of unhappiness in personal or relationship life

_____

_____

_____

_____

Changes to make:

1. _____
2. _____
3. _____
4. _____
5. _____
6. _____
7. _____
8. _____
9. _____
10. _____

© Patrick J. Carnes, PhD 2018

Exercise 3.1

Happiness Versus Reality?

Most who complete the Happiness Funnel find contradictions. You may have found that some of the things you love doing, you are not doing. Or you find work or other issues in the way. You may also notice that what you spend most of your time doing does not bring you a sense of well-being. Some of that is reality. In a prisoner of war camp, there are no real choices. A chronic illness in yourself or a loved one can become all-consuming. There is no doubt that some realities are irrevocable. Recovery in addiction and family dysfunction brings one to the point of awareness of how much is unchangeable suffering.

The truth for many is resistance. Steven Pressfield uses the word resistance to describe the many ways we sabotage and keep ourselves from realizing our talent and dreams. He authored the novel *Bagger Vance* and produced the movie based on the novel. The story tells of how an extremely talented golfer, through trauma and addiction, lost his motivation and confidence. For Pressfield, it was a metaphor for realizing and regaining your talents. Another of Pressfield's books is the *The War of Art*. In it, he states that any activity that requires talent, commitment, or creative effort hits resistance. He describes this as an inner war that takes many forms. One of the leading forms of self-sabotage that he identifies is addiction. Being lost in the energy it takes to feed an addiction and the loss of reality it takes to stay in the addiction bubble undermines belief in yourself and your dreams and your very real talents. There is that endless cycle of making promises to yourself to change and failing, which erodes all confidence in trusting yourself to finish anything.

There are many paths that this resistance can take. Past traumas create poor coping and lack of confidence under stress. Surrounded by people who believe what you want is impossible or unreachable will undermine your "call." Burying yourself in activities and business with no time to take stock of where you are is an endless treadmill of resistance. The more pie plates in the air, the better. Add in taking care of everyone's needs but your own plus major financial stress, and you have a recipe for losing yourself. Recovery means letting go of "old rabbit holes" that go nowhere.

Once in recovery, you start reclaiming, inch by inch, your reality. You learn about how your distorted thinking was part of your addiction. You become clear that you kept using solutions that did not work for you. The picture of how you became addicted informs you further about the things you do not want to repeat. As the dust starts to clear, you make decisions that stabilize your life. Yet, you ask, what do I do now? You hear about answering some "call," but you do not feel you know what that is for you.

As stated already, a path to start on is to notice what makes you happy and what interferes with your happiness. You start remembering your early childhood and what inclinations you had that were, for whatever reason, contained or put off-limits. The next step is to open your mind to re-engineering your life to be and do the things that will feed your soul. An essential portal for this "recovery" of ourselves is the Vision Table.

The Vision Table parallels the Decision Table in *Recovery Zone I*. You will remember that on the Decision Table we used the approach of Leonardo Da Vinci of making a "mind map" by putting everything on one very large surface so you can make sense of it in its entirety. Recall how you put all the decisions you were facing in front of you so you could prioritize the most immediate and pressing issues as you initiated recovery. At the beginning of this volume, you revisited the Decision Table and laid your issues out in terms of hard choices and paradoxes. It was the same format, but your Inner Observer provided a different perspective.

The Vision Table is similar. You write down all that you want in your life. This includes those things you want to achieve, experiences you dream of, things that make you happy, relationships you want to have. Above all, you should list the activities, events, and processes that really matter to you. You must set aside the "voices of no" that cry out to you that the things you want are impractical, unrealistic, and impossible. The question here is, when your life is over, what would have made it worthwhile? Ultimately, this thought leads to the question of what you wish your legacy to be.

As stated earlier, in chess, a primary strategy for winning is that you must control the middle of the board. From this perspective, you track where the important current and potential moves might occur. You first used the Decision Table to sort what you needed to focus on in the immediate future (what needs to be in the middle of the worksheet for you). Now you have examined some of the dilemmas in your life. Contained in this knowledge are the truths of who you are and who you wish to become.

Controlling the middle of the board in your Decision Table is seeing where the best moves are. The Decision Table is always a tool available to you when overwhelmed by the choices before you. This strategy is now a viable part of your recovery. The Vision Table allows for the same comprehensive focus and sorting but with the perspective of your remaining life and of your long-term recovery. Focusing your vision on your "best" moves is critical to who you are.

Your Vision Table

Vision work is not new. Aristotle observed that humans think best in pictures. Both Greek and Roman thinkers noted that what you pictured in your mind often found its way into reality. In more contemporary times, it was the business community that really focused on the power of visualization. An oft repeated story relates the famous proposition made to Napoleon Hill by Andrew Carnegie, a pioneer in 19th century business. Carnegie said that he would introduce Hill to the greatest business innovators, such as Henry Ford, and technology builders like Thomas Edison and Alexander Bell if Hill would write a book so that every person could build their dream. Carnegie himself had a vision of a network of colleges and junior colleges throughout the country making the United States the center of innovative thinking. Coupled with this very large-scale thinking, he wanted a book on how average people could change their lives and build their dreams. Carnegie believed that any person who was willing to work could build and innovate no matter how big or small. So he challenged Hill to write the book, but to do so without funding. Hill accepted.

Hill took on the assignment, interviewing some of the most accomplished people in the world with the result that these giants of success shared one common strategy: real change occurred through vision. If you read Hill's books or listen to his tapes made in the 1920's, the instructions are quite specific and similar to instructions modern psychologists use. As I listen to Hill today, I am amazed at how comprehensive and precise his writing was without all the new knowledge we have today about the brain and change.

Hill was followed by Charles Haanel, who developed a "master key" system based on the same concepts. Almost a hundred years later, there are many investment, development, and science companies who state that they are a "master key company," meaning they use Haanel's concepts on vision as part of their operations and creative planning.

Today, of course, we know more about why vision systems work. For example, psychologist Wayne Dyer showed that Olympic athletes who visualized their performances performed better than those who did not. When you picture yourself performing complex moves, the neurons that fire in the brain are the same neurons used during actual competition. So, where did Dyer pull his strategy called "visual motor rehearsal"? He borrowed it from NASA, where visual motor rehearsal was a core piece of training for astronauts. Today, visualization in health care is used in diverse areas including pain management, trauma treatment, and sports medicine. Brain researchers, using brain imaging, can identify how visualization activates various parts of the brain to create a spatial map, which empowers performance.

The case this book makes is recovery is built on a zone that does not occur without a guiding vision. It is the same message of Admiral Stockdale, Victor Frankl, and Mihaly Csikszentmihalyi. Leaders who have explored the value of meditation and mindfulness also agree that visualization works, mostly because of the power of explicit intention. In the integration of top-down thinking and bottom-up thinking, intentionality is critical to changing habits and growing abilities. In recovery, being intentional about intimacy and meaning expands our consciousness so we operate out of our values and self-regulation, and not from an "out of control" reward process. To do that, we also have to be mindful of what matters and what makes us happy.

There is also the matter of quantum physics. We know that all matter is really energy. We human beings are more responsive to vibrational energy than we think. Our sense of self and our thinking embedded in our story we tell ourselves is the electric energy flowing through our neurons. Without that "soul," those neurons are just atoms and molecules. Those patterns and ideas that float on the grid of our brain are about energy. Rhonda Byrne writes about what some have termed the Law of Attraction:

> Our job as humans is to hold on to the thoughts of what we want, make it absolutely clear what we want, and from that we start to invoke one of the greatest laws of the Universe, and that is the law of attraction. You become what you think about the most but you also attract what you think about

The common denominator of those who write about intention is the alignment of energy so it is consistent with flow in life and fits with your personal "call." That energy appears to be a two-way street in that what we focus on calls us to make that happen, while synchronicity starts to occur helping the reality to be. When *Out of the Shadows* first appeared, it had the title *Sexual Addiction*. As a new author, I of course was nervous how it would be received. Even in my personal and professional network people worried and were even antagonistic about it. My first workshop on the book was in Washington, D.C. I expected it to be filled with critics. Instead, the attendees were either therapists who had a patient for whom they wanted to find more help, or people who had the problem themselves. It was an exhausting but rewarding experience. The fact that I could offer help to people who needed it validated being in the storm of doubt.

On the flight home, the last thing I wanted was to talk more about sexual addiction. The man who sat next to me, however, asked me what I was doing in Washington. I made an ambiguous comment about work. He pursued the conversation by asking what I did. I told him I was a psychologist and I'd just done a workshop on sex addiction. I added that I had a new book on the topic. He looked at me and said, "I know this book, and in fact, I have it with me." He pulled it out of his case. He went on to tell me that he was a publisher, thought that it was a good and very important book, but that my publisher had made a very significant marketing error that could bury the book. By titling it *Sex Addiction*, we'd made the book difficult to buy because it was like an admission of guilt. He said that he'd actually thought of calling the publisher and suggesting retitling it. He asked me for my editor's phone number and for my permission to call.

He was true to his word. Three days later my publisher called to tell me that they as a staff had spent a whole day talking to my fellow traveler by phone and that they recommended retitling the book *Out of the Shadows: Understanding Sexual Addiction*. They asked if I was comfortable with the change. This was in a day when such a change meant huge typesetting and marketing costs. I was amazed at the effort and expense they were willing to go through to help me. I immediately told them yes. The change made the book a bestseller over time. For me, it was a spiritual synchronicity. I had a workshop that validated my vision of writing the book. Despite the misgivings of those around me, it was the right thing to do. Then what were the chances of me sitting next to perhaps the one person who could propel the book to success?

We use the term "call" based on Joseph Campbell's scenario of the hero's journey, but our life is a collage of calls, some are quite big while others can seem minor, important only to you. Mindfulness pioneer and author Jon Kabat-Zinn tells of his father building by his own hands a boat in which he and his whole family sailed around the world. That trip shaped Kabat-Zinn and the rest of the family profoundly. Then his father, in his spare time, started building small wooden models of various sailing vessels. Late at night, Kabat-Zinn would sneak down the stairs overlooking his father's workshop and watch his father focus on building ship models. His father was happy and in the zone, which helped Kabat-Zinn understand how focus could be meditative. That same focus created a major adventure that bonded the whole family, but also became a rewarding and meaningful focus hobby for his dad.

In recovery, clarity of intention is critical. Intention guides and shapes our lives. The Vision Table helps with the sorting out of priorities. It does that by allowing you freedom of context. So, think about something that all of us have done. Have you ever gotten up to get something in another part of your house, and when you walked into the room you thought it was in, you forgot what you were looking for? This does not mean senility is setting in early. What happens is that from the brain's point of view, you changed perspective. You are now in a different context. What you meant to get was clear in the room you left, but you lost focus on it when your perspective changed. A helpful strategy is to touch the doorframe before you enter the other room to keep your focus on your quest for what you need. Otherwise, you must return to where you were to remember, "Oh yeah, I was looking for...." Thus, perspective can affect your intent.

Another example is Einstein's observation about relativity and trains. If you are on a train and you walk from the sleeping car to the dining car, it parallels how we experience life a moment at a time. Life is experienced as moving from one car to another. But if you were on a hill overlooking the train passing by, you would see the whole train at once. In this case, you would be looking at your life as a whole. When your life is complete and over, what does it look like. How did you use your time?

In 2005, I was hospitalized with a disease called Valley Fever. The infestation was in my lungs, and it is often fatal. I remember waking and being barely able to open my left eye. The faces of my daughter Erin and my wife, Suzanne, were inches from mine. It was an instant reaction on my part. I realized I did not want to go and I would fight to stay. It was an ordeal that changed me.

As I walked out of the Mayo Hospital in Scottsdale, Arizona, there was this lovely garden. I had walked past it many times without stopping to notice. This time, I stared at it with a deep resolve. I had spent so much time doing things that really did not matter. I was mired in busyness. I had not done things I desperately wanted to do, and the time-wasting activities were like Styrofoam. They took up space but had no substance. At times, I did not notice the beauty of the world because I was not present to it. My resolve at that moment was not to spend time on anything that did not matter. My perspective had changed. When you show up in the moment, you start to align yourself with the energy of the world and the universe. Many meditation programs and religions tell us to start meditating by just focusing on a flower. Think of Christ's urging to look at the lilies in the field.

Earlier, we mentioned Randy Pausch's classic book *The Last Lecture* about having just one year to live and wanting to give one more lecture (which today is a classic YouTube video). In the book he talks about how everything changed in terms of what mattered. I urge you to take the same journey. Consider your life. If you were told you had twelve months to live and that you'd have your physical abilities for only nine months, how would you spend your time? Many things probably would cease to be a priority.

The Vision Table allows for multiple perspectives. This maximizes your ability to focus your intent. You can focus on a year, five years, or a lifetime. You will learn that visualization can even be a rehearsal for a difficult conversation that day and how you intend that experience to go. It can be a rehearsal for a speech you will be giving in three months. It can also help you learn to track your ideas and maximize effectiveness. There is quite a lot of literature on how to develop these skills and the management of your focus. The bibliography provides a key reading list that you may wish to explore as you go forward.

The Vision Process is important in recovery because good recovery means discovering or rediscovering what matters, what is rewarding, and what makes us happy. At the same time, we need to focus on our recovery practice so it becomes second nature to us (i.e., an expert system that raises our brain function and quality of life). In fact, we need to grow our brain by creating new neural networks that work for us. Finally, there are changes and things to clean up from our addiction life so we do not carry them forward. This all takes about a year.

The Vision Table can help organize and implement that work. **Figure 3.2** is a visual graphic of what we have done and need to finish.

Vision Table

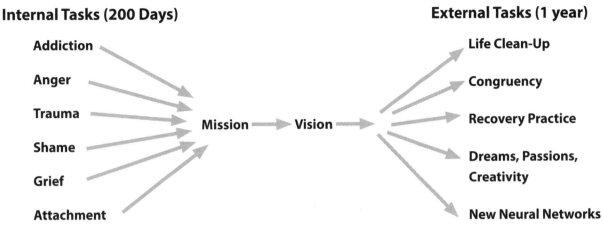

Figure 3.2

Start with a large, empty sheet of artist paper. Draw a circle in the center about ten inches in diameter. Now think of all the things you want in your life. Draw some symbol of each one that seems important to you. Please do not use words. You do not have to be a great artist, but do try to draw details that will help you remember what that symbol represents. The goal is that each symbol represents your desires, talents, and happiness. This may take hours or even days. As you do this, it starts a mental process that keeps refining and adding to the picture. When finished, there is an array of options to stimulate your thinking and planning.

Spend some time reflecting on your work. Ask yourself what symbols are the most important. Circle the ten symbols that are most important to you and that you could achieve in the next five years. Choosing that ten does not rule out others. You're simply identifying those that mean the most. In the middle of the circle, record a list from one to ten. Now write out what steps you will have to take in the next year to make those ten key symbols real in your life.

A second stage that many use (and that your therapist may ask you to do) is to do a poster board. To start, find a large piece of "tag" board or poster board (available at any office supply store). Then assemble a variety of magazines, newspapers, or even pictures off the internet. Find pictures that fit your most important symbols. The advantage of this approach is that the images are more concrete, which aids your visualization.

For example, if I ask you to have a fantasy about buying a new car, you could do that relatively quickly and simply. But you might struggle if I asked you to fantasize all of the following steps.

- Picture yourself walking into a car showroom
- Walking through all the models on display

- Finding one you like and walking around it and noticing the quality of build, design, and color
- Sitting in the driver's seat and smelling the "new car" smell
- Playing with and noting the features and gadgets on the dashboard
- Talking with the salesperson and staff about the purchase, costs, and delivery
- Taking delivery and allowing the feeling of it now being yours to sink in
- Starting the engine and driving out of the dealership

In effect, the fantasy has much more detail. The richer the detail, the more effective the visualization.

Also, you can change up how you place yourself in the visualization. You can imagine yourself in it or you can watch yourself in it. You can focus on different pieces of the process. Most important is to have the feelings that occur as if you had actually experienced it. Tracking your feelings is critical to the bottom-up integration of your intent, and important not to neglect. The advantage of cut-out pictures is they are richer in detail, making you more precise in the picturing of what you want. Going through the process of making a collage of pictures may also impact what you select and the priority you give it. It may in fact be different than when you did the mind map of it.

The use of pictures in expressing your intention is very important. One of my desires in life was to find a mahogany boat from the late 1940s, such as the boat that appeared in the movie *On Golden Pond*. I found an eight-by-eleven picture of a 1948 Chris-Craft glistening in the sun as it cut through the water. Each year I would staple it to the front of my daily journal and planner. It took about five years, but I found that identical boat in a barn forty miles west of Minneapolis. The farmer had used it to store wheat. Of course, the first task was to dig out all the little kernels of wheat. Then we had to clean it, refinish it, get it to stay afloat, and finally to start. Today, more than 70 years after it was built, it runs smoothly and is a joy to my family. And in many ways, I have that picture to thank. That picture kept me focused on the search.

Vision Table Worksheet

You may use this space below to draw out or paste images of your Vison Table with as much detail as you can provide.

Exercise 3.2

In visualization and mindfulness, when what you intend appears, they call that manifestation. But just because you picture something does not make it happen. The intent and the focus are critical. Planning and effort are also essential. Jack Canfield and Mark Hansen are the architects of the *Chicken Soup for the Soul* series. They tell the story of taking their first book to over eighty publishers, all of whom turned them down. Finally, when they found a publisher who got the concept to do the series, they got a contract for the first book. They vowed to each other that in the first year they would do four radio shows a day to get the book promoted. This involved incredible sacrifice, but they kept to their plan. Today over 250 Chicken Soup titles exist, over 100 million copies are in print, and the books have been translated into 46 languages.

Wayne Dyer, who perhaps more than anyone else brought visualization into modern psychology as well as the business world, made an important observation. He noted that falling short of your visualization can also be a lack of inner coherency. He observed that if you have unresolved personal darkness of some sort that you hold on to, it will be hard to transform your desires and dreams from vision into reality. As part of our process, you were asked to look at shame, grief, trauma, and other aspects of the dark side of yourself. Before finishing, the Recovery Zone process will push for clarity and currency in your intent. The unfinished and unattended must be part of integrating vision into powerful focus. It is an important element of alignment with the energy that is you floating on the grid of your brain.

Every time I write a book, I visualize holding it, looking at the cover, hearing the reactions of readers and having that feeling that "I did it." Every author struggles with resistance, and I certainly do. It helps me to see people use the materials and test things out. But I still have to get it done. Every book brings me to my knees sooner or later, and for sure the *Recovery Zone* series has been no different. In that sense, a book is like any other ordeal.

On the next pages, we ask you to focus on your four most important goals. Draw a detailed picture in each quadrant. Share with your support group and therapist your process of selecting these four image targets to visualize. Discuss what truths reside within each if you are to make them manifest.

Top Four Vision Table Priorities

Vision priority one:

Vision priority two:

Vision priority three:

Vision priority four:

Exercise 3.3

Optional Assignment: Write a Letter To Resistance

You may find that resistance will find clever ways to undermine your true intentions and desires. If you find that happening, it may serve you well to address resistance directly. Write a letter to resistance about how you see it undermining your best efforts. You will have other opportunities in our process, but if you see the efforts of resistance already, face it directly now! Read your letter to those you trust.

Exercise 3.4

Chapter 4 **The Financial and Work Disorders**

In our time and culture, the battlefield of life is money. Instead of horses and chariots, guns and fortresses, there are banks, checkbooks, credit cards, mortgages, salaries, the IRS. But the inner enemies remain the same now as they were in ancient India or feudal Japan: fear, self-deception, vanity, egoism, wishful thinking, tension, and violence.

Jacob Needleman in *Money and the Meaning of Life*

I started a family-oriented addiction program in the mid-1970s. The program was unusual at the time because it took all members of the family down to age six. There were many skeptics, especially as a service of a classic surgically oriented hospital. With time, however, it grew, and we extended services beyond alcoholism and drugs to include eating disorders, sex addiction, and consultation. We received a grant from the National Center for Child Abuse and Neglect and had 150 families in ongoing programs. Plus, we were one of the primary contractors hired to design Family Support Centers for military families.

My salary for this was $43,000 a year. I was married with four children. I had a Ph.D. and knew that a fresh graduate with a master's degree in hospital administration and no experience started at $150,000. One afternoon, I was sitting in a board meeting for our program and realized that I was no longer happy running the program, and that I needed to stop.

I resigned at the end of the year, telling everyone who asked that I was taking a year off. There was controversy about that because many people believed I had been recruited to another hospital. The truth was that I somehow intuitively knew I needed to stop and take a break. Another truth was I did not know if I had enough funds to last six months, let alone a year, so I needed to improve my situation financially. With the program, I had done what I set out to do seven years earlier, and now my family needed me and I was no longer excited about going to work. I had a book I wanted to work on, but no specific plans.

My first few days of freedom were busy, as I focused on setting up a home office. I also started organizing my book process. Then the pain hit me. I was having feelings of loneliness and thoughts about how replaceable I was. So much of my identity was wrapped up in being in charge of the program and all the people who worked there. Who was I without all that "busyness" around me? I joked that now I had to make my own coffee and run off my own copies. Like many jokes, mine contained more truth than merriment. The bottom line was that my self-worth was tied to being the founder of a program and a leader of 250 employees. Without all that activity, who was I really?

I thought maybe a change of scene would help, so my family and I took a trip to Palm Springs. In order to appreciate how I felt at the end of our trip, you would need to know that at that time there was a TV series called *Kung Fu*. In the show, the hero (a Shaolin monk played by David Carradine) was traveling in the early wild west. He was also an expert in martial arts. In each episode, there was a moment when some profound wisdom story was told. Periodically, the monk would flash back to his youth with his master at the monastery. The master always called him "grasshopper" and taught him some symbol or story relevant to the episode. The master always seemed to come out of some sort of mist before imparting his wisdom.

So, the first morning of our vacation, it was misty out. But I was an inveterate runner and, undaunted, started stretching for my morning run. As I was warming up, a figure came out of the mist. An older man, perhaps 65 or older. "Do you mind if I join you?" he asked. I told him he was welcome and I would enjoy the company. The feeling was like two old friends who had run together for years.

The first thing I noticed is that the pace picked up. I realized that although maybe thirty some years older than I, he was in better shape. The next thing I noticed was that being with him was like being with someone whom I knew from long experience to be trustworthy—even though we'd just met. Within a few minutes, he said, "So how are you doing today?" With that, I poured my heart out about the whole hospital story, my identity issues, my uncertainty about what I was to do, and even my joke about making my own coffee and copies.

He nodded and listened. And we continued to speed up. Then he said, "I have done that seven times. I started an oil company, a publishing firm, and five other ventures, and have felt what you are feeling almost every time." Then he looked at me and said, "Do you want to know what the rules are?" I was immediately transported into the *Kung Fu* series. It was like he'd asked, "Grasshopper, do you want to know the rules?" Still, I was sort of taken aback that there were rules. The best I could do was to nod my head and say "yes."

He started by saying to never do anything longer than five to six years. Any time he'd stuck around longer than that, he regretted prolonging the experience. His second piece of advice was to never make a change like this without taking a year off in between because you often do not know what is going to come to you.

You need to let your mind make sense of what you just did and create clarity about your next effort. He told me the temptation is always there to shorten the time off, and every time he'd done so, he realized it was a mistake. He also said it's okay to return to the same type of business or even the same company, but the role and challenges have to be different. He also told me that halfway through my year off, it would become clear what I was called to do next.

After that run, I never saw him again. He returned into the mists of masters. I had no way to trace him or even thank him. However, this grasshopper was listening. What he said to me has helped me repeatedly over the last forty years. The first lesson I learned was that writing another book was the right task for me. By April, several projects emerged, and with them came some income. First, I was commissioned by Bantam to write *Don't Call It Love*. By the following January, I helped to open the first inpatient unit for sex addiction at Golden Valley Health Center, a 110-acre medical complex west of Minneapolis. And I found that I loved what I was doing.

Through this experience, I also learned that some things are constant. Exercise is constant. Writing and meditation are too. Music fits in this category as well. However, the one year off fits the process of brain change we described in Chapter One. Neuro-relaxation is key according to Doidge. We must allow the top-down, bottom-up flow to integrate our learnings. Wayne Mueller in his book *Sabbath* writes about finding moments of rest and stillness throughout the day and even taking a day or week to do the same. The one year off concept, he compared to the farmer who learns to let fields lie fallow periodically to get maximum production over time.

When I bring this up to patients, there is an immediate resistance. The most oft cited reason is, "I have to get back to work." Next, they bring up money issues. So I ask if they had a heart attack and were told not to work, could they find a way to survive financially. I further ask if their family knew that they had a choice to do what they wanted versus what was best financially, what would their family advise them to do. Then I remind them that by entering recovery, they have already begun the process of living a happier life, and their family is all for it. Lastly, I point out to those that have made plenty of money and have been incredibly "busy" as they did this, that they also have left a trail of hurt and pain with their addiction.

There is a joke on the Gentle Path campus about the "Dr. Carnes year off club." However, those that do take the time report that taking the one year was pivotal to changing their lives. If money is an issue, there are certainly ways to reduce activity and give yourself the gift of time. I also ask patients if they have enough money to go a year without working. If not, it is a worthy priority to have that level of cushion. Even when there is not enough for a whole year, people will nearly always find the money for the rest. Usually, that person sees the benefits and figures it out.

A very important lesson for all of us is to create a life with multiple streams of income. That being done, if you wanted to stop, you could. For sure, that is another worthy goal, and with thought there are numbers of ways to make that happen. But it needs to be part of your plan.

I often hear people say that they feel that they do not have a "call." My guess is that they have not drilled through the layers of other people's expectations to remember their early desires. For that, they need time.

The quest for a zone of living that brings happiness and supports recovery inevitably requires a self-examination of how we work and what we do with money. As we have learned, addiction thrives in excess and deprivation. It is no surprise that these two extremes would be woven into our pre-recovery lives and require changes critical to making recovery work. The following self-assessment asks a series of questions about financial and work styles. Not all questions will apply and not all categories will fit. Read the questions carefully, however, scanning for issues that might apply to you. When they do, record where you see problem areas and note examples of how your balance and your life have been affected. In each category, there is a space provided in which you can record what your family taught you about work and financial management.

Your therapist may have access to an instrument called the Money And Work Adaptations Stress Index (MAWASI). If so, after you have completed your self-assessment questions it can be very useful for your therapy to take this validated and comprehensive survey. Other assessments can be also extremely useful at this point, so ask your therapy team about the options. However, first start with the following questions about your money and work patterns.

Financial and Work Disorders

Spending — In what ways has buying been a solution to emotional upset or anxiety? Have you obsessed about things you wished to buy? Have you experienced a pattern of binge and purge by purchasing and then returning merchandise, land, or businesses? Have you acquired just to acquire? Do you have trouble knowing what is enough? Or, how much to spend on others? Has your spending jeopardized your financial viability? Have you consistently spent more than you could afford? Spent money on self-destructive things and not on life enhancing things (because you could not afford it!)? Is compulsive spending connected with other addictions?

What has been the impact of your family on your spending patterns?

Debting, Hoarding — Do you find yourself putting off things you really need because "they are too expensive"? Buy poor quality merchandise to save money? Go without your needs being met and feeling superior or safe? Do you stockpile goods that you will never use? Have you ever had so significant a debt you felt constantly impoverished? Have you seen skimping as virtuous? Have you had significant resources and still did not take care of your needs? Do you consistently neglect yourself? Has anyone called you miserly? Do you feel deprived and therefore vulnerable to other addictions?

How has your family impacted your ability to care for yourself financially?

Compulsive Working — Do you find it difficult not to be at work? Do you return home and start working on home projects? Do you have periods of rest when you are focused on a goal or task? Does your work involve any of the following: High excitement and intensity? Public visibility? Power over others? Risk and stress? Long hours? The real issue for many is the inability to give up the mood alteration of work. Is your work a way to avoid problems, alter mood, and escape from family issues? Does your work involve caretaking of others and has that become compulsive? If people did not know what you do, would you still do it? Is your work solely about money? If you have other addictions, are they connected with your own work style?

What lessons did you learn in your family about working?

Compulsive Underearning/Underachievement — Are you significantly overqualified for what you do for a living? Are you not working to your full potential? Do you struggle with procrastination and inability to get things done? Do others in your immediate family have success, and achievement somehow eludes you? Does fear of failure paralyze you? Do you find yourself fantasizing about some windfall such as winning the lottery or some job falls in your lap that solves your problems? Are you compulsively working at unrewarding, mind-numbing tasks? Does underearning affect other addictions or mental health issues such as depression?

What did your family teach you about achievement, work, and duty that keeps you stuck?

Money Obsession — Are you preoccupied with money or the acquisition of money? Do you worry about money you have? Do you obsess about your money and worry you do not have enough—when in fact by most standards you do? Do you spend an inordinate amount of time checking accounts, e-trading, or reviewing your portfolio? Do you obsess about retirement and having enough? Does obsessing about money affect any other obsessions?

What did your family teach you about money as a solution to life problems?

Money Avoidance — Do you have money and feel guilty, resentful, or fearful about what you have? Have you consciously rejected any signs of affluence in your life? Are you skeptical of people's motives if they have money? Do you base your lifestyle so as not to be tied to financial concerns? Do you have difficulty managing your finances such as problems with records, balancing checkbook, or getting taxes filed? Do you avoid money issues to explore higher or spiritual values? Do you feel inadequate around money matters and simply ignore money problems until they become a crisis? Do you have other people handle your finances so you will not have to deal with them? Do you manage your own personal accounts successfully? How has your attitudes toward money affected other mental health issues such as self-esteem and lifestyle balance?

What lessons did your family provide which might make you avoid money issues?

Exercise 4.1

Deferred Life Plan

In Randy Komisar's book *The Monk And The Riddle*, the author refers to the "Deferred Life Plan." Basically, this is a process where a person feels they have to do what they have to do, and then they get to do what they want.

Do you find yourself saying that when "_____" happens, then I will be able to do what really matters to me? In other words, are you deferring life until you have enough money, an inheritance, or meet some other threshold?

Make a list of what you currently are deferring that would make your life more fulfilling.

1. _____

_____

2. _____

_____

3. _____

_____

4. _____

_____

5. _____

_____

6. _____

_____

7. _____

_____

8. _____

_____

9. _____

_____

10. _____

_____

Exercise 4.2

Stress Maker II

You will remember that you were asked in *Recovery Zone I* to draw a picture of your stress maker. The point of the exercise was to show that trauma victims and those that live in toxic stress create ways to stay stressed. The hormones that flood the brain when in extreme challenge are hard to give up. So these individuals will re-create situations similar to the original trauma or bring other sources of chaos and drama into their lives to continue the hormonal influx of neurochemicals.

Michael Singer, in *The Untethered Soul: The Journey Beyond Yourself*, refers to this process as collecting Kamsaras—cycles of pain and fear that you recycle. When you are addicted to your own intoxicating hormones and enzymes, the idea of a year off can seem very threatening. Or worse, pursuing the concept of meditation and the seeking of personal stillness can be dismissed as useless or unachievable or unrealistic. Actually, such dismissive attitudes could be a layer of unacknowledged terror.

Hopefully, when you drew the picture of you as making your own stress it helped make explicit the trauma reenactments that partnered with your addiction or mental health issues. In *Recovery Zone I* you also completed your trauma egg. Your therapist may have asked you to also explore the *Post Traumatic Stress Index—Revised* (PTSI-R) or other measures of traumatic patterns. Those drawings become powerful metaphors of the work to be done. Now it is time to integrate your growing awareness of your internal world with how you have handled money and work. Look over all the categories you just completed and integrate that information with how you have used them in dysfunctional ways to serve the Kamsaras of your life.

A good example comes from Debtor's Anonymous (DA). More than anyone else, this fellowship has pioneered in compulsive underearning (not using your abilities) and debting (using debt as a way to keep oneself in chaos and stress). This is the origin of the well-known phrase, "fear of the mailbox." In other words, work and money become inordinate sources of stress.

A personal example for me came when one of my daughters went to treatment. During family week, the treatment staff had our family do a family sculpture. My daughter positioned me walking around and focused on the ceiling while repeating the phrase, "I have so much to do." That image was both very painful and very accurate. A constantly overwhelmed state was a good way not to notice what was going on around me. So that image rippled through my understanding of what I was presenting to the world. My daughter gave me a great gift that day.

This assignment asks that you further explore how the work and money adaptations you have identified might look like to others. Draw a picture of yourself portraying how you bring excessive stress on yourself. Remember that when you did your original Recovery Zone map, you drew ways that you could overstress yourself with some activities and avoid challenge, which brings other stressors to yourself.

You can use the space provided in the book, but, as always, bigger sheets of paper provide more space to work with. Try to capture your learning about both work and money. Remember the power of image as your family would see you.

Doing this now will give you a picture of the ordinary world as you have lived it. You now have the choice of knowing what you do not want. You also have a choice to start using your vision skill to discover what "yes" is.

Stress Maker II – Work and Money

Draw a picture or pictures that portray some of the features that affect your career and financial success. Remember, this is not about being a great artist. Rather, pictures and symbols become another way the brain integrates learning. You may also wish to add dimension to the drawing by depicting how you learned to handle work and money. What was your family's impact? Further integration occurs as you show your work to others, including your therapist, who may notice additional connections. Remember, you can use large sheets of paper to do this.

Or you can do your immediate versions in the book and a more elaborate version on larger paper.

Stress Maker II – Work and Money

Exercise 4.3

Purpose and Call: What Your Talents Can Tell You

There is no part of the brain in which we can cut out a part and say that "this is you." There is no part of the brain in which the "self" resides. However, there are few things more indicative of who you are than how you spend your time. Also, spending your time in ways that are rewarding, challenging, and meaningful is indicative of your mental health and your resilience. Without those ingredients shaping your "zone" or flow, successful recovery will remain elusive.

Donald Super is regarded by many as the father of industrial psychology. For sure, he moved the goal posts when thinking about careers and how people invest their energy and time. He described work as a constantly changing process over the lifespan. People learn from their experience and circumstances and those life happenings shape them developmentally into the "self," or who they become. This parallels the "grasshopper lesson" from earlier in this chapter. Put another way, experts predict you will probably have seven major jobs in a lifetime. These jobs may be in the same industry but most likely they will not. They may be in the same profession, such as medicine, but they will shift in terms of focus, innovation, administrative responsibility, and scientific breakthroughs. What attracts you at age 20 will be different at 40 and 60. Digitalization is also changing how we do a lot of things. In short, your work and life experience will change.

That means, in turn, that recovery is a major life recalibration in terms of where our energies and time go. There is a fuse that is lit with recovery and none of us know how long we have. All of time is precious. More than likely, you will have other moments of recalibration such as you are now experiencing. Nancy Duarte, who's graphic that we used earlier to describe the hero's journey, repeatedly makes the point that we will often repeat the whole process (denial, mentor, new special world, special skills, and re-entry into the ordinary world). This may occur many times in our lives. At this writing, I am in my mid-70s and I wonder at all the changes that have occurred in the last eighteen months. My self-talk goes: "Now that I have all these things out of the way, what will I finally do with my life?" What all this reminds me of is the classic science fiction fantasy by Brandon Sanderson, *The Stormlight Archive*, a tale of talented knights working to renew a devastated planet. One of their guiding phrases is, "It is the journey, not the destination." This is kind of like Frodo when he trepidly took the ring in *The Lord of the Rings*, although he did not know the way.

This process of our changing lives and keeping our talents and skills matched with what matters requires a different concept in order to mobilize all of our brain's abilities. An example exists in how the military handles complex logistics. The problem is matching resources in crisis or urgent situations. For example, they create what is called a motor pool. In it are a wide range of vehicles ranging from jeeps, cars, and trucks to more specialized vehicles like armored personnel carriers and Humvees. In other words, they have an inventory of specialized vehicles and capabilities that could be called upon at any moment.

Similarly, our brains have an inventory of special talents and interests that can be called upon in a moment's notice. We may not even think of them as relevant to career, happiness, or focus. Yet the reality is each of us has an inventory of "expert systems" that could empower us. In order to think about this inventory, we need to think about our lives and our expertise in the same manner as when we used tables for decisions and focus. Amongst our talents exist another why underneath the why. In our constantly evolving history, skill sets reside underneath categories we do not see as currently relevant—or even as expert systems. This "brain pool" needs to be disinterred for the rapidity of changes in our lives.

One of my most embarrassing moments professionally was my first time ever in front of an audience speaking about mental health. I was teaching a course called Parent Effectiveness Training (PET) developed by Tom Gordon. I was in graduate school in counseling psychology and had been trained as a PET instructor. After introductions, a man raised his hand and asked what was my experience that qualified me to teach about raising kids. I only had a two-year-old at home and most of these people were facing teenagers. I was so nervous that I blurted out that I had trained dogs professionally for seven years. Taken wrong, it could have been perceived as an insult. Fortunately, they perceived it as a joke and laughed, thinking that I was intentionally creating some humor. The truth is that I learned a lot from training dogs and found some incredible parallels with teenage kids. You first have to have a relationship with the animal or the defiant teen. Next, if you set a boundary, both the dog and the teenager have to know that you mean it. Looking back, however, I could have been much smoother in my intro.

The dog training thing is true. However, it obscures some expert system issues. My Dad had been training dogs for 25 years. His specialty was hunting and field dogs but he did circus work, security work, as well as basic obedience courses. He was good at it and built a profitable boarding and training business. He had a weekly column in the Minneapolis newspaper and several outdoors programs on television. In his late 40s, he realized he did not want to do hard physical labor for the rest of his life. He reinvented himself by learning the basics of electrical engineering and working with companies to solve their lighting and advertising issues. He ultimately was successful at that and started other businesses, which also went well. To finance this career shift, he leased the kennel business out and used that money to launch his new efforts. It was basically the money upon which our family depended.

In the spring of 1962, the man who leased the kennels came to my father and admitted that the kennel business was failing. My father and mother were both fully engaged in the new venture, which was on the cusp of making money to support the family. They came to my sister and me; she was fourteen and I was seventeen. I was starting college in the fall, but neither of us had a summer job. They asked us to take over the kennels and said they would help us rebuild it. Unfortunately, they had little time to help. There were 13 dogs in house, and only seven were paying customers. Much of the buildings, fencing, and grounds were in disrepair. We rebuilt the business for six years. At the end of four years we handled up to 125 dogs a day and had eight people working with us. Before long, the business was once again providing the income stream to support the family. It also paid college tuition for both my sister and me.

Yet the experience was very difficult for both of us. Almost every summer day and holiday, including Thanksgiving and Christmas, we worked long hours. Later my parents would reminisce about that time as the best in our family's history. My sister and I would look at each other in profound disbelief. For myself, I could never have a normal date because I had chores early every morning and I worked late each day. I envied my friends who did fun teenage things and could stay out late. At least I could go somewhere as a collegian while my younger sister was more trapped. Both of us felt damaged by the process. Today, I really appreciate my sister and how she made things fun as opposed to just bearable.

What did I learn? I learned to handle field dogs. I learned how you teach a 200-pound St. Bernard to balance on a one-inch bar. I learned about dogs. I developed skills most farm kids learn including how to repair fences and run machinery. In addition, I had a learning curve in customer service, what works and what not to do. I learned problem-solving, vendor relationships, and staff issues. These efforts did not bring us closer as a family. We hardly saw each other. For sure I mastered compulsive working and other obsessions. When I went to college, for example, I worked in several 21 credit semesters. I also learned that there was a dark cloud called depression in me, and that I was capable of using compulsive behaviors to escape.

That all sounds pretty awful, but I learned profound life lessons as well. I learned that you could take a business that is in the hole financially (worse than a startup) and make it work. I know that adversity can be overcome—especially if you have the right partner. I learned that if you treat people well and give them more than they asked for, they will come back. I learned that whether you are working as hard as you can is not enough or even necessary—and that done compulsively it is a way to avoid unspoken pain.

All of us have talents more or less floating in our brain. How we acquired them can be a mixed bag. But we have them.

The next series of exercises have proven useful in helping sort through the abilities you have on tap for use in your zone or flow. Start with the next exercise, Talent Pool One, which assumes you have had lots of experiences, both positive and negative. A way to sift through your assets is first to list your talents, abilities, and gifts. As you list them, think also about your confidence level. If you have a good singing voice but at this point have little confidence that you could use it, on a scale of one to ten you would give it a low number. But if you are comfortable performing in public, give yourself a high rating. If you have experiences in business, living in foreign countries, or military training—any experience from which you have learned something unique, record those experiences and how unique you think they may be. Finally, think of your skill sets. List what skills you have and rate how valuable they are to you or to others. Then reflect on the lists and think through what expertise or specialties you have. In other words, make a list of the expert systems you know you currently have.

Talent Pool One

First, start with your innate talents and gifts, some of these abilities you are really confident about and even enjoy, while some may be unused, and/or you have little confidence in them. Another category is experiences you have had that provide perspective and some valuable knowledge that is unique. Finally, what are your skill sets? Simply put, what are you good at? Reflect on how valuable these skills are to a possible redesign of your future. On the right-hand side of the graphic, we ask that you list existing expertise or specialties in which you may have already integrated certain abilities, experiences, and skills. List in some detail what it is that you already are really good at.

Talent Pool One – Talents, Experiences, Skills

Talents, Natural Abilities, Gifts

Confidence Level

1. _____   1 2 3 4 5 6 7 8 9 10

2. _____   1 2 3 4 5 6 7 8 9 10

3. _____   1 2 3 4 5 6 7 8 9 10

4. _____   1 2 3 4 5 6 7 8 9 10

5. _____   1 2 3 4 5 6 7 8 9 10

6. _____   1 2 3 4 5 6 7 8 9 10

Experiences

Uniqueness

1. _____   1 2 3 4 5 6 7 8 9 10

2. _____   1 2 3 4 5 6 7 8 9 10

3. _____   1 2 3 4 5 6 7 8 9 10

4. _____   1 2 3 4 5 6 7 8 9 10

5. _____   1 2 3 4 5 6 7 8 9 10

6. _____   1 2 3 4 5 6 7 8 9 10

Skills

Valuable

1. _____   1 2 3 4 5 6 7 8 9 10

2. _____   1 2 3 4 5 6 7 8 9 10

3. _____   1 2 3 4 5 6 7 8 9 10

4. _____   1 2 3 4 5 6 7 8 9 10

5. _____   1 2 3 4 5 6 7 8 9 10

6. _____   1 2 3 4 5 6 7 8 9 10

Expertise/Specialties

1. _____

2. _____

3. _____

4. _____

5. _____

6. _____

7. _____

8. _____

9. _____

10. _____

Exercise 4.4

In *The Last Lecture*, Randy Pausch tells the compelling and moving story of how he recognized from all his trainings what his call was. He was a very successful engineer on the faculty of MIT. Clarity came, however, when he learned of his terminal cancer:

> And then, there in the waiting room, I suddenly knew exactly what it was. It came to me in a flash. Whatever my accomplishments, or the things I loved were rooted in the dreams and goals I had as a child ... and in the ways I had managed to fulfill almost all of them. My uniqueness, I realized, came in the specifics of all the dreams—from incredibly meaningful to decidedly quirky—that defined my forty-six years of life. Sitting there, I knew that despite the cancer, I truly believed I was a lucky man because I had lived out these dreams, in great measure, because of things I was taught by all sorts of extraordinary people along the way. If I was able to tell my story with the passion I felt, my lecture might help others find a path to fulfilling their own dreams.

Pausch and his family struggled over his need to give one more lecture. His book is the perfect illustration of the paradoxical conflict between being true to self and true to family. Ultimately, his passion brought his family together. He gave that lecture and today it is memorialized on Youtube, and his book is a classic statement about finding your call.

Unfortunately, not all of us have those moments of clarity, nor are the childhood memories retained. Internationally known family psychologist Shefali Tsabary calls this the "Great Forgetting." She observes in her book *The Awakened Family* that every child has moments filled with grace when they laugh and play and delight in what they are doing. Yes, they may go to school, have chores, and have the inevitable things they are made to do. Yet all have moments of doing something they love when they feel most themselves. They may shout in delight. Laugh when they get it right. Put time into it and find that time flies by as if it were mere moments. They improve and people can see the talent and the skill acquisition. These "talent allies" teach and help as we search for our call. These are the genuine moments of joy.

But shouting, inventive, and energetic children are not convenient in families and schools. Words like "behave," "practical," "mature," and getting into a good "school" are the tips of resistance to what our true nature was and is. Tsabary talks about the principal problem of parenting as the fact that parents' expectations are more often about them as parents. In this pattern of parenting, the child's success reflects on the parent as well as the parent's goals. In other words, they have not come to grips with their own identity and are living their own expectations and desires through their children. It is the problem that Paulo Coelho described in the introduction of this volume of *Recovery Zone*. Remember his comment about an essential confusion about what love is. Love ultimately is about loving family members (both spouses and children) enough to allow and to assist them in becoming who they are meant to be.

At the beginning of this book, I described my time with granddaughter Kiran after Suzanne's death. Kiran knew already that she was special, and she needed to know that it was okay for her not to be on the same path as her extraordinarily successful sister. She needed support to be her unique self. You too, have this knowing of what you are blessed and called to do. Yet I hear all the time, "I don't know what my call is." For these people, it seems like some magical or mystical thing that happens to some people but it is not happening to them. They even think it is great that people hear their call but add, "I am not one of them." Not true. They know the voices of "no" that flood their minds and ask for their loyalty to parental destinies. Yet, their true voice feels lost. The clouds of addiction, family dysfunction, and associated allies further obscure personal purpose.

Earlier, I described the conflict with my father about reading. To him, it meant I was to become some feckless dilettante who was too lazy and too defiant to get down to business. This meant facing reality. His reality was not mine. Many moments I felt like I was being self-indulgent. But today I love and collect books. I write them, too, and that work has put me and my children through school. But for years I struggled with my love of books and writing.

Sometimes people give up the struggle and get comfortable. They settle for good enough. They are making money, their family seems happy, and they have moments of satisfaction. Yet, when they start their day, is it with joy about what awaits? Are they excited about the challenges of the day? Do they keep improving and adding novel dimensions to their lives? Is their life bigger than they imagined?

When you completed your Happiness Funnel exercise, did you list any items that you did as a child? All children have a "discovery zone" in which they experience wonder and joy. Did any of those types of moments appear on your list? We see discovery as essential to the Recovery Zone. If you understand the word recovery, it is most often used when we "recover" something. Like in the early days of space travel and a capsule containing astronauts plunged into the sea, we would "recover" what we lost or were separated from. In health care, recovery has an intonation of getting back to normal. This interpretation is not the same as reclaiming our health. Or reclaiming our balance. Our intent is to live our lives in more coherence with who we are as people. We recover what we have lost. This means remembering what we lost in the "great forgetting" and discovering our innate talents and desires.

Doc Childre writes in his book *Heart Intelligence* about how meditation brings the brain to a new level of "knowing." For many, he suggests that "early on our sense of purpose can bounce around and shape shift at times. This is because, as our heart's intuition starts to increase, this raises our vibration and awareness which often changes the course of our desires and directions." In the HeartMath Institute laboratories, extensive research shows how the meditation process sharpens intention and even intuition. When heart and mind have inner coherence, purpose emerges, whatever the life experiences have been.

The reason behind this quest is that our sobriety and quality of recovery depends on it. It is like buying a car or a coat that was cheaper rather than getting what you wanted. Maybe even you settled on less quality because it was at a discount. Is your life a discounted life? Is your sense of self discounted? To return to the issue of living in the zone, Mihaly Csikszentmihalyi's fundamental insight was that by focusing on activities you are good (or expert at), you can keep improving, and this will make a difference to you. In other words, what you are doing matters.

Dan Siegel in his book *Mindsight* describes this zone as an integrated harmony of activities, as in the confluence of a river. Dan Goleman called this state of focus the "portal to happiness." Even in high-risk situations such as a surgeon, pilot, athlete, business leader or a performer of any kind, there is a sense of control. Facing risk with confidence in your choices and abilities is core to resilience. Failure is only a setback and part of the journey.

Ironically, as an addict, trauma survivor, or affected by the toxic stress of family dysfunction, you used your best abilities, at times, with dangerous outcomes or real consequences. Yet you also felt you could control what happened. However, addiction is a phantom optimum and the rewards but illusions. Escape strategies never satisfied, fear became terror, and the danger and consequences were real. The very best protection against relapse is to redesign your life, so that you are part of a river of energy that matters and makes you happy.

Sometimes that means dramatic changes. Recovery means putting careers, jobs, money, lifestyle, people, and sources of happiness all on the table. This can be disruptive and threatening to those you love. But it's worth it. Recovering people who slow things down to consider this notion of a calling have been proven to do better. I recommend taking the time (12 to 18 months) to reflect on your life purposes or call. Also, this is a good time to acquire skills that you can integrate into a recovery practice. These practices unite your efforts like the confluence of the flow of a river.

Success at anything requires starting with fundamentals but increases in complexity and ease of use. We call this an "expert system." We have used the example of the quarterback having an expert system where he has accumulated skills and experience. When the play starts, he has a plan, but when the plan does not pan out, he looks down the field and "knows" immediately what his best options are. It is the "bottom-up" part of his brain that does not have to think about it but knows what will work best. Similarly, in learning a language or an instrument, it is awkward at first but with time you develop an "unconscious" competence. Recovery is in fact an expert system with fundamentals that you integrate into a way of life.

More than likely, you already have "expert systems" that you know how to execute without thinking. These are things you are better at than most people. You simply have to stand back with your Inner Observer (and people who know you) and do an inventory. That shift of perspective and the consequent integration of what you are good at and what you want to be good at becomes a platform for a recovery practice and a phenomenal life.

All of this perspective brings us to the talent pool.

The metaphor is pooling things together. In nature, streams and springs pool together to create small bodies of water, which are naturally calibrated to become larger bodies of water and rivers of consequence. This mechanism creates extraordinary harmony by cleansing, nourishing, and replenishing the Earth. Within each of us there is a "talent pool" residing in our brains, which, when collected and integrated, will create extraordinary results. It is time to reassess your talent pool.

First, you started with your innate talents, gifts, and abilities (Talent Pool One). Some of these abilities you are really confident about and even enjoy, but some may be unused, and/ or you have little confidence in them. Yet you know you have some built-in gifts. All of these parts of you can contribute to your well-being. Another category is experiences you have had that provide perspective and valuable knowledge. Living in another culture or being raised in a family that was "musical." Some of these may in fact be unique and add a dimension to what you bring to a task. They may also be common but nonetheless useful, such as time in the military or experience in startup companies.

Finally, you record your skill sets. Simply put, what are you good at? You have accumulated specific skills which you may or may not use now. Reflect on how valuable these skills are to a possible redesign of your future. On the right-hand side of the graphic, we asked that you list existing expertise or specialties in which you may have already integrated certain abilities, experiences, and skills. The idea is to use your Inner Observer, your therapist, and recovery support people to reflect on these lists of expertise and determine what "expert systems" you already have and what you need to focus on to expand your bottom-up brain's bandwidth of expertise.

In the graphic **Talent Pool Two**, start by listing your existing areas of expertise (both career and non-career related). These are areas you may or may not be very accomplished at, but you have them. In front of the list under the column labeled "R," place a check next to those that are rewarding to you. Under the column with the "$" (dollar sign), check those that are currently financially necessary for you. At the end of each expertise you list, a column is provided for you to place an estimate of the percentage of time you used this set of skills just prior to recovery. Then there is a scale (1–10) in which you rate how much you now would like to use this set of talents. If little or not at all, use a 1, but if you would like to be spending a maximum amount of time in this activity, rate it a 10. The in-between numbers are for your best assessment of how much you see this set of skills as relevant in your future (both professional or as a recovering person).

For example, you have an intuitive golf game and even have placed in some local tournaments. You have had little time to work on it but when you do, it is so much fun for you. Or you are a competitive golfer whose livelihood depends on winning tournament points.

You love the excitement and the crowds, but hate the press. However, there is a spirituality in the experience that is meaningful to you. Or maybe you are very good at it, very successful financially, and you dread every moment of it.

The second list asks you to list those areas of expertise you wish to develop both career and non-career. In the "R" column, check those you think would be rewarding. Check the "$" column if you think this would play a role in your financial well-being. In the "%" column, determine how much time, if any, you devote to developing this expertise already. Rate from one to ten your best estimate about how this expertise would enhance your recovery. On the right-hand side are two boxes for you to write your thoughts about whether you feel a call for any of these activities. Note then how recovery has changed your thinking about your talents and desires.

This work at first can seem daunting. There are these lists and rating scales that may seem overwhelming. Take your time and allow yourself some stillness. This process has been, for many, an important method of realigning purposes. Doc Childre says to listen to your heart: "My heart's guidance was the most important step in manifesting my purpose, regardless of how my vocational choices and life played out." This step allows you to look at what you know to be true.

The final worksheet, **Talent Pool Three**, refines this process by asking you more specifically about the skill sets you wish to develop. These are areas you are willing to focus on to integrate into your expert system. The list is where the rubber meets the road in terms of how you wish to challenge yourself. You list the areas in which you wish to grow and how to accomplish that growth. When the list is complete, select the three most important skills and note why they are important. Then select the three most rewarding skills and specify why you made that choice. Some of the same items may make your priorities clear while identifying rewarding areas of focus work.

The last step is critical. Randy Pausch in *The Last Lecture* speaks persuasively about lists that start with, "If nothing else, I will ...." This is a way of making the most meaningful and important things happen. So, if you think in terms of a year of focus work to change your life platform for recovery, make concrete at least five steps to include in your planning. No matter what the distraction or the inconvenience, here is what you will make happen.

Talent Pool Two

List your existing areas of expertise. Under the column labeled "R," place a check next to those which are rewarding to you. Under the column with the "$," check those that are financially necessary for you. Estimate the percentage of time you used this set of skills just prior to recovery. Then there is a scale (1–10) in which you rate how much you would like to use this set of talents now. There are two boxes for you to write your thoughts about whether you feel a call for any of these activities

Talent Pool Two – Expert Systems

What do you sense has been your call?

How has this call changed?

Expertise on Board (% Time) **Utilization Now**

R $

1. _____ ( ) 1 2 3 4 5 6 7 8 9 10
2. _____ ( ) 1 2 3 4 5 6 7 8 9 10
3. _____ ( ) 1 2 3 4 5 6 7 8 9 10
4. _____ ( ) 1 2 3 4 5 6 7 8 9 10
5. _____ ( ) 1 2 3 4 5 6 7 8 9 10
6. _____ ( ) 1 2 3 4 5 6 7 8 9 10
7. _____ ( ) 1 2 3 4 5 6 7 8 9 10
8. _____ ( ) 1 2 3 4 5 6 7 8 9 10
9. _____ ( ) 1 2 3 4 5 6 7 8 9 10
10. _____ ( ) 1 2 3 4 5 6 7 8 9 10

Expertise in Develop (% Now) **Recovery Related**

R $

1. _____ ( ) 1 2 3 4 5 6 7 8 9 10
2. _____ ( ) 1 2 3 4 5 6 7 8 9 10
3. _____ ( ) 1 2 3 4 5 6 7 8 9 10
4. _____ ( ) 1 2 3 4 5 6 7 8 9 10
5. _____ ( ) 1 2 3 4 5 6 7 8 9 10
6. _____ ( ) 1 2 3 4 5 6 7 8 9 10
7. _____ ( ) 1 2 3 4 5 6 7 8 9 10
8. _____ ( ) 1 2 3 4 5 6 7 8 9 10
9. _____ ( ) 1 2 3 4 5 6 7 8 9 10
10. _____ ( ) 1 2 3 4 5 6 7 8 9 10

Exercise 4.5

Talent Pool Three

List the areas in which you wish to grow and how to accomplish that growth. When the list is complete, select the three most important skills and note why they are important. Then select the three most rewarding skills and specify why you made that choice.

Talent Pool Three – Focus Work Up

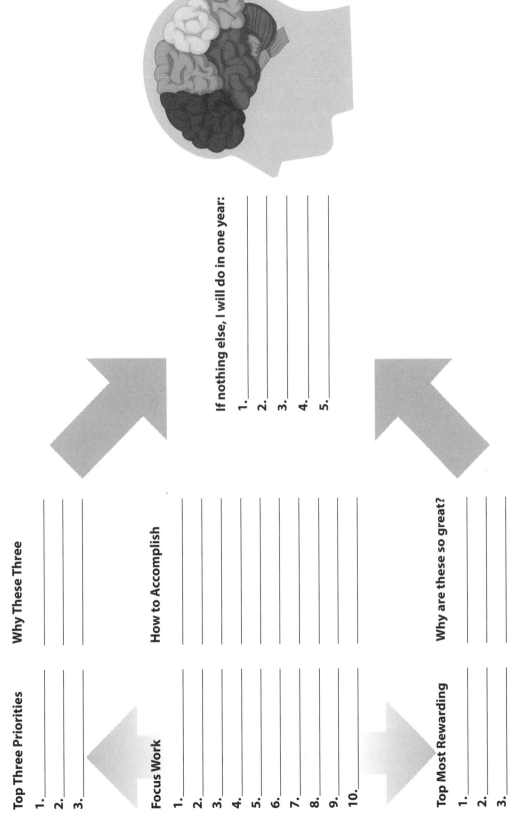

Top Three Priorities

Why These Three

1.

2.

3.

Focus Work

How to Accomplish

1.

2.

3.

4.

5.

6.

7.

8.

9.

10.

If nothing else, I will do in one year:

1.

2.

3.

4.

5.

Top Most Rewarding

Why are these so great?

1.

2.

3.

Exercise 4.6

Remember that Dan Siegel says in *Mindsight* that this integration of strengths becomes a confluence like a river, which he compared to "flow." Whether it is a motor pool or in nature, an aggregate of flows becomes a powerful force. Clearing out the wreckage of a life gone awry provides a space in which to integrate issues of money, work, and lifestyle. However, it is a tough moment because you do not know how the complexities of change will work out. If you are unsettled and unsure about the future, that is natural at this stage. The truth is you are between knowing what did not work and creating what will. You are in-between.

We are always in-between. The myth we all share is that we have stability. We do have degrees of stability. In periods when stability is higher, we can look through euphoric lenses at those times as better or even the best, even when they were not. The reality is that instability often results in bringing new ways of living that indeed are better. Meanwhile, a period of consolidation can in hindsight appear as "stable." We do remember the whitewater periods when cascading forces made for fearful moments that changed the course of our lives. But even in the rivers of life, a placid surface can belie the deep, powerful currents underneath. Never is change not happening.

The Great Idea ....

Every reader will identify with having an idea that everyone around you thought was crazy, impractical, or even dangerous. Yet you did it anyway. And you found that everyone around you was right. It is one of the most common experiences people with "medical conditions" have. They go against their doctor's advice, family wishes, and the warnings of trusted friends. It is the nature of addiction and mental illness to think you are right. So relying on support groups and others is key to recovery. You do this because you learned how your best ideas brought you and maybe others serious harm. But herein lies a very significant paradox.

Consider the movie *Star Wars*. George Lucas insisted on keeping creative control despite extreme skepticism of the concept and prolonged financial struggle. Eleven of the best directors turned him down, so he finally directed the film himself. His integrity changed our culture and a profound paradigm shift occurred. He literally introduced quantum physics to the masses, as well as the wisdom of Joseph Campbell, who was the model for the character Yoda.

Financially, the series has become one of the most profitable film ventures of all time. Money was not the motivation for Lucas. The "Great Idea" was. He had this rudder that told him he was right to take the risks. Dan Goleman in his book *Focus* describes Lucas as an example of an "inner compass, a North Star that steers one through life according to the dictates of one's deepest values and purposes." Goleman's description of the brain's process of keeping this focus is important as we reflect on the brain pool of our talents:

The decision rules derived from our life experiences reside in subcortical neural networks that gather, store, and apply algorithms from every event in our lives— creating our inner rudder. The brain harbors our deepest sense of meaning in these subcortical regions—areas connected poorly to the verbal areas of the new cortex but richly to the gut ....this inner radar holds the key to managing what we do—and just as important, what we don't do. This internal control mechanism makes all the difference between a life well lived and one that falters.

Sometimes this process uncovers passion about a great idea. The reset button is there. What does this guidance system tell you about how to spend your remaining time? Remember Doc Childre's caution that your passion can remain elusive until you allow yourself the stillness and have the courage to listen. Remember that the Great Idea will test you, and, for those of us in recovery, the paradox awaits. To be true to ourselves despite the risks and challenges, or play it safe? Can we trust our recoveries and take a deep dive into something and hope it is not a rabbit hole or an old behavior? The truth for us in recovery can be a very thin edge. Remember, to implement a great idea requires a certain level of personal coherence. Having a great idea can occur at any stage of personal disarray. Chaos invites the leap. Yet no creative act occurs without focus and emotional certainty. The great idea always disrupts others. Focus is how those who have created success for themselves summoned the level of effort, discipline, and vision to overcome the inertia that awaits all change. Focus stimulates solutions and harnesses necessary pragmatism. But it emanates and is sustained by the deep passion of the self. It is never accidental, although it counts on the spontaneous. Seldom is success of the idea about one's ability, although such contributions come from those able to mobilize ability. Nor is it only about discipline and planning, although being willing to prioritize is key. Otherwise, boredom kills the spirit. In short, focus requires the commitment of the self—to help the self.

Chapter 5 **Smoke and Mirrors: Showing Up**

> *When you look at the dark side, careful you must be. For the dark side looks back.*
>
> Yoda, *Star Wars*

Pastor Joel Osteen challenges people to complete the "I am..." statement. What he asks for is a statement that is true and indicates what is important to you. In this book we have talked about the "separated self," the image you project that may contain some truth but papers over the real you. Many times, the separated self is what you think other people want or expect you to be. In *Recovery Zone I*, for example, we asked if you were a different person with your family than with your friends. Later in the same book, we asked you to think about the role of shame and how you tailor your "image" to cover some of your behaviors. The Osteen challenge, of course, has deep biblical roots in the Old Testament, going back to when God answers the question Moses asked of who he was with "I am who I am."

Osteen talks about the importance of being who you say you are. He also cautions that when you complete the "I am..." statement, you should be careful because that "I am" may come back at you. If there is something hidden that no one knows about, you must live with the contradictions. Most people will put it in a compartment so they do not have to contend with it. However, sooner or later the compartment leaks and what you've been hiding emerges as shame or self-disgust.

Compartmentalization creates a split in the self. The "work to be done" here is sewing together the one true self. That integration allows for a level of presence that empowers the self and deepens the capability to stay in stillness. That presence becomes the "ground of our being."

There are lots of ways you can tell when people are really genuine:

- Usually they do not monopolize conversations and respond in conversations by keeping the focus on them.
- They may have accomplishments but not engage in too much elaboration or exaggeration.
- They make themselves vulnerable by owning flaws and quickly acknowledging missteps and mistakes.
- They are good listeners and have the ability to be in your presence in total silence with no anxiety.

- They do not gaslight, which is deceptively misleading others to alter others' perception of reality.
- They accept anger, criticism, and collaboration without feeling diminished.
- They are grateful and not presumptuous.
- They have the courage to consistently express an unpopular opinion or point out disappointments.
- They tell the truth no matter how inconvenient or even dangerous.
- They have the courage to be congruent with their values both publicly and privately.
- They do not have a sense of entitlement or exploit others.
- They do their best to do what they say they will.
- They have empathy for others.
- They are aware of and know how to affirm and care for others.
- They are "impeccable" with their word, meaning they do not denigrate or judge others, nor do they attack themselves with hurtful or self-critical statements or self-talk
- They do not "fall in love at first sight" because, for them, relationships and reputations are earned.

There is a famous phrase in the *Big Book* of Alcoholics Anonymous: "Some of us cried out, it is too great a task." And that may be true with "I am" statements. None of us can achieve all of those signs of being present all the time. But a healthy person lives within that bandwidth. They are not wallowing in despair, in feeling victimized, or in feeling fundamentally defective. Nor are they affected by an inflated sense of importance that causes them to appear desperate for excessive attention and admiration. They make available an image that reflects the state of their life and their being. They are looking in a mirror and seeing their truest "I am" looking back.

The idea of narcissists searching for themselves in their own reflections opens many lenses for thinking about life. The analogy of vampires not seeing themselves in the mirror and then finding victims to fulfill their hunger by sucking them dry is classic narcissism. Rokelle Lerner points out in her book *The Object of My Affection Is in My Reflection* that narcissistic wounding affects all of us. We all have the pain of not being validated.

The Wicked Queen in *Snow White* consulting the magic mirror as to who is the "fairest" in the land is straight out of the narcissist's quest for validation. The problem the narcissist has is if anyone spoils their image of themselves, they tend to overreact, which in turn makes them hard to live with. The classic narcissist has a hard time understanding their impact on others.

However, most of us have looked in the mirror at a critical moment of truth and faced ourselves. Therefore, looking in the mirror can provide us with various "reflections" upon which to see the truth about ourselves. Since we have learned that mirroring is key to a sense of self, let us explore various types of mirrors and ask the fairest questions we can. We have created various mirrors for you to think about. If you were looking in the mirror or truth right now, what would look back at you? Portray that by drawing the "I am" that looks back. Remember, the goal is not a perfect drawing; the goal is to convey a sense of the truth about yourself.

- **The Fun House Mirror** — In the movie *Mask*, about a boy whose face is lionized (because he has craniodiaphyseal dysplasia, a disease that deforms the face), several characters go into a fun house in which mirrors distort reality. In the fun house distorted mirror, the boy's face looks ordinary. He sees how handsome and attractive he would have been without his disease. He is overcome by sadness and grief about everything he has gone through and all that he has missed. In his family's craziness, his problems of appearance were overlooked and normalized. No one was there for him in his loneliness and pain. Imagine a fun house mirror and ask what distorted, crazy, or even abusive images were made to look normal in your family? How do you look in this mirror?

- **The Mirror of Erised** — The Mirror of Erised is the mirror in which Harry Potter saw himself interacting with his parents, his deepest desire. This is because his parents were murdered when he was a baby and so he never knew them. The headmaster of Harry's school, Albus Dumbledore, had kept the mirror hidden because he knew it could be dangerous. When he discovered Harry using the mirror, he explained that Erised is "desire" spelled backward. He then explains that people can get lost in the mirror, even though the mirror did not represent truth. It was merely an image.

     This is similar to addiction. Addiction to an unavailable fantasy is one of the easiest ways to lose yourself. In the series *Star Trek*, there was a holodeck where you could live out any fantasy. Some who went in to the holodeck never really came back. Crew members described this as holodeck addiction. Look in your personal Mirror of Erised for your deepest desire. How do you look in this image, and what does the desire do for you?

- **The Mirror of Righteousness** — Look in this mirror for scenes of your personal righteousness. When have you felt superior or "one up" or "better than," only to later learn that you were in error? Even our most well-intended purposes can become stiflingly self-righteous. Timothy Keller's book *The Prodigal God* used the example of the eldest brother in the parable of the prodigal son. In the parable, the elder brother held on to his rage toward the younger brother, and this was a barrier for reconciliation in the family. Keller's point is that righteousness is another way to avoid reality and pain. At many points we have underlined in this series how dark feelings can be obsessional and interfere with integrating the self. Such anger becomes a barrier to being present. How do you see yourself in the mirror when you have been righteous and rejecting?

- **The Mirror of Intimacy** — Family therapists often place a mirror between family members so they can see their own face as they give feedback or their version of the truth to their partner or family members. This provides perspective on what their family sees. What images would reflect how your family sees you? Is that what you want? What must change?

- **The Mirror of Internal Perspective** — Picture your Inner Observer and how that particular part of yourself looks. Picture your true self that is emerging as you grow. Explore how your interaction with your wise self looks at this time. Are there any barriers present or special qualities that exist?

- **The Mirror of Reflection** — What are the images your Inner Observer wants you to attend to in your life? This exercise is another form of visioning and is part of the vision table process. Use the Mirror of Reflection to further refine what you want in your life. What would you look like and what would your life look like when congruent and in the "hum"?

- **The Mirror of Validation** — Most importantly, we must hold a large space for the Mirror of Validation. What images would finally validate you so there was quiet in your soul? How would you know you were empowered and comfortable being in the "flow" and "hum" of your personal recovery zone?

Within each mirror, try to use images (rather than words) to describe what you see. Words may be necessary but focus on the images and what they mean to you. Remember in all this work to keep your feelings and words "impeccable." This concept to keep your internal and external dialogue impeccable comes from the book *The Four Agreements* by Don Miguel Ruiz. The concept is that you not allow yourself to be judgmental or negative not only with others but also with yourself. That means you must look at what is real and not shame or put yourself down. Shaming yourself corrupts the process and creates barriers within yourself. Take time with each mirror and note your reactions. (Before you do this exercise, it is highly recommended that you finish reading the chapter. Getting the full scope of the chapter will help your work.)

The Fun House Mirror

Imagine a fun house mirror and ask what distorted, crazy, or even abusive images were made to look normal in your family? How do you look in this mirror?

Exercise 5.1

The Mirror of Erised

Look in this mirror for your deepest desire. How do you look in this mirror, and what does the desire do for you? Where do your think this desire comes from in your life?

Exercise 5.2

The Mirror of Righteousness

How do you see yourself in the mirror when you have been righteous and rejecting?

Exercise 5.3

The Mirror of Intimacy

Imagine placing this mirror between yourself and your partner or a family member so you see your own face as you gave feedback or your version of the truth. What images reflect how your family sees you? Is that what you want? What must change?

Exercise 5.4

The Mirror of Internal Perspective

Picture your Inner Observer and how that particular part of yourself looks. Picture your true self that is emerging as you grow. Explore how your interaction with your wise self looks at this time. Are there any barriers present or special qualities that exist?

Exercise 5.5

The Mirror of Reflection

What are the images your Inner Observer wants you to attend to in your life? This exercise is another form of visioning and is part of the vision table process. Use the Mirror of Reflection to further refine what you want in your life. What would you look like and what would your life look like when congruent and in the "hum"?

Exercise 5.6

The Mirror of Validation

What images would finally validate you so there was quiet in your soul? How would you know you were empowered and comfortable being in the "flow" and "hum" of your personal recovery zone?

Exercise 5.7

Presence to Self and Others

In some ways the mirrors parallel a process used in many businesses and training institutions called a "360." Five or more people are selected, and they usually represent a mix of people who you supervise, who are your peers, and people to whom your directly report. They ask for their frank evaluations of your performance and then the feedback is summarized. When a 360 is presented, people often are surprised by what they hear, whether it is positive or negative. The more congruent people are, the fewer surprises there are that emerge from this exercise. The 360 evaluation process, as applied here, is an effort to help you with your recovery work by giving you perspective from all directions.

The purpose behind the mirrors exercise is to help you access your own wisdom about yourself. Like so much of recovery and therapy, it is about uncovering what you already know. The mirrors help you to think through a 360 evaluation of yourself. However, sharing drawings with others can generate a lot of useful information. Your sponsor, peers, family members, and therapist all could talk with you about what is revealed in the mirrors. Long-term committed friends who have seen you over the years in various contexts can be extremely useful. The goal is to unite the self and eliminate the fragmentation that occurs in people's lives.

If we were to go to a business that sells mirrors and ask them to repair a broken mirror they would say it is not worth the trouble because they would have to fill and polish the area—and still a slight ripple would follow the crack and cause something of a distortion in the reflection.

They would advise us to get a new mirror.... It is the mind that is the mirror and not so easily disposed of. By looking into the fracturing of the mirror of the mind and regularly noting the fissures on its surface ... we can begin to polish with mercy whatever incompletely repaired reflection distorts our world view.

—Stephen Levine, *Unattended Sorrow:*
Recovering from Loss and Reviving the Heart

The key to this process, Stephen Levine observes, is the dialogue between the heart and the mind (remember top-down and bottom-up).

Out of that dialogue an inner voice emerges (wise mind), which will guide us to healing.

However, you are on the sharp edge of a paradox. The paradox is that who is viewing you matters. One way of measuring character is by what one does when no one is looking. If your loved ones could see everything that you do, would you continue all those activities? Even if you knew there would be sharp reactions to your behavior, would you engage in that behavior in front of them? Or would you keep some things hidden because they violate your values and commitments and you fear rejection by those that matter to you? If you would keep some things hidden, you have fragmentation of the self.

The other side of the paradox is that if you go out of your way to do something that really helps someone or makes the world significantly better, would you let the knowledge of the good you did remain secret? Or would you let slip to a few individuals your good deed? Would you not reveal anything of your involvement to those you helped? Or would have a need for validation for your effort, even if it diminished some of the good you accomplished? Sometimes to be effective it is best to let your intervention go into that exceptionally large category of "nobody else's business." Another measure of character is doing things that simply are worth doing and "letting go" of the need to be acknowledged. No one needs to know you helped.

In meditation, the starting goal is to be present to the moment. The example that is often used is looking at something in nature that is beautiful. For example, you can take a flower and appreciate its beauty. If you start to think about a color or the type of flower it is, or its purpose in nature, you start with a label (such as purple) and that puts an idea (a barrier) between you and your immediate focus on the flower. That cognitive act reduces your presence.

In the same way, to be helpful for someone in pain or grief, sharing your similar experiences (I had that happen to me and what I did was...) or giving advice or even sharing how sad you are about the situation may not be helpful. Simply being present is all that may be necessary—or helpful. The phrase often used is "showing up," and keeping your focus on the other person is the priority.

Flowers or cards are customary after tragedies or significant loss. But who is the person still checking in months later? Who remembers your surgery date and time with a text of encouragement? Who sends a collection of grief candles months after the event to acknowledge that you probably still struggle?

In therapy, the relationship with client and therapist is key. Therapists are most effective when the client feels their presence. They sense when their therapists "show up" for them. For therapists, the problem is the "diagnosis." Diagnostic criteria and understanding the underlying causes and traits of their patient's problems help them plan effective help for the client. This is a "label" that can affect being fully present to the challenges the patient faces. Like categorizing a flower, it can be a barrier. Good therapists must at times step over the barriers created by their knowledge of psychological disorders. The best predictor of successful therapy is when the patient believes the therapist would do or has done what is being asked of the patient. My belief is the best therapists and the longest lasting therapeutic relationships are based on the presence of both parties.

The patient must show up, too. I frequently see patients with their therapists or case managers. When I see significant progress, I ask the patients if their therapists have been helpful to them. The responses are always emphatically yes. I then ask if they have thanked their therapist for all the energy and effort on their behalf. "No" invariably is the answer. So, I ask them to take the time now to do that. I also request the patients to be very specific about how the help was provided.

Usually, we all are in tears at the end because the gratitude on both sides means so much. Remember the therapist, like the teacher described in an earlier chapter, is gifted by learning from the patient. Please note: Always thank your therapist at some point. It is one of the many ways to make gratitude real. And therapists are great to practice this important skill with.

Henri Nouwen, a gifted theologian who wrote on attachment and spirituality, observed that three essential stages occur. First, you come to trust yourself. Trusting yourself means keeping your promises, living in truth, and doing what you intend to do. In other words, the inside and the outside match up. When you sense the integrity of the self, then you more deeply trust others. Up to that point, your view was through a fragmented lens (like a fragmented mirror). You viewed others as keepers of secrets and people who would not come through for you. We call this "projection" when you project onto others what is true of yourself. When you know you are trustworthy, and you find others worthy of your trust, you reach the third stage, where you start to trust at a "spiritual" level. You believe that your higher power will be there for you and take care of you. If the first two are not present, wrestling with the larger questions of a spiritual life is a bridge too far.

Earning trust and living in trust is not "too great a task," but it is difficult. The paradox of being true to yourself and being faithful to others inevitably creates conflicted goals—much like Randy Pausch in *The Last Lecture*. Jung said this "rub" in relationships provides some of the most spiritual moments in life. Why? You must trust you can work it out. Relationships often contain inconvenient truths.

Sometimes loving someone is a series of wake-up calls. The attractive idea is of a soulmate who is a preordained match for you and who brings immediate mutual understanding and enduring passion. There are no issues to resolve in this narrative or, if issues do exist, they are easily resolved. Frankly, I am a bit of a romantic. When the Hallmark Christmas romance shows come on, I love to watch. I even can be moved to tears. We all have this "deepest desire."

Yet it is mythic. One of the founders of family therapy, Carl Whitaker, described marriage as an inevitable struggle. The task is to find the best struggle you can. It was a comment meant to be humorous, but it contained truth. Loving someone over the long-term eventually creates spots of soreness and pain. Intimacy is like the rest of life and certainly recovery: there are always moments of whitewater in which you can be bruised.

When my wife Suzanne died, I had a therapist friend send me the following quote from Elizabeth Gilbert's book *Eat, Pray, Love*. It provides a different take on what a soul mate is:

People think a soul mate is your perfect fit, and that's what everyone wants. But a true soul mate is a mirror, the person who shows you everything that's holding you back, the person who brings you to your own attention so you can change your life. A true soul mate is probably the most important person you'll ever meet, because they tear down your walls and smack you awake.

But to live with a soul mate forever? Nah. Too painful. Soul mates, they come into your life just to reveal another layer of yourself to you, and then they leave. And thank God for it. Their purpose is to shake you, drive you out of your comfort zone, tear apart your ego a little bit, show you your obstacles and addictions, break your heart open so a new light could get in and then they leave.

The description of a soul mate is certainly different from the vision of soul mate in the prevailing culture. While harsh, there is some truth in it. It is obvious to say, but we do tend to forget this truth: the people who love us and live with us know us best. Our contradictions are obvious to them and we can learn so much if we allow them to say their truth and trust ourselves to handle their honesty. The result can transform and nourish our souls—or polish the mirror.

Think of being in the optometrist's office when the doctor asks, "Better with, or without?" If you are weighing in your mind whether you are better off in or out of your relationship, you may not be "seeing" the problem at all. So not only soul mates but all those who love you can become a mirror.

In relationships, start with the concept that problems have owners. There are those issues you bring to the table. Then there are issues that really are about your partner. And finally, there are issues that the relationship owns, like coming to agreement about child-rearing issues, or sex, or money. Let us start with when it is on our side of the table.

When my wife Suzanne was in her battle with cancer, she had a period of intense chemotherapy. Her oncologist took me aside and told me that Suzanne would also receive strong doses of steroids to help her body take the stress of the chemotherapy. The oncologist predicted that for two or three days after each treatment, Suzanne would experience severe emotional volatility. And that did happen. She would easily become enraged over minor or even imaginary issues. My psychiatrist friends used the term steroidal psychosis.

These were difficult days and I found it hard to take. For over twenty years I had known her to be a kind and gentle person. Now, suddenly, she would have tirades over things that did not happen or were just minor incidents, and they were hurtful. None of us, including our adult children and myself, were spared during this time. Still, we cared deeply for her. Then, afterwards, she would calm down and feel remorse over it all.

However, embedded amongst all the anger, Suzanne said things that came from deep inside her that had the ring of truth. She brought up issues about me I recognized as accurate. It was hard to sort out, given all the rest that was said and said with such force. But when I really listened, I recognized that she had been trying to get my attention on some issues for a very long time.

In the months after Suzanne passed, I had the opportunity to clean out her papers and journals. In her journals, I saw myself through her eyes, and I realized how much I misperceived what she was telling me that she needed.

I did not like what I saw reflected in this mirror. I thought (and still think) the marriage was solid and successful with deep love on both sides. Yet, through Suzanne's eyes, I finally saw some of the flaws that I had overlooked. This pushed me into some profound changes, and I am a much better partner and person today because of this acknowledgement of my flaws. I just wish that it had not taken her drug-driven anger to get my attention. This example illustrates why the mirror concept is so helpful.

How about when the problem really belongs to the other person? One of the great stories about relationships comes out of medieval times and King Arthur's court. One of the members of the Knights of the Round Table was Sir Lancelot. His legend was about the quest for the Holy Grail, the cup Christ had used at the last supper. Supposedly, whoever found it and drank from it would become immortal. At one point on the trail of the hidden cup, Lancelot heard about an old hag who lived on the edge of the forest in Arthur's kingdom. Not only was she old, but she looked like what we often see ugly witches depicted as on Halloween. Lancelot went to see her. He told her he had heard that she knew where the Holy Grail was. She said that she did not know where it was, but she knew how Lancelot could find out where it was.

However, if she were to tell him, he must first do her a favor. She was very enamored with another knight in Arthur's court named Sir Gawain, who was one of Lancelot's close friends and very handsome. She would give him the secret to pursue his quest for the Grail, but first he had to convince Gawain to marry her. Lancelot approached his friend and said that he could find the Holy Grail, but only if Gawain were to marry the old hag. Gawain knew of the old woman and had to think it over. Finally, he told Lancelot he would do it. I have often thought that this was a lot to ask of a friend.

So, Sir Gawain went to her hut at the edge of the forest to ask for her hand in marriage. Seated in front of the hag's hut was a stunning, beautiful woman. She said to him, "This is not what you expected." Gawain admitted that he was incredibly surprised at her appearance.

She asked Gawain why he was there. He told her about Lancelot and that he had come to seek her hand in marriage. She replied that she would marry him but that he had to make a choice. For half the day she would be beautiful for him and half the day she would take on the appearance of the old hag. Did he want a beautiful woman on his arm at Arthur's court during the day but then he would sleep with the old hag at night? Or did he prefer the reverse with him sleeping with her as a stunning, beautiful woman at night, but an old hag in front of his friends and members of the court. Gawain responded quickly, saying, "I think that is your decision, not mine." The woman smiled and said, "Then I shall be beautiful at all times for you, for you have given me dominion over myself."

This is one of the fundamental truths of relationships. Separating from the other and letting them be themselves is the great challenge. We must recognize that the other is not an extension of ourselves. It is one of the hardest lessons of marriage, parenting, and even friendship. When we apply pressure and manipulation of the other to be what we want, only confusion and resentment result. Happiness and intimacy are most likely when both parties feel they can be themselves.

However, when being true to both yourself and the other, there can be immense differences. Therefore, in intimacy there will always be moments of struggle.

When the problem is owned by the relationship, the problem can be difficult to resolve. Often, when people get stuck in their relationships, it feels like it does not matter what they do, they will always lose somehow. Decisions can seem like choosing the least of the worst options, even though each choice is a legitimate path. At such times, it is important to remember that it is in struggle that we find what our truth is and who we are. This is what Jung means when he says that pain and suffering are often the most spiritual moments humans experience.

In Chapter Three we described when the relationship has the problem as the intimacy paradox. The good news is there are strategies that make these issues easier to work through. First, in couples recovery groups the word "currency" has special meaning. It means keeping current in all things and not putting off the unpleasant. The phrase is often used when you have made a mistake. You stay current when you promptly admit it.

Recovery means that in your circles of intimacy, you keep them "current" about all that is going on—the good and the bad. Constantly checking in reduces overwhelm, accumulating baggage, and loss of transparency. In fact, the whole premise of the eighth and ninth steps is to make amends to those whom you have harmed. This is not just about apologizing; it is also about taking responsibility and creating currency in your life. It is the very spirit of the serenity prayer because you have done all you can. Peace comes into your life when you are not anxious about unaddressed issues in your life.

A parallel principle involves accepting your limits as a human being who makes mistakes. We constantly have to evaluate what we can and cannot do, and this includes relationships. When I was a young father, I read an article that said most humans could only handle seven intimate relationships at one time. I figured I had a wife, four children, and two golden retrievers, so there was nothing left over for others. Personally, I found the observation partially humorous and partially accurate, but also incomplete. There were moments where the only place in the house I could find total positive acceptance was with the dogs.

Behind trying to fit into this model of bandwidth in intimacy looms a much larger truth. If you want the following, you must be intentional about your relationships.

- To be transparent and true to yourself.
- To show up and be true to others.
- To be in the Zone and be your most talented self.
- To have a platform of a recovery that becomes your default way of confronting difficult moments.

Again, you must be intentional about your relationships. Intentionality is key to translating all you have learned internally into your ordinary, everyday world. Being intentional is vital in restructuring the relationship and intimacy constellations around you. The remainder of this chapter and the next chapter provide frameworks for getting current and sifting through all your relationships, which is at the core of all the goals we listed above.

Once you're in recovery and you establish some traction in your therapy, you realize that cleanup is necessary in some of your relationships. In the interest of currency and healthy intimacy, the following process will be helpful. Called the Critical Closure Planning Process, these steps have proven to be useful in organizing this cleanup in a systematic fashion.

There are eight categories in which to list tasks that can heal and focus your relationship life:

Critical Closure Planning Process

1. **Those Harmed** — While many of you have completed an eighth and ninth step by now and made amends, this process is often a matter of timing and the result of much reflection about appropriate action. Actually, the process can go on for some time. This space is for what you know you have left or what is on your front-burner in terms of action.

2. **Current Dishonesties** — Sometimes clarification or even disclosure can take up a great deal of time. Some issues are simple but need to be dealt with. Others can have repercussions but also need to be dealt with. Remember, this task is not just about inevitable truths emerging but also what you can live with.

3. **Difficult Conversations** — Recovery exposes real problems and differences in relationships, problems that require problem solving or resolution. This space is for those discussions you know you need to have but have delayed for a myriad of reasons. Ultimately, you have to have the conversations, so list them so you can plan and keep your integrity.

4. **People I Support** — In this category, you have to consider who needs your support and attention. While you may be actively doing this, it still takes up bandwidth and you have to consider how to continue the appropriate level of support or in fact increase it.

5. **Unfinished —** Some situations are convoluted enough to be considered unfinished. Some may even require therapy to get out of or to continue. Either way, you will need help. No matter what these are, relationships simply cannot remain in limbo as unfinished matters. Sooner or later, inaction on your part will further unravel in ways you do not want. It is best to make a list of unfinished issues so you can take them off your table as an energy drain because you obsess about it.

6. **Let Go, It's Beyond My Control —** The serenity prayer forces you to get out of the way and stop attempting to fix things. Listing issues you cannot fix helps you understand your own limits and what your control issues cause you. Inaction can be a legitimate goal.

7. **No Longer Matters** — We all have relationships that sap us of energy and, in return, bring nothing to us or the other person. In this category, list the relationships that are going nowhere or that remain for unhealthy reasons.

8. **People I Neglect** — There are people who do matter, who are priorities for you and you cherish. However, you neglect them. You need to list them and ask yourself why. Remember, we always think we have more time to get to them and usually we really do not.

Exercise 5.8

Creating these lists will also help you in reviewing your work on the mirrors. Again, this is all material to share within your therapy and recovery groups. We have provided space for you to record the eight lists of the Critical Closure Planning Process (Exercise 5–8). Remember, however, if you think you need more space, use a large sheet of paper.

Chapter 6 **The Ultimate To Do List**

Some people end up like Tolstoy's character Ivan Ilyich who anguished on his deathbed, "What if my whole life has been wrong?" A fearsome scene....

—Wayne Dyer, *You Are What You Think*

Psychologist Wayne Dyer inspired millions of people by urging them to clarify their intentions, transform those intentions into viable visions, and translate those images into reality with concrete steps. An example is his work with the Israeli Olympic team proving that athletes who use psychomotor visioning of their athletic challenges perform better than those who pour all their energy into intense practice. Dyer's work proved that practice plus imaging makes for optimum performance—or flow. Athletes are more likely to get into their optimum zone with imaging as part of their routine. Dyer also assisted astronauts in NASA's quest for landing on the moon. His primary message was if you can picture it, you can do it.

This is the same message we introduced in *Recovery Zone I* with the formula for getting the life you want: A + B + C = your optimum zone when:

- A = A vision or model of what you intend
- B = A commitment or passion to change
- C = A plan to make it happen

Today, if you did not get done what you intended to do because you responded to the needs of others, did things that were not necessary, or were more about appearances, or worse, none of the things you did were important, you have wasted your day. That time is gone. And if you live your life this way, you will end up like Ivan Ilyich, wondering what happened and what you did wrong.

Recovery Zone II is designed to help you make your outside world match your inside world. For this, you have to use the strategy of altering your perspective on your life. Einstein's challenge to modern physics and systems—his theory of relativity—is a perspective you use as you do this.

Here is where the analogy of the train helps again. If you are on the train, your perspective shifts as you go from the dining car to the sleeping car. You are in the here and now of life of the train. However, by observing the train at a distance from the top of the hill, you see the train in its totality. You also can see where it came from and where it is going. How you think about the train is relative to where you are.

Relativity is in part about using multiple perspectives to make sense of it all. Looking at your life from the top of the hill, you see the entirety of the train, its cars, engine, and crew. You know how it got there and where it is going in that moment in time. When you look at your life from beginning to end, the vision from the top of the hill helps you to see what happened in your life, so you can ask if that is what you intended. Plus, you now can imagine that train's look, destination, speed, and purpose. It is the opportunity to "true" up as engineers say, so that the person inside the train is also viewing the entire train.

Have you ever had the experience of receiving the same message from a number of different, unrelated sources at about the same time? You can write it off to coincidence. But once you understand how connected we all are to the energy of the universe, such synchronies are important to notice.

I did not fully understand that concept in the fall of 2004. After all, I was only 60. What did I know at 60? Anyway, it took a near death experience to get my attention.

As I said before, over the winter I'd contracted a disease called Valley Fever. It is a fungus that inhabits the desert sands. Breathing this fungus into your lungs can be deadly. Think of the curse of King Tut. When the early explorers of his tomb started dying in large numbers, it was attributed to a curse by the ancient emperor. In reality, they had disturbed the desert floor and inhaled the fungus. What happened for me was that my next-door neighbors finally had decided to start building their new home—disturbing the desert sands. I became very ill from inhaling the dust and had great difficulty breathing.

I remember lying in my bed in the Mayo hospital in this nether space, gazing into great peacefulness and feeling how simple it would be to leave earthly cares and physical pain behind by crossing over. I opened my left eye to a mere slit. There, inches away from my face were the eyes of my wife, Suzanne, and my youngest daughter, Erin. I knew instantly I wanted to stay and be with my family. Thus began a painful four-month recovery. My lungs still have the scars.

During my recovery, I had plenty of time to think about things. Previously, I had been in a group of healthcare leaders who were working on their leadership skills. I had been an active member for two years. So, my colleagues in that group were now friends who knew me and my story.

A few months before my illness, one of the group members looked at me after I had shared about my current struggles and said, "I have heard this story from you before. And I am not sure you really want to succeed. At this point, I can't really tell what your endgame is. There is no way it hangs together for me. I see you working hard, but I'm starting to wonder if you're just spinning your wheels and avoiding getting what you want." I was angry and hurt. I had spent two years with him refining my goals and purposes, and I still did not make sense to him. I felt very judged.

Two weeks later at a board meeting for a charity that focused on addiction research, I got the same message. At that time, we had a member who had been a long-time sitting congresswoman. She was the first person elected to Congress who had gone to treatment for her alcoholism and then been re-elected. She was a great board member, very skilled, and also very direct. She said to me, "I love this board and what we do, but frankly it is you I can't figure out. There are so many things going on with you, but why? When we are at the end, Pat, what have we got? What did we actually get done?" So basically she raised the same question that the group member had raised. And the very same feelings I had in my group came back.

As I had time in recovery from Valley Fever, I sat at my chess table and took the time to really think about my life. What would it look like as a whole? Something was missing, and people were seeing the lack of a coherent, explainable whole. I spent almost four months working on this issue as I could. I realized that the question being asked of me was about the impact of all my efforts. What really was important? What did I really want and what was I willing to sacrifice to make that happen?

The crucible of Admiral Stockdale's paradox suddenly made sense to me. The prisoner of war survivors he described did two things to focus: first, they totally immersed themselves in the present moment. Second, they became completely committed to a vision whose every detail was etched in the purpose algorithms of their brain. Plus, most importantly, both are absolutely necessary and completely true. Both demand your full attention. I finally understood that the essence of the structure of the universe is found in spiritual paradox. In other words, we are on the train and we are at the top of the hill watching the train at the same moment in time.

As a therapist, I used the words "here and now," believed I understood them, and practiced what I thought they meant. Yet I needed to learn that being in the here and now is more than just paying attention. The practice of being in the here and now really means paying attention to what is important, for there are no "ordinary moments." It is one thing to notice, quite another to "show up." Every moment is valuable—and once gone, it is gone forever.

When I walked out of the Mayo Clinic and noticed the beauty of the poppy garden, which I had seen many times before, I asked myself why I had not noticed the garden's beauty. I suddenly realized that I had allowed myself to be involved with time-consuming activities that really did not matter. I was not taking in what was in front of me. The vow I made that day was not to spend time on activities and involvements that did not matter to me.

Intentionality is the bedrock of resilience. Resilience is the essence of recovery and core to all success. If you need a book on this, try Lynne McTaggart's *The Intention Experiment*. In the book, she summarizes the science that has led to the importance of being intentional. Intention leads to vision and purpose. And vision leads to the goals that manifest in the steps that make for achievement, success, and the implementation of dreams.

Mihaly Csikszentmihalyi also notes that in the process of getting into purposeful flow, happiness ensues. I realized that in focusing on what matters and what fits for me, I was defining what my legacy was to be. Some use the term "call," but in reality, it is answering the questions, "Why do this? What is my life about?" I started writing about this and used the term "legacy statement" or, more euphemistically, the ultimate to do list. My chess table morphed from a vision table to a legacy table.

As I have shared this process, I have often, at some point, had a participant—clinicians as well as patients—stand up, hesitate, and then say out loud, "The defining moment of this whole experience and maybe even my life was the Legacy Statement and Ultimate To Do List." That moment can still bring me to tears because it was true for me too.

Many people will say, "I do not feel a call," like in the hero's journey scenario. Actually, though, it is in there. They simply must search for it. The process of the legacy table starts a fundamental rewrite of the bottom-up brain. True north in your emotional constellation is lit up for you if you do this carefully and conscientiously. Once done, it is parallel to becoming pregnant. You either are or you are not. If you are, you must deal with the reality. There is no going back.

Once you know your true north and emotional compass, you may want to stray, but there is no going back. You now know too much. This is why in *Recovery Zone I* we speak of the significance of the word "over" as part of grieving. When something is over, it is over and you focus on "next." It is as Stephen Levine describes it, the "war" of grief.

"In the world within and around us, heaven and hell are constantly warring for our approval. The war-torn heart longs for a moment's peace. The less we make peace with our pain, the more we tend to make war on others."

Most of the readers of this book have been through a war of some type. Addiction, trauma, dysfunctional relationships, or some sort of chaos has caused you to seek recovery. For you, "over" and "not going back" are not incidental. Thus, the remainder of this chapter is devoted to making out an Ultimate To Do List and creating a statement of legacy.

To help you, we have broken this process into five phases. Each phase involves a lot of thinking and time. These phases are not something you can complete in a few minutes and say you have done the work. Each phase takes time, effort, and thought. More importantly, the process works best when you have companions who are asking the same questions. The five phases are:

- **Phase One** — Look back through *Recovery Zone I* and the exercises in this book to distill the intents and discontinuities of your life. This helps you see the dots that you need to connect.

- **Phase Two** — Admitting and affirming to yourself the genuine achievements and progress you have made in your life already. This can help you see what does in fact matter to you.
- **Phase Three** — Distilling from Phases One and Two the essential goals and values that raise the bar by which you measure the future. This helps you match your insides with your outside, including realities of the external or "ordinary world."
- **Phase Four** — The Ultimate To Do List connects the dots in four essential categories: (1) What remains to be done, somewhat like a universal bucket list; (2) How to make currency exist in your life, so when you leave it is clear to everyone what was important; (3) What new frontiers of growth are imperative to keep your momentum; and (4) How to translate this work so it rests on a platform of real recovery.
- **Phase Five** — Create a legacy statement. Explaining this statement to others so they can help you clarify it is fundamental to success. Plus, it is not a value or goal if you cannot describe it to the important people in your life.

This chapter is pivotal to the remaining chapters that can transform your life. It is your ticket to walking through the portal of being in the one true zone for you.

Phase One – Gathering the Dots

The patient leaned back and was speaking of a twelve-step meeting he was about to speak at that week. He described that he went back to the journals he wrote during the perfect storm. And then he reread the assignments he completed in treatment. He then said, "I could not believe how bad it was and how distorted my thinking was. That was a helpful perspective on how far I have come. The other thing was that the crisis made clear to me what was most important in my life to me then—and what still is."

Crisis and hardship make clear what we need the most in our lives. It is helpful to: (a) keep an ongoing record of your progress, and (b) to periodically take the time to reflect on the past. The gold when you make your Ultimate To Do List (UTDL) is the clarity your experience gives you about what matters and who you really are. I highly recommend that you carve out time to revisit your early work in recovery as you start the UTDL process. After you have done this, record at least five things that were the most important things that mattered to you by virtue of going through the turmoil of your life falling apart. What do you never want to forget about your life ever again? In *Recovery Zone I* we referred to these as "imperatives"—those moments that we would never repeat.

Recovery Zone I is a journey through your interior world and how to navigate changing to a zone of peace, meaning, and excellence. The journey was about teaching you strategies and helping you untangle the many contributing factors to that perfect storm. From the perspective of the eye of the storm, you have a picture of what not to repeat. Many of the exercises contained statements about what long-term items mattered in your life. Examples would include your mission statements for your personal covenant, action steps to use your grief, and the mission reclamation work you did around shame.

In the section below entitled *Recovery Zone I* Reflections, the first column asks you to make a list of what mattered. The next column has the heading Commonalities and Trends. These two columns can help you see that the same desires and passions emerge repeatedly for you. Then you are asked to synthesize the items that emerge repeatedly into categories, listing at least five but no more than seven of these common purposes. Lastly, there is a parallel column that asks, "Why is this important?"

As you review your internal Recovery Zone work, you will trip over items that are really not goals or strategic enough to rank as a life achievement. But they are still tasks that you do not wish to forget to do. They are usually things that are important but got lost in the process. Examples might be something "unfinished" out of the Grief section or an important amends out of the Relationship critical closure process. At the end of this chapter is a section called "The Forget Me Not Clipboard." Keep track of these items by recording them on your clipboard.

Early Recovery Reflections

Notes from the crisis and hardships that caused this "melt down." What still matters to you and is important to your life?

Exercise 6.1

What Matters?

Phase 1.1 Exercise

Looking back over your work in *Recovery Zone I* and your previous recovery work, you can uncover the statements and themes of what stood out to you. In the exercise below, fill out the 20 spaces of what matters to you. The first ten are from *Recovery Zone I*, the last ten could come from any part of your recovery work. Please list your reference and where it came from. It could be additional *Recovery Zone I* exercises, work with a therapist, or journaling.

Exercise	What Matters?
1. The Decision Table	
2. Best Moments	
3. The Grievance Story	
4. Intuition Insight	
5. Your Hero Map	
6. Your Place in the Family	
7. Mission Reclamation	
8. Sorrow: The Unfinished	
9. Mission Statement	

10. Covenant Letter	
11.	
12.	
13.	
14.	
15.	
16.	
17.	
18.	
19.	
20.	

Exercise 6.2

Commonalities and Trends

Phase 1.2 Exercise

In reviewing your previous exercise, "What Matters to You," you will notice there are commonalities and trends regarding what matters to you. In this exercise, you are asked to take the proceeding exercise and create at least five but no more than seven common categories, purposes, or trends of what "What Matters" to you. (This is what you want your life to reflect of who you are.)

Commonalities and Trends (of what matters)
1.
2.
3.
4.
5.
6.
7.

Exercise 6.3

Why Is It Important?—The Why Behind the Why

Phase 1.3 Exercise

In this exercise, record why you currently believe the items on your list of What Matters to You are important to you. You may also apply what you have learned early in *Recovery Zone II* about the "Why Behind the Why" and what that may be for you at this time.

Why Is It Important?
1.
2.
3.
4.
5.
6.
7.

Exercise 6.4

Phase Two—Legacy Focus: Lifetime At A Glance

Let us return to Einstein's hill. That perspective allowed us to see where the train came from and where it was going. As a perspective, it is also a filter through which to measure and forecast progress. From a lifetime perspective, it is an illuminating "glance" at your whole life.

The first part of the process is to affirm what you have done that matters to you. This recognition is not easy. I struggled with it on many levels. For example, in the category of achievements, an event that I was proud of occurred in my freshman year in college. We were all required in the Vietnam era to participate in the Reserve Officers Training Corps (ROTC). On the first day of class we were introduced to the basics of close order drill—how to march as a group. We were divided into squads of eight. We were also instructed on the basics of how to march with an M1 rifle. Randomly, people were selected as "squad leaders." I was nominated for that task in my squad. We were told to practice on our own, and the following Saturday there would be a competition involving the whole battalion of students.

I talked to my classmates in my squad and we agreed to practice two nights that week and to make the best of it. None of us knew what we were doing. What we did not know was that we were one of the few squads that did actually practice. Come that Saturday, we were inspected and marched all day. During inspection, I brought my rifle up so fast it hit the bill of the cap of my inspecting officer. It was not exactly an auspicious start. Yet at the end of the day, our squad scored dramatically higher than any other, and we won the battle group competition.

Immediately I was harassed as "gung-ho military" by some individuals I did not even know. Here is what I did know: I was a farm kid (politically pretty unaware) who took my assignment seriously, got cooperation from seven others who were like me, and the results of my efforts showed. Today, there is probably no one alive who even remembers that day. But it mattered to me. And that is the trick I learned to this assignment. No matter how incidental it seems, if it matters to you, it counts. Your goals emerge out of achievements both big and small. They have consistency and coherence of their own.

Here is another example in the same category of looking at your achievements. I made a list of all the programs, companies, and organizations I started. Out of 24, 15 were still functioning. Nine of the programs had ceased to function. What I heard in my head was what my father often said about how he had to work to keep me from getting a "big head," which meant I should focus on the programs that had not succeeded. To say I started 15 existing entities sounded egotistical and arrogant. Yet I was trying to follow the protocol I had set out for myself, which required listing my accomplishments. Listing my failings and failures would have been lots easier. But the goal was to see the accumulation of what I actually had done—which direction was the train coming from that was consistent with where I wanted to go.

Achievement is the first category. You are asked to list your genuine achievements. Raising children is an achievement. So is a successful marriage, a college degree, and overcoming failure. Anything counts if you had the grit to get it done. It is easy to criticize but hard to build. Then you are asked to switch the valence, the value assigned to an object, behavior, or consequence, and think about what you still would like to achieve in your life, whether it be a hobby, retirement, or career-related. Maybe there is a book to finish, an idea you think might work, a new business, or even a business that can be brought to a whole new level. What would you enjoy and find challenging and have the skills to accomplish?

The second category is legacies. Are there family heirlooms you wish to pass on to future generations? Are there treasured family lands, cabins, or farms to be kept in the family? Are there traditions meaningful to people? Is there something philanthropic you have helped start? Is there writing, memories, organizations, or research you contributed to that will continue your impact on the planet? Is there something you have done that will touch people long after you have gone?

People often have problems with this category, even if they have had significant impact in many ways. Sometimes in therapy or in a group everybody else sees it, but the individual either does not or minimize their impact on others. If it is hard to think about, give yourself time to think through what you can still do, for being intentional about legacy can have incredible impact. This second category is extremely important since it is a category in which you do something you like, are capable of doing, and may matter greatly.

The third category is Best Experiences. Best Experiences are more like the ultimate bucket list. If you think of experiences you have had, what does your mind keep going back to as the most fun, eye opening, exciting, rewarding, and renewing experiences you ever had? The problem with this category is that it is easier to think about events you would still like to create for yourself or your family. The answer: You do not have time. The reason so many adventures or places linger on your bucket list is that you did not have sufficient passion to plan. You let life and money make the decisions.

Get them down on your list and we will figure out how to make these things happen later. Notice what you have done. What can you learn from what you have done?

The fourth category is Best Relationships. Best Relationships may be the most important of the categories. You are asked to identify the most important, best relationships across your life span to date. Use any criteria that matters to you: the most fun, the most productive, the most learning filled, the most supportive, the most engaging, the most humorous, the most loving—all these different factors can go into the Best Relationships category.

I have been blessed to know some of the most interesting, intelligent, dedicated, creative, hilarious, and productive people on the planet. At this writing, I am 76. And as I look around me, most of my most treasured relationships are with people who are now deceased. So for me, the perspective on top of the hill changes.

I am doing a much better job of honoring those people who are still here. I am keenly aware of the value of all my kin—young and old. And I am looking for people with whom to have relationships. The point is that I really understand who I am looking for. Grief, I believe, is our number one teacher. I bet you believe this too. This is why the second half of the Best Relationships category asks the very pointed question: In the time that is left to you, what relationships do you need? List those and think about why.

1. _____

_____

2. _____

_____

3. _____

_____

4. _____

_____

5. _____

_____

6. _____

_____

7. _____

_____

8. _____

_____

9. _____

_____

10. _____

_____

ACHIEVEMENTS – What are the achievements in your life?

Phase 2.1 Exercise

Look back over your life and list the things you view as genuine achievements. Raising children is an achievement. So is a successful marriage, a college degree, and overcoming failure. Anything counts if you had the grit to get it done.

Think about what you still would like to achieve in your life, whether it be hobby, retirement, or career-related. Maybe there is a book to finish, an idea you think might work, or a new business, or even a business that can be brought to a whole new level. What would you enjoy, find challenging, and have the skills to start and/or finish?

ACHIEVEMENTS	ACHIEVEMENTS—To Be Done
1.	
2.	
3.	
4.	
5.	
6.	
7.	
8.	
9.	
10.	

Exercise 6.5

LEGACIES—What are the legacies in your life?

Phase 2.2 Exercise

Are there family heirlooms you wish to pass on to future generations? Are there lands, cabins, or farms to be kept in the family? Are there traditions meaningful to you and others? Is there something philanthropic you have helped start? Are there writings, memories, organizations, or research you contributed to that will continue your impact on the planet? A legacy can also be something small and personal just between you and someone else. Have you taught someone how to fish? Or how to bake your family's famous pies? Big or small, is there something you have done that will touch people long after you have gone?

Give yourself time to think through what you can still do, for being intentional about a legacy can have incredible impact. This is extremely important, since this is a category in which you do something you like, are capable of doing, and that may matter greatly. List the legacies you've made and that you would still like to make below.

LEGACIES	LEGACIES—To Be Made
1.	
2.	
3.	
4.	
5.	
6.	
7.	
8.	
9.	
10.	

Exercise 6.6

GREAT EXPERIENCES – Experiences you have had to date

Phase 2.3 Exercise

The best experiences are more like the ultimate bucket list. If you think of experiences you have had, what does your mind keep going back to as the most fun, eye-opening, exciting, rewarding, and renewing? List your Great Experiences below. Notice what you have done. What can you learn from what you have done? What great experiences would you still like to have?

GREAT EXPERIENCES	EXPERIENCES—To Still Have
1.	
2.	
3.	
4.	
5.	
6.	
7.	
8.	
9.	
10.	

Exercise 6.7

BEST RELATIONSHIPS –
List the best relationships you have had to date

Phase 2.4 Exercise

Best Relationships may be the most important of the four categories. You are asked to identify the most important, best relationships across your life span to date. Use any criteria that matters to you: the most fun, the most productive, the most learning-filled, the most supportive, the most engaging, the most humorous, the most loving—all these different factors can go into the Best Relationships category. List the best relationships you have had to date. Then think about the time that is left to you and the types of relationships you still want to make. List those and think about why they are important to you.

RELATIONSHIPS	RELATIONSHIPS—To Be Made
1.	
2.	
3.	
4.	
5.	
6.	
7.	
8.	
9.	
10.	

Exercise 6.8

Phase Three – Goals, Values, Meaning

Think of a big red arrow pointing to this next piece of work. In this moment, you can step out of your history and into your destiny. At this point, your future belongs to you.

Looking through all the work you have done for Phases I and II, commonalities and themes should be obvious. From a hilltop perch, it is important for you to distill out of the reoccurring incidents, passions, and wishes to create your top five goals. These goals should be stated concisely yet should be big enough to include all of your vision.

In my case, my two top goals were: (1) To help create a body of knowledge about addiction so that people could get help (in contrast to how little was available when I needed it), and (2) To create a group of clinicians who knew what to do with non-substance addictions. Both of those are specific yet wide enough to include the various activities that I envisioned. A third goal was to create events and space for my family to enjoy their lives together. Again, note the clarity of purpose that is broad enough to contain a variety of ways to meet the goal.

Your purpose now is to review what you have done and what you have envisioned and craft five statements of purpose or goals. Let your wise mind help you sift through the streams flowing through your brain, determine what matters to you, and, when it is all over, what you want to happen. In the space provided, describe as best you can these five legacy categories. Do not worry about wording at this point because you will have several chances later in your process to refine and rewrite these five life purposes.

Next you will note a space entitled "What You Want Said." The idea here is to picture your funeral or graveside service. Reflect on each of your goals. What statement would you want said at your funeral that causes everyone else to nod their heads in agreement about you living up to that purpose. My number one purpose was to create a body of knowledge. About that goal, the statement I hope people will say, "He lived as he taught." Another way of phrasing it would be, "He practiced what he preached."

Sometimes these phrases have deep roots in your family history. My grandfather died pheasant hunting in North Dakota. A pheasant was flushed, and he raised his gun to shoot but had a heart attack that instantly killed him. He never pulled the trigger. When my father picked up his Dad's gun, he noted that the safety switch was still on.

As my Dad told this story at the funeral, there were tears in his eyes. Every young person who learns to hunt is told that you do not ever take the safety off until you are a nanosecond away from pulling the trigger and sure what you were shooting at. So many hunting accidents and deaths occurred because people take their safety off too early. Obviously, my father had learned that lesson from his father. Equally obvious was that it had deep meaning for my father in terms of the way my grandfather lived his life. My Dad was sharing deep meaning in the story (like all stories), even though it may have seemed minor to many. As grandpa died, he was living out the rule he taught. This represented deep importance to my father. More importantly for my purposes, it represented how I wish to live my life.

When finished, you should have five goals matched with five phrases or sentences that you would hope to reflect your purposes—a phrase that could be said about you when you pass. Embedded in each combination of goal and phrases is a value. Ask yourself what the common value is. Record it as simply and concisely as possible. For me, the value was that I would be true to what I say is true about me.

Ultimately, your five goals and five values will be the standards of your true north. Everything you place on your Ultimate To Do List must fit within this framework. Remember, resilience and recovery depend on intentionality.

FIVE STATEMENTS OF PURPOSE OR GOALS

Phase 3.1 Exercise

List five goals or purposes matched with five phrases or sentences that reflect your purposes—things that could be said about you when you pass. Embedded in each combination of goal and phrase is a value.

PURPOSE OR GOAL	What you would like said about you regarding your goals?
1.	
2.	
3.	
4.	
5.	

Exercise 6.9

FIVE CORE VALUES

Phase 3.2 Exercise

Embedded in each combination of goal and phrase is a value. List five values that reflect your five goals and purposes.

FIVE CORE VALUES
1.
2.
3.
4.
5.

Exercise 6.10

Phase Four – Creating Your Ultimate To Do List

The first decision to make is the format you choose for your UTD list. To help you, worksheets for creating your UTD list are laid out in this book. However, by now you likely know that such an important document is best done on large worksheets. Your therapist may ask you to complete large worksheets with all the accompanying graphics as part of their materials they received for teaching Recovery Zone as a curriculum. Or you can go to Gentlepath.com and get your own set. Another option requires—you guessed it—a large table to work on. Like the Vision Table, this "Legacy Table" work lends itself to working on large artist pads or easel paper. These are available in any office products or craft store; it just depends on how you prefer to do your list.

Many may still prefer to work in the book because it keeps the material close and flows with the logic of the process. That said, the preprinted forms are inviting and help to create your work in larger spaces. The large artist paper provides you with the most space, lending itself to more of the being on the "hill" experience. The next thing is to note or make four separate sections or quadrants. Each section becomes a focus of your Ultimate To Do List. Start with the upper right quarter of your paper or follow the sequence as we present them in the book.

Life Completion – Your Life Priorities and Legacy Table One

In the first section or option, list all those items that you realize you still want to do or have. To start, return to your earlier work in this chapter entitled: The Legacy Focus: Life At A Glance. You will remember we asked you to look at what you still wanted to have happen for Achievements, Legacies, Experiences and Relationships. Legacy Table One is to summarize a "bucket list" of your remaining priorities in your life in each of these lists. In addition, there may be things you wish to do that do not fit in any of those categories. We use the term Special Goals for these unique items. Review your vision table and the other exercises in *Recovery Zone II* and record what you want to accomplish yet in your life. What ultimately matters to you? This allows you to do both option expansion and option selection. We again have provided you with space to acknowledge your most important accomplishments so you see the momentum of your life.

Systems Theory tells us that the strongest systems are those with the widest range of options. Our evolution as a species shows that we were successful because of our ability to adapt more easily than competitive versions of early humans. In other words, to have what you want, you have to look around at all your options and abilities. Then you begin the refining process to knit together a plan.

We use the hummingbird as an example. It has the ability to stop and hover. It is also capable of moving in any direction (up, down, forward, backward). But when it decides the route to take, it is decisive and quick as well as fierce in its commitments. This metaphor is useful to keep in mind as you select your options and craft a final vision of what you are seeking in your life. One way to do that selection is to review your life goals and values. Place an "X" in the space provided on those items which most closely match your goals and values statement.

Life Completion – Your Life Priorities and Legacy Table One

Transcribe your life priorities in each category. Place an "X" in the small box next to those that most match your life goals and values.

Achievements	Legacies	Great Experiences	Best Relationships
TO DATE:	TO DATE:	TO DATE:	TO DATE:
1			
2			
3			
4			
5			
TO BE DONE:	TO BE MADE:	TO BE EXPERIENCED:	TO BE DEVELOPED:
1			
2			
3			
4			
5			

Exercise 6.11

Exit Strategies – Your Life Obligations: Legacy Table Two

The concept of "currency" comes out of twelve step programs. Staying current means keeping people informed, not letting resentments build, and not procrastinating on critical aspects of recovery. If you make a mistake, "promptly admitting it" is an example of currency. If you have made amends to everyone on your list but something new happens, you take corrective action and make amends as soon as possible. If you slip, you do not sit on that information. You immediately seek support. In your old life, you were on the "deferred living plan" with rationales like "finding the right moment" or waiting until some task was done. Or there always was putting things off until people were in the right mood.

Keeping current means facing tasks most of us would like to defer. Probably at the top of most people's obligation list is their written will. If you do not have a will, have a will that is not current or does not match your situation now, or you have not thought through all that could happen because of it, you will be doing a great disservice to people you love. No matter what your age, there is an important duty here. There are few things that can happen that are more destructive to family relationships than an ill-conceived will. Writing down who receives what needs to be clearly detailed. A family farm, a lake cabin, special possessions, valued keepsakes, or ownership of a family business can immerse loving siblings into profound, ugly conflict that can last for generations. I have witnessed the destructive nature of no or poorly specified instructions over and over. But a thoughtful plan can alleviate heartache and allow for grieving and appropriate healing sorrow.

An example is a friend who had a nice cabin on the seashore. His son told him that he wanted to inherit the cabin. None of his siblings at that time wanted it. (Although you would be amazed how those preferences can radically change post-funeral.) My friend said to the son that he could buy it and keep it in the family. They established a market price that the son paid. The money paid was part of the estate to be divided equitably. No one lost because one member got the cabin. Those kinds of arrangements, worked out ahead of time, can save a lot of anger, bitterness, and heartache. Similarly, family possessions of special meaning should be designated including cars, jewelry, and collections, basically anything to which people might be deeply attached. Even very young adults would be amazed at what would be important to others in the family—if they were asked.

Making a will is a good prioritization exercise for you. When your life is over, "what does it look like" comes into sharp focus. We accumulate so much stuff that a will forces us to review how much we hold onto that we no longer need. Remember Yoda's famous comment from *Star Wars* about the need to "Train yourself to let go of everything you fear to lose." Creating a will also makes clear what would be still worth acquiring for whatever purpose.

A will is ultimately an act of caring and, in many ways, it can also be a statement. It means that it matters to you not to leave a mess for the people that you care for. Most of us should review our wills quarterly. I am amazed at how often adjustments need to be made. Do not assume you know how things will work out no matter what your age is.

Making a will is the tip of the spear in some ways. Closely behind it are your medical instructions and your plans or instructions for celebrating your passage. I do not recommend relying on others to "figure it out." My deceased wife and I went through quite a process because she did not want to do it and would only do it if I did mine as well. I am so grateful for that. First, when she thought about it, she wanted things I would never have guessed but in retrospect could see as very important and meaningful. Second, our children had different and conflicting ideas as to what would be best. Ultimately, of course, her list trumped everything and saved lots of conflict.

In the days after a passing, there are cards, letters, and flowers but loved ones are pretty numb. The sorrow really sets in about three to four weeks later. As you strategize what you want to have happen, include some rituals or actions that are further out in time. It is in the long haul that grief needs tending. For example, a letter can be written with the request not to be read for a certain period like first anniversary of the death or the next birthday.

Humans have built-in mechanisms to dissolve a blood clot, but those mechanisms may have to work over a long time. Clots of sorrow are the same. Bit by bit, the sorrow dissipates and becomes adsorbed. We don't stop loving just because we had a funeral for them. So support is just as important down the line as in the immediate aftermath of someone's passing. What are your strategies to extend support to loved ones over the long haul? What can you do now to provide comfort and love? Do you have letters you have written that can be collected and then rediscovered? I am asking you to think thoughtfully beyond your own funeral.

For certain, two things will occur in your life. First, the time of reckoning will happen at a speed that is hard to believe. Second, it will happen before you expect it.

In my life I saved many things from the growing years of my four children that I wish them to have. Almost all of it they now have so they can choose their own memories and keepsakes. I am down to a single trunk, and piece by piece it becomes less crowded. There are some things I just want to keep because every now and then I want to touch them or look at them.

This brings us to additional issues of currency. The river of life does not stop. You will change things. Maybe you will take my recovery advice and take a year off, sell the family business, or start a new one. You may have a dream home or a novel to finish. What strategies do you need to have on deck now? What about the unexpected? Going back to an earlier chapter, do you have enough money to live a year without income? What preparations do you need to make for the remainder of your life and for the life of your loved ones after you leave?

All of these considerations bring to mind planning for life transitions. If you are going to make major life changes, you have to plan for transitions (like taking a year off) and preparations (what is retirement for you?). You cannot duck the realities of these issues. Plus, how do you take steps to care for yourself? Do you need to lose weight? Get further education? Take care of physical issues? What key boundaries do you need to bring into your recovery and therapy work? What do you need to do to make sure people cannot invade you with identify theft?

Henry Cloud, in his book *Boundaries: When to Say Yes, How to Say No to Take Control of Your Life*, brought the word "boundaries" into modern therapy made an astute observation: Once you have surrounded yourself with good boundaries, you feel safe enough to forgive others. Much of therapy is about the deconstruction of our abusers and detecting how our identities were stolen. It is like you have to be the real, vulnerable you, but also have a strong shell that sheds life's chaos. As part of the covenant with self, you must take care of yourself step by step. In this way, life is not about the exciting or dramatic moments, it is about putting one foot in front of the other.

Our image for this section of your Legacy Table is the turtle. The hard shell (read boundaries) protects the vulnerable self. Slow and steady progress is the theme. Not making assumptions, not taking things personally, not rushing in, not taking things or situations for granted, and never stopping in terms of persistence—all are necessary character traits. This is a critical part of things for your Ultimate To Do list. Keeping focused and doing what you must equals a purpose-driven life. Notice that out of the species of the earth, turtles are among those who live the longest. Want to live a long life? Think "currency."

The following exercise helps you to focus on Exit Strategies and Planning: Legacy Table Two. Space exists for you to list what is done. You may already have thought through your will, for example. Yet, as before, it provides space for you to list what remains: will considerations, funeral planning issues, transition plans, and preparations for the rest of your life. Again, once you have thought this through, mark an "X" next to those items that most closely match your life goals and values.

Exit and Planning Strategies: Legacy Table Two

Transcribe your life priorities in each category. Place an "X" in the small box next to those that most match your life goals and values.

Will:	Funeral:	Transitions:	Preparations:
TO DATE:	TO DATE:	TO DATE:	TO DATE:
1			
2			
3			
4			
5			
TO BE DONE:	TO BE DONE:	TO BE MADE:	TO BE MADE:
1			
2			
3			
4			
5			

Exercise 6.12

Lessons: Legacy Table Three

Lessons. The telling of a story is more than reporting events. As a parent, many times I would be retelling a story to a sleepy child who would perk up and say, "You forgot the part about...." If the kid knows the story as well as you do, why are you telling it again? It took a long time for me to learn, it is not the story that is important. Story telling is about bonding. The story is core to attachment—which is critical to intimacy and to happiness.

For over 40 years it was my privilege to be a part of a group of men who went to recovery together, and also hunted and fished together. In short, we had a history. At holiday dinners we always told the stories of our adventures. Some were funny, some were about challenges, some were about dangers, and some clearly were about losses. After some time, our wives began adding to or even completed the telling of the stories about us—even though they were not there at the original event. But they became part of the storytelling. It became their story, too. At times, all of us would laugh until tears came. Sometimes it was just tears.

I realize that what was happening was about the power of story. As we shall see, storytelling is crucial to our understanding of the brain and recovery. For the moment, though, we need to focus on meaning and story as part of our legacy. For example, one night I had two of my grandsons with me at a hotel that had a vast pool with play equipment. We had a great time. Later that evening I noticed that the light was on in the boy's bedroom in our suite. I went in only to find my oldest grandson up, in tears, and wanting to call his mom. We did and my son asked if I wanted him to pick the boys up. I told him to let me work with this for a while.

In the ensuing conversation with my grandson, I found out this was his first night away from home and he was lonely for his parents. So, I told him this story. My great-grandfather left Sweden at the age of 16 (I emphasized the "left his family" part) to come to Minnesota. He learned the language and two years later contacted his childhood sweetheart, who then "left her family," not knowing anyone but my great grandfather. As he had done, she crossed the ocean and made her way to Minnesota. Together they had a farm, other businesses that also were very successful, and by all reports a very happy marriage. At that time, I had the gold pocket watch given to my great-grandfather by his parents with a gold chain and an 1870 issue of a Swedish coin. The gift was to remind my great-grandfather of his roots and that he was loved by his family. (I also have the original trunk that my great-grandmother traveled to American with.) In it were all that she possessed in the world—other than her immense faith in the young man she was to marry. Sometimes people ask me about the trunk I keep my last keepsakes in. You guessed it. It was my great-grandmother's.

The boys were familiar with the watch because it was in a case on my desk. I added that I was going to pass it on to their father. "Great!" he said, "I am the oldest kid so I will get it." He went promptly to sleep as I realized I created a potential problem.

The next morning my son joined us for breakfast. I told him the whole story of the previous evening and he and both boys listened intently. I made it clear that the gift was to my son and the ultimate inheritor of the watch was his choice. The expression on my son's face said, "Thanks a lot!" So then, to make it fair, I went to an antique watch dealer and bought another pocket watch with a great story that was also over a hundred years old. I carried it to many of the key moments of my career, as I had done with the other watch. Then I passed both to my son so each of his boys would have their grandfather's pocket watch. My son will figure out who gets which watch. He always figures these things out. It is one of the many reasons I like him so much.

The story of the watch and the trunk are synecdoches. A synecdoche is when something means much more than what it is. Yes, at one level we are talking about an old pocket watch that is not really very convenient. Still, it runs very well. The old trunk still works too but is way too heavy by today's standards. On a deeper level, however, both items represent individuation and becoming a courageous young adult.

Leaving your family in order to carve out a new life for yourselves is a personal epic. It is about answering a call and making a path where there was not one. My ancestors did this. I want us to be like them. Successful therapy and recovery is acknowledging the many synecdoches that already exist—or could.

In the opening pages of this book is my description of talking to my granddaughter about what I witnessed in her deceased grandmother. I was a witness, but I also added to her story. We are always teaching. We surround ourselves with symbols that mean a great deal to us—but if unshared, the synecdoche dies. As does our impact and purpose. Much of therapy is figuring out the symbols we live by and the meanings we attach to them. When you wrote out what you wanted said about you, where did that come from and why did it matter? Otis Green writes about making a legacy:

> As social creatures, we have an impact on others, leaving impressions that will survive us. The question is how conscious we are of our transient nature and how conscious we are of the legacies we leave behind. Many traditions encourage the development of an awareness of our mortality, so we may use our days more wisely. Those who are inattentive to the potential of death may face the end of their lives with a realization they have not lived in ways they want remembered. (Otis Green—2003)

A refining process occurs when we live with awareness of what ultimately matters. We are constantly invited, pushed, and expanded to see messages, possibilities, and paths open to us we would have missed. By thinking of how we impact others, we are impacted because the bandwidth of our conscious awareness expands, causing us to live our lives more truly as ourselves, to achieve an excellence and a happiness that otherwise we would not have known, and, no matter what happens, to live our lives fully even with all the world's suffering.

We use the dragonfly as a symbol of this part of our work. For traditional peoples, dragonflies were "message bearers" about being true to ourselves. A dragonfly sighting was a symbol to stop and ask oneself, *What am I missing?* Sometimes it is the obvious we overlook. All of us have had misgivings and even warnings about something and proceeded anyway. The reciprocal is also true. All of us have had hunches, messages, and beliefs we failed to follow, only to profoundly regretted our inaction later. By living intentionally, aware of our impact in legacy, we sharpen our intuitions and self-knowledge, forging the courage to do the next right thing.

Lessons: Legacy Table Three asks you to reflect in a conscious way your impact on others you love over the life span. Are there **gifts** you can leave with others which embody important meanings and synechdoches? Are there stories or events which you have witnessed but never shared? If you are in recovery and made it this far, you have stories—that maybe need to be told. What **symbols** matter to you? In earlier times family symbols were integrated into a family shield. What is on your shield and do your kids, spouse, and even parents know them? As a family exercise, one of my daughters proposed that each member name an animal that they were most like. That exercise has been a source of many discussions over the years.

If you were to think about the most valued learnings you have about life, what would be on that list of **teachings**? Have you ever shared them? What have you passed on so far? Consider what you have taught and know you still want to pass on. When and where would be a good opportunity without it coming across as "preachy." Before my mother died, she asked my help in writing a short book called "Rosie Remembers." In it were amazing stories none of us knew. As her "editor" she also told me about what she left out, some of which was markedly more important than what she included. The whole process was a gift to us all. And I am going to make certain that some of what she left out gets integrated into our family story.

Lessons: Legacy Table Three

Transcribe your life priorities in each category. Place an "X" in the small box next to those that most match your life goals and values.

Gifts:	Witnessing:	Symbols:	Teachings:
TO DATE:	**TO DATE:**	**TO DATE:**	**TO DATE:**
1			
2			
3			
4			
5			
TO BE DONE:	**TO BE DONE:**	**TO BE MADE:**	**TO BE MADE:**
1			
2			
3			
4			
5			

Exercise 6.13

Recovery Legacy: Legacy Table Four

For those of us who have been pulled back from the edge and into recovery, there is also a **Recovery Legacy.** All who enter that door are grateful but there is a rather harsh truth about staying in the process of change: You have to pass it on. Alcoholics Anonymous never would have happened if the founders had not discovered the importance of sharing their stories. The real dividends of significant change occur when you are of service to others. In the twelve step communities, the basic life of the fellowships depends on people rolling up their sleeves and becoming of service in some way. To go to meetings and therapy, gaining the goodness and value of those actions, and then to go on as if there is no further obligation is skating on very thin ice.

The other part of this equation involves shame. Whatever the reasons why you entered a recovery process, shame about your issues can become a barrier that gets in the way of reaching out to others. Writing a check (although important) is not the same as helping others get out of a hole that they are in—especially when you know what it takes to climb out. Helping them may actually mean joining them in their darkness so they can see there is light.

Sometimes our shame prevents others from even knowing that there is help. No disease entity ever got the support needed until people who had the problem stood up. People hide behind anonymity. Please note, the intention of anonymity in twelve step programs was to not compromise others; every member was free to witness and speak about his or her own experience. AA would never have gotten off the ground were it not for people sharing their stories in articles that appeared in *Reader's Digest* and *The Saturday Evening Post*.

Whatever brought you to the safety of a meeting, there are others who need to know what could be possible for them. This means that in small ways and large ways you must speak your truth about what it takes to recover from relational dysfunction, trauma, toxic stress, and addiction. Are you willing to let others know your story as a way to be a witness to the value of living in recovery? It is one of the hardest questions in the legacy bucket. How are you going to make it better for others who are desperate like you were? One answer exists only: Get involved in passing it on.

Also the field of recovery will not get better without financial support. Meetings and literature are there because of donations large and small. Organizations that exist to support recovering people do not just happen. Remember that no disease ever got better until people who had the problem got involved. They spoke up about the needs of people in recovery. Financially, they supported research about mental health and addiction and most effective ways to help.

Our animal symbol for this section of the Legacy Table is the dolphin. They travel in pods and work together in intelligent ways to get food, protect themselves, and raise their young. Being together is about bonding for mutual benefit and life. A twelve step or similar group is the same. You cooperate, share, and solve problems. To be in such a group has its joy and humor. Typically, the recovery groups do the same. Fun and laughter are a sign of a healthy group. Think about what you contribute to your pod.

Legacy Table Four asks four questions: 1. What ways can you be of service to your support organizations or to their leadership? 2. What ways can you model what good recovery looks like such as sponsorship and volunteer service? 3. What ways can your witnessing of your life help others in a meaningful and even public way? 4. What concrete financial support can you make to help the process for all of us?

Recovery Legacy: Legacy Table Four

Transcribe your life priorities in each category. Place an "X" in the small box next to those that most match your life goals and values.

Service & Leadership:	Model:	Passing It On:	Tradition:
TO DATE:	TO DATE:	TO DATE:	TO DATE:
1			
2			
3			
4			
5			
TO BE DONE:	TO BE DONE:	TO BE MADE:	TO BE MADE:
1			
2			
3			
4			
5			

Exercise 6.14

To assemble your Ultimate To Do List (UTD list), take each section and list the things that fit into each category. For some categories, you may have to think through what you might do. Remember, the list is to get a picture of what you would like your life to look like in the end.

This process has been provided to help you sift through your list. After you finish making your list, allow yourself some time. Think about it. Add to it. Strike out those items that are not in alignment with your goals and values. This process takes many days and perhaps even longer periods to achieve full clarity.

Setbacks

I have listened to the things that people typically say at this point and realized that they are telling essentially the same stories. And as I've listened to those stories, I've discovered there is also much more to them. So I made a list of what I thought were the most common issues that tend to be blockages for people. Many people have setbacks or something has happened to them which knocked them for a loop, and they find they cannot do what they need to do (or used to be able to do) to get going again.

On New Year's Day, I fell and severely sprained my ankle. I was walking down to my office at the lake. It was a cold and snowy mid-winter day in Minnesota, and although the steps were sanded, I slipped and ended up with my left foot wedged under a rock. When I fell to the ground, my head narrowly missed another rock by a few inches. As I look back, I realize that if I would have hit that rock, then my whole story might have a different ending.

My son, who is 50 years old and quite conscious in his own way, always feels very compelled to help his father continue to learn in life and he said, "Dad, don't you feel gratitude about this?" I told him, of course I felt lots of gratitude, but that wasn't what I was really thinking when I managed to catch my breath after I hit the ground. I was thinking I wasn't going to get up again. I couldn't breathe, and my question was, "Why am I still here?" I thought that must mean that perhaps God is saving me for something, and right then I just didn't know if I was up for it. My son said, "Dad, that's not the answer that I was looking for." And I said, "Yes, but it's the truth."

What you may learn and what my experience has been is that almost all of my process of development has been to give things up. This is one of the hardest lessons for all of us: learning to let go and give up things. Learning what is important to keep and what is important to let go of. For example, as a therapist, you may love doing one-on-one sessions with clients as much as I loved teaching the Training Modules for IITAP's Certified Sex Addiction Therapist (CSAT) program. My daughter once told me, "You can't do both modules 1 and 3. We've got to get you out of module 1; you're traveling too much." I really hated to give that up. Then there was a point where no time existed to teach in the training modules at all. I also used to see every patient individually. Today, I see the patient community as a group. And there are plenty of other things that I'm giving up; it seems like there's always something that I have to give up and let go of. And so it is: In letting go when you have a setback, there is the ability and freedom to come back.

One of the essential resilience factors we work on in *Recovery Zone* are the comebacks. You're going to continue to have setbacks, so how do you begin to mobilize internally so you can have a comeback? It is more than just resilience. There is a lot more to it. The ability to be able to mobilize the comeback is critical. Many people come to *Recovery Zone* because they have hit a wall and they don't know quite how to pick themselves back up.

Shame

Shame is common to our stories and a lot of those stories revolve around worthiness. Am I worth the sustained effort? Am I worth having something work better for me?

There are two ceilings that many people have.

- The **Ceiling of Complexity**. This is where you have so many things going that you can't possibly manage them all. The ceiling of complexity is very connected to the issue of shame.
- The **Shame Ceiling.** This revolves around how much you feel you deserve in life. How much do you value yourself? How much do you love and have passion for yourself?

People who have these issues may be very close to success but will not allow themselves to cross the finish line. Abundance of all types may be intolerable. Is there a voice from the past to whom they are listening? Is there a loyalty to a role in the family that rules out pulling off a comeback?

Balancing too many pie plates is a great way to come up short and stay loyal to those voices from the past. So, ask if you are ready to succeed. Remember the Chinese proverb about having 10,000 things in your mind being your own roadblock? What can you let go of? The other issue here is your commitment. Another Chinese aphorism is picking yourself up eight times when you have fallen seven. The lesson life continues to teach is that very often, less turns out to be more. Less sometimes means letting go of favorite things, activities, and work.

Making A Plan

Now we start to craft a plan. When I started, I thought I could accomplish my goals in five years. The reality is it took 15. In doing this with clinicians, patients, and recovery groups, 10 years seems to be the optimum. So, we start with a 10-year timeline. The focus then shifts to the first year, which I think is the focus year of recovery in which you practice the skills you will have accumulated by completing this book series. Then a less detailed approach in worksheets for the second and third years of recovery. When finished, you will have the beginning of a map of your ultimate purposes—starting with the focus on the now and then the long term. The following worksheets can be templates for your thinking. Having a plan is key to comebacks. I

TEN YEAR TIMELINE				
YEAR:	LIFE COMPLETION :	EXIT STRATEGY:	RECOVERY LEGACY:	LESSONS:
20___				
20___				
20___				
20___				
20___				
20___				
20___				
20___				
20___				
20___				
20___				

Exercise 6.15

ONE YEAR TIMELINE BULLET POINTS: Out of the Ultimate To Do List, list bullet points of what you should do in the next year if you want "_____" to happen in your life in the next three, five, or ten years?

	Quarter 1	Quarter 2	Quarter 3	Quarter 4
LIFE COMPLETION	▪ ▪ ▪ ▪	▪ ▪ ▪ ▪	▪ ▪ ▪ ▪	▪ ▪ ▪ ▪
EXIT STRATEGY	▪ ▪ ▪ ▪	▪ ▪ ▪ ▪	▪ ▪ ▪ ▪	▪ ▪ ▪ ▪
RECOVERY LEGACY	▪ ▪ ▪ ▪	▪ ▪ ▪ ▪	▪ ▪ ▪ ▪	▪ ▪ ▪ ▪
LESSONS	▪ ▪ ▪ ▪	▪ ▪ ▪ ▪	▪ ▪ ▪ ▪	▪ ▪ ▪ ▪

Exercise 6.16

TWO YEAR TIMELINE BULLET POINTS: Out of the Ultimate To Do List, list bullet points of what you should do in the next year if you want " _____ " to happen in your life in the next three, five, or ten years?

	Quarter 1	Quarter 2	Quarter 3	Quarter 4
LIFE COMPLETION				
EXIT STRATEGY				
RECOVERY LEGACY				
LESSONS				

Exercise 6.17

THREE YEAR TIMELINE BULLET POINTS: Out of the Ultimate To Do List, list bullet points of what you should do in the next year if you want "_____" to happen in your life in the next three, five, or ten years?

	Quarter 1	Quarter 2	Quarter 3	Quarter 4
LIFE COMPLETION				
EXIT STRATEGY				
RECOVERY LEGACY				
LESSONS				

Exercise 6.18

It is obvious from the preceding paragraphs that things happen that can interfere with your intentions. Yet, by holding your intentions close, your course will be clear. Some things will appear that enhance your life, and some things you will not get to. For example, I learned some extremely important lessons while on bed rest after heart trouble and my sprained ankle. One thing I learned was about how to rest, including the important skills of emptying my mind and staying in stillness.

Your job is to keep yourself in alignment with staying in your zone and plan. This becomes a gigantic step toward a life that reflects your true self. To organize an intense immersion into your focus during the first year, take each of the four quadrants of your UTD list and make each a quarter of your year. Obviously, some things will have different immediacy. But if you can keep to the themes of each quadrant, you can set into motion practices that will bring you to the inner and outer coherency you seek.

Because you're balancing the work of the first year with the long term, your second and third year plan is more about bullet points and priorities. Then, at the end of the first year, you repeat the process of a detailed next year and think through the next two years.

Use the process of planning a year in depth, with the following two years in a more general way, and stay withing the ten year plan you have envisioned. Once your recovery practice (expert system) is on board, your Ultimate To Do List will be integrated into the alignment with the algorithms and paradigms of your "bottom up" brain. Intentionality will help you live and stay in your zone.

In Chapter Ten, I suggest ways to organize your Ultimate To Do List so you can work on your legacy focus over a year's time as well as "immersing yourself" in refining the expert system (habits, skills, and strategies). Dedicating a year for this process of changing your focus and integrating new tools to use will increase your resilience "intelligence." However, this will require concentration over the year. But at the end you will have a new map to your story and perhaps a new picture of what you will have at the end of your story. First you have to pull together what you have learned and integrate it into a system. That is the process in which "wash on – wash off" becomes an integrated system to implement your plan. Then we shall put them together.

Between now and the next chapter, you might wish to experiment with the special learning opportunity we outline next. You might find some wording for how you are feeling right now.

Writing A Legacy Statement

After you have completed the planning process, you can write your Ultimate To Do list and the plans that go with it. For me, this ended up as a 30-page document plus addendums. While difficult and personally taxing (for example, working through describing what my achievements were, and editing my father's edits in my head), the process made me think about my plan.

After I'd created this document, people read it and gave me some really good feedback. Moreover, it made available to others what I wanted my life to look like in the end. I have posted it for you to look at on PatrickCarnes.com. Sometimes I am surprised by how much of it actually has happened. When I included the final strategy of doing work on the DNA of sex addiction, I knew that was the logical ending, and that work is what I am involved with now. At the time, however, I wondered if I would ever get there.

I encourage you to use this process as a way to further integrate the actual visions you have for your life, and to explore some of the whys behind the whys. Remember, the overarching goal is to take your recovery out of the New Year's Eve resolution that went nowhere category and transfer it to your life purpose. In the last chapter, we will help you organize this thinking into a doable process. For the moment you have made a platform of intentions of how you want your life to look when it ends. There is a lot to do. But how to get it all done? Piece by piece you assemble it. The next two chapters will provide you an overall strategy to meet your goals. Recovery is really based on an "expert system" and habits which are core to the resilience you will need. Your legacy work provides the motivation and intentionality to go beyond a New Year's resolution. An expert system clearly starts with intentionality, which is where we start in the next chapter.

The Forget Me Not Clipboard

As you review your internal *Recovery Zone* work, you will trip over items that are really not goals or strategic enough to rank as a life achievement. But they are tasks you do not wish to forget to do. These are usually things that are important that may have been lost in the process. Examples might be something "unfinished" out of the grief section or an important amends out of the relationship critical closure process. Keep track of these items by recording them on your clipboard.

Forget Me Nots
1.
2.
3.
4.
5.
6.
7.
8.
9.
10.
11.
12.
13.
14.
15.
16.
17.
18.
19.
20

Exercise 6.19

Special Learning Opportunity

This is a fun but also very thoughtful and meaningful exercise. Throughout the *Recovery Zone* series, we have mentioned the influence of Joseph Campbell and the hero's journey. His most famous book was *The Hero With A Thousand Faces*. Basically, he made the case that we all live the hero's journey. For sure, it is the story of recovery.

Campbell heavily influenced George Lucas, the primary author and producer of the movie epic *Star Wars*. Lucas struggled for years to get backing for *Star Wars*. When it was being made, the bets in the film industry was that it would be a major disaster. Lucas persisted anyway, eventually creating one of the most influential movies ever made. However, the challenges he experienced were right out of the hero's journey. Here is the learning opportunity:

11. Go to a site (such as jcf.org) that has assembled the best quotes of Joseph Campbell. Print a set of those quotes.

12. Go to a site (such as starwars.com) that has the most often quoted sayings of Yoda, the 900-year-old Jedi Master in *Star Wars*. Print a set of those quotes.

13. Read through each. What themes do you notice? Do any of them inspire you? Are there quotes that apply to you and your journey now? Allow yourself to be inspired by the impact these two individuals have made on all of us and how that occurred.

Chapter 7 **Creating an Expert System**

Is the system going to flatten you out and deny your humanity, or are you going to make use of the system to the attainment of human purposes?

Joseph Campbell

When we lose a computer file but are able to retrieve it, we say that we were able to "recover the file." When we get sick and then get well, we recover our health. In other words, when we have lost something that we had and it is then returned to us, we use the term "recovery."

Throughout the *Recovery Zone* series, we talk about the identity theft that occurs in families. As we fight through the layers of judgment and trauma, our "recovery" is regaining the true self. Authors like Randy Pausch in *The Last Lecture* and Paulo Coehlo in *The Alchemist* underlined for us that truth is the core of therapy and recovery. They tell us that often we knew as children what our call was and who we were to be. The work for us as adults is casting off what has distracted us from who we really are so we can make our lives reflect our true self.

Many times, even therapists who have worked very hard on themselves in training and their own recoveries will make a suggestion to a patient, yet internally, unspoken in the therapist's mind, is the thought that if they followed the advice they were giving to their patient, their lives would improve as well. One of the gifts of being a therapist is that, after a while, you are constantly nudged towards further congruency and improvement. In fact, after seeing hundreds of patients and families, therapists start to keep a list in their head of things that work in their own lives.

In 1997, after a long week of training, a group of 46 therapists and I made a list of such things. There have been many changes in the world and in clinical practice since then, but the basic summary of their observations, I believe, still stands. **Figure 7.1** below is a list of those common observations. Note that the theme is learning about and being your true self.

The Lessons of Therapy – the Revised Standard Version

Admit your mistakes and flaws and have no secrets from those close to you. Such disclosure is the most honorable act for humans, especially with your children.

Lies, omissions, denial, and blame cover the essential life reality: You are responsible for your behavior. Consequences, however, come from others, so take charge of your life or someone else will.

Healthy people do three things with the past: they forgive themselves, they forgive others, and they learn. Life can be a recreation of childhood, however, so any unfinished business may be reenacted.

Unhappiness in a relationship is often about oneself but projected onto the other. So fight fair, be accountable, and respond joyfully to you and your partner's needs. But never violate your soul or distort what is true about you.

Do all that you can to make your relationships work. The quality of your life is contingent on the quality of your relationships.

Sexuality is intertwined with the soulish place, so handle carefully. Acknowledge that sexual fulfillment begins in the brain, not the body, and with yourself, not your partner.

Enduring, satisfying, and fun sex depends on enduring, satisfying, and fun intimacy. Sex without intimacy almost always hurts someone.

Live within your means and have no unsecured debt. At the same time, do not hoard money and live in deprivation. Nor should you hide your money from your partner. Never threaten or exploit others with your money. Life is about abundance, not scarcity.

Money issues, sexual issues, and relationship issues are often the same issue.

Work is the implementation of self, so do it with passion, balance, integrity, and joy. Work that separates you from yourself, from others, or from the planet is an empty, soulless path.

Self-nurturing and self-loving may need to be learned, so practice regularly. Honor your own conversations with self as well as your commitments to self.

Life is precious, difficult, and designed to bring the best out of humans. To make it work requires deep connectedness. In other words, we must have a spiritual life.

The primary connection is with the process and all living things. Disconnection or the exclusive focus on goals brings out the worst in any of us. Some describe this as a loss of grace.

You do need to have a plan. Most people cannot get there from here without one.

Do not forget that problems and solutions are like matter and energy—an infinite exchange. There is always a solution. Most people's problems are really solutions that are not working.

Greed, control, self-destructive attachment to things or ideas, exploitation of others, addictions, and other ways to distort reality are about the loss of yourself or, as some would say, a wound to the soul. They are signs of an unexamined life.

A successful or soulful life requires you to cope with disappointment, to make meaning out of suffering, to convert loneliness into solitude, and to create with passion and joy.

Mental health is the acceptance of reality at all costs. The lessons will be repeated until learned. If ignored, the lessons become harder.

The lessons we must each learn teach us about human limitations and our interdependence with all.

The Fall Institute
The Meadows
November 8, 1997
Patrick J. Carnes, acting secretary

Figure 7.1

These revelations are not just found in the therapist's office. In Kristin Hannah's book *The Nightingale*, quoted earlier, the core teaching is that love tells you what you want but war tells you who you are. The hero's journey is all about difficulty and overwhelming circumstances refining the truth about oneself.

Abraham Lincoln fought a war that cost more US lives to date than any other war the United States has experienced. Lincoln was also (probably) bipolar, so he had his own internal demons to face. He said, "Every man is born an original, but sadly most men die copies." The purpose of recovery is to no longer be a copy of someone else's vision. So the question remains: Once you start this thing called recovery, how do you weave all of this into a meaningful life that lasts?

In the last chapter, we explored how your intentions could impact your life. You made an Ultimate To Do List and the five values that govern the goals of your life. But having goals does not always translate into reality. The classic New Year's resolutions are like the promises of addicts, the traumatized, and dysfunctional people everywhere. They don't lead to lasting real-world change Thus, our increasing self-knowledge makes the question, "How do I do this in a lasting way?" cut even deeper.

And the answer is that you **intentionally create an expert system.** Throughout this book you have learned various aspects of how to recover the self that has been separated, and how to implement those original facets of yourself back into your life. "Wax on, wax off," Mister Miyagi said to young Daniel in the movie *Karate Kid*. But how does it come together? Concentration, focus, danger, conflict, and success are a part of it, but, above all, there is the weaving together of what you have learned into new habits that govern your life, especially when there is no time to contemplate.

We need for the bottom-up brain to have a network of intuitions and best guesses that are more accurate and consistent with our values and goals: i.e., our intention. The bottom-up brain incorporates new habits—the habits of recovery.

The top-down brain needs to know what it really wants. (My suggested readings on this are Daniel Goleman's book *Focus* and Dan Siegel's book *Mindsight*.) The tools the top-down brain uses to do this reengineering are the tools of focus. There also must be the courage and the consequent willingness to put the time in to make it all happen. All expert systems (physicians, quarterbacks, languages, parenting, etc.) require focus and time. But it starts with knowing your intentions.

Expert System Habit One – Intention

At the end of the day, often in your daily log, you have to ask yourself if the day turned out the way you intended. The most important part of knowing your goals is that you actually get something done towards accomplishing them. However, some days are so filled with the unexpected, so your nightly reflection may have to be, "Did I get anything done that I wanted?"

Life can be easily filled with distractions—the sand that keeps you from your goals. Interruptions are legion in a time when the average adult looks at his or her cell phone 225 times a day. If your goal is to only put your energy into activities that matter, there are many ways time can evaporate on you. There is also the resistance factor. Were you avoiding what you knew you had to do? If your goal for the day was getting badly needed self-care time, but the day went very differently and you did not get the rest and restoration you planned, what boundaries collapsed that caused this?

Learning to live intentionally is one of the hardest consciousness habits to cultivate. It is helpful to notice your morning and evening work, your reflection practice, and your goal-setting. These are all mechanisms of attention in which time is a highly valued currency. If you spend time in ways that do not help you reach your goals, you cannot get that time back. What you can do is resolve to stay more focused and present each day. Towards that end, visualization skills are key.

Your Vision Table provides the ultimate purposes that you picture on a lifetime scale. But, your yearly, quarterly, weekly, and daily recording and reflecting on your goals is the way to make the changes happen. Linking tools to what really matters in your life deepens the role of not letting yourself slip into old habits and the erosion of your identity and happiness. Or, as President Lincoln said, it stops you from becoming a copy of other people's perceptions and wishes.

In the morning, envision how you want the day to go—whether it be rest, task, or conversation. Take the stress out of the day by picturing it. Gain perspective in the evening by reviewing how you could have made the day turn out differently. Once your bottom-up brain integrates this, it is no longer time consuming, and it is very helpful to your inner coherence.

This applies to your relationships as well. Many readers will be familiar with the Awareness Wheel pioneered by Sherod and Phyllis Miller in their books on couple's communication. In the Awareness Wheel, the first awareness is what your senses tell you. Seeing, hearing, smelling, tasting, and touching are how we "see the field" in our relationships. On those awareness points we make assumptions. What I observe in my partner, I often infer conclusions on those observations. Often, both our observations and conclusions could be in error, and then we have feelings that may be unwarranted. This unexamined process can lead to dark moments in a coupleship. We have to check out and evaluate our assumptions—remembering that is what they are! Therapist's will often ask their patients to use a phrase such as "What I make up about that is..." to ensure common understanding. Remember that the book *The Four Agreements* cautions against making and living on the basis of assumptions.

Whatever our feelings and thoughts are, they lead to intention and action. Throughout the process, in every relationship, even the incidental ones, our feelings and thoughts demand awareness and discussion. This discussion is the essence of intimacy. Showing up and being present, when integrated into your expert system, is transformative because you are paying attention—being conscious of yourself and others in your life.

Intention is the easiest habit to leave out of your awareness and your conversations. We historically have gone from feelings to action without being aware of or examining our intent. When we suspend our reactions to decide what is to come next, we're allowing time to choose our reaction—even if it is only to review our assumptions or observations before we react.

Remember the work you did on your "Window of Tolerance?" It is a tool for visualizing different responses and being consistent with the person you are. Partners who notice behaviors that are not consistent with what is intended can help each other achieve inner coherence.

A problem exists when the discrepancies between what you want to do and what you actually do stay consistent. This may mean more than a New Year's resolution that did not have sufficient resolve. It can mean that your brain's old default patterns are stronger than you thought.

All of us, whether addict or not, have these fallback systems in the paradigms that float in our brains. Not reverting to these etched-in neural algorithms can be a struggle. What works is an "examined life" in which we use our consistent attention to make what actually happens match our intent. It sounds like a lot, but with initial effort and establishing consistent rhythms it works. So, you can do the work, or you can let life circumstances push you around. In their classic book *The Spirituality of Imperfection*, Ernest Kurtz and Katherine Ketcham caution us that the work does not stop. We can imagine perfection but never achieve it. They also point out why storytelling is so important to the search for meaning. Or, as we have termed it, changing the narrative. The more accurate the story is, the more it gives us a measure to our progress. To borrow from one of our great writers, Ralph Waldo Emerson, "It is the journey, not the destination."

Expert System Habit Two – Self-Care

People trying to help others who have suffered through trauma, sickness, or tragedy seem to always ask, "Are you taking care of yourself?" After a while, that question becomes obnoxious, given that they are doing everything that they possibly can and the assumption is that they would neglect themselves. When you are surrounded by therapists (as I am), they add the "meaningful stare," which they learned in graduate school. I do believe there is a course offered in graduate and residency programs which teaches varieties of different stares to help the process. The meaningful stare, in this case, implies that they know you are probably not doing enough self-care. Usually, however, what is needed in friendships and from therapists is for them to show up for you. Not recommendations or advice, but rather company and listening.

When my mother died under very difficult circumstances for me, it was an emotional body blow. I could not do anything, but I had a hard time accepting not being busy or useful. After a week, I thought I would return to work and maybe experience some normalcy. I went into The Meadows on a Monday, and Pat Mellody, one of the founders of The Meadows, came to my office at the end of the day. He asked, "Did you accomplish anything today?" Pat was someone you could not dodge easily. I answered honestly, "No." He responded, "Then go home. You are not helping anyone here and you are not helping yourself." Another learning about my personal tendency of running to help others as a way of avoiding my own pain.

Self-care is the bedrock of a recovery expert system. When you finished *Recovery Zone I,* you made a covenant with yourself to care for the self. Part of that contract was about trusting your emotional and physical processes and giving your body and psyche what they need to weather turbulence, being willing to live in the eye of the storm, even if that means being still while in the presence of great upset and pain. This is the paradox of doing and being: what may feel like self-indulgence is actually self-care.

Paying attention to your body is the key. If you do not have your body as a platform, you have nothing. Exercise, weight management, and physical healing is essential to caring for yourself. In this day and time, there is a wealth of evidence about the importance of physical exercise and being in the appropriate weight range. They use the term body mass index (BMI). Being overweight or obese is contrary to recovery. A high BMI would indicate compulsive or addictive eating and possible depression. Therefore, knowing your BMI is like other basic health statistics like blood pressure, heart rate variability (HRV), and other circulation measures.

As we have learned, everything you do for your heart, you also do for your brain. Remember, much of your brain is located surrounding your heart. Moreover, the brain is highly integrated with all your organ systems. Your system responses come from here. When you work on mindfulness and emotional regulation, you focus on sinus rhythm and heart rhythms, which ultimately affect your heart rate variability because heart variability is the best indicator of your health, both physical and mental.

Psychiatrist Daniel Amen has talked for years about the connection between body health and mental health. He uses the term "Brain Warrior" and in his book *The Brain Warrior's Way* he asks the question, "If you don't know why you have to get healthy, you will never do the 'what' of brain health." The whole focus of living in a recovery zone is to be happy because you have achieved a coherence between what you do and synching it with what matters. Amen states:

When people begin the shift ... they start to think and behave differently. They become more serious about their health and understand the importance of making good decisions; they stop complaining about giving up the treats, they stop saying 'everything in moderation,' and they stop taking the month of December off from their health plan. This mindset shift is one of the most critical aspects of success. Without it, you are doomed to yoyo dieting and falling back forever.

Recovery is a purpose-driven life—because you never want to go back there. Amen adds, "If you know your purpose at a deep emotional level, you will refuse to be a sheep and you'll arm yourself with a sheepdog's attitude of being serious, guarding and fighting for your own life and the lives of those you love and serve." This means being thoughtful about what you're eating and about your exercise patterns. You do not put off needed procedures, visits to the doctor, needed surgeries, or taking your medications.

One of the turning points in therapy is having your own brain scanned. You see how trauma, addiction, and dysfunctional living has affected your brain. The resolve deepens. Two years later, if you made that shift, have the scan repeated and see how areas of your brain rendered inactive by your out-of-control life have filled in. It is like losing eight to ten inches off your waistline. The difference is undeniable. The new habits of self-care are measurable.

Expert System Habit 3 – Accountability

A part of the *Recovery Zone's* covenant is to be true to yourself. We have noted that only when you trust yourself do you really start to trust others. When that trust comes, one starts to "trust the process." The concept of a Higher Power remains elusive when no such trust exists. We have this ritual in January of making resolutions, but they often fall by the wayside. When you do not keep your resolutions, self-trust erodes. Will that be the fate of your five goals that are listed on your Ultimate To Do List? To make sure you keep all your promises, the following actions are helpful:

- Share in your support groups, with your therapist, and, if appropriate, with family members. A goal is not real unless you have said it out loud and you have witnesses.
- Break it down into smaller timeframes such as ten years, the next year, or by months and weeks so it is in manageable pieces.
- Rewrite the goals quarterly and yearly. You will find they morph and become more refined. Try to do the rewrites in your own handwriting.
- Ask what you will have to give up to achieve your goals. Also plan rewards that are significant enough to you that when you succeed, it is worth keeping those promises with yourself and others. Also make it clear what not achieving your goals will mean in terms of what you lose.

■ Ask what your word means when you make promises, which in turn makes the agreement clearer to yourself and those who believe your promise. This is the evolving covenant with the self.

Frequently, the problem is that "things come up." A great exercise done by Stephen Covey and his staff teaching *The Seven Habits of Effective People* is to keep your priorities clear. They give each of their participants a glass container with a layer of sand in the bottom. Then they provide them large rocks which represent their priorities. The instructions are then given to get all the rocks into the container. Of course, they cannot fit the rocks in. The trick is to take out the sand and put the rocks in first. Then pour the sand in. The point is that it can all fit if you start with the priorities.

Each of us has interruptions, distractions, and the unexpected. Plus, there are the unexpected barriers, with the virus COVID-19 being a classic example. I am very sure that during the pandemic you may have had days when you were not able to do anything you had planned. The trick in these situations is to recognize and separate the sand from the rocks. Refocus on the priorities. Being accountable to others helps here, for often the perspective of others gives us new strategies to get our priorities accomplished. However, we must keep focus on what does need to happen to keep our promises. This means daily, sometimes hourly reflection—our next habit.

Before proceeding, try the following. In Exercise 7.1 you will find five rocks. Write your ultimate five goals in the space provided. Next to that is a drawing of a container labeled SAND. Think about the sand as distractions in your daily life. Discuss this with your support networks and think about how to keep your priorities in the forefront of your life. You do not have to figure this out alone, and your success depends on your transparency.

PRIORITIES (Rocks) – Five Ultimate Goals

Write an ultimate goal by each rock.

1. _____
   _____
   _____
   _____

2. _____
   _____
   _____
   _____

3. _____
   _____
   _____
   _____

4. _____
   _____
   _____
   _____

5. _____
   _____
   _____
   _____

Sand

Think about the sand (distractions) in your daily life. Discuss this with your support network and think about how to keep your priorities in the forefront of your life. What is the "sand" in your life?

_____
_____
_____
_____
_____
_____
_____
_____
_____

Exercise 7.1

Before proceeding to reflection, I highly recommend Steven Pressfield's book on resistance, *The War of Art*. He talks about identifying the enemy, and suggests that the enemy is us:

Resistance will unfailingly point to True North—meaning that calling or action it most wants to stop us from doing... The more important a call or action is to our soul's evolution, the more Resistance we will feel toward pursuing it.

Using accountability and support will make resistance a compass to keeping our dedication on course.

Expert System Habit Four – Study

In preparing this book and its supporting materials, we did a series of test retreats and weekly groups with patients. I remember an older man in one of our meetings who spoke up and said, "I hated reading the books because I do not like reading. What I learned the most from *Recovery Zone* was the realization that when you read a recommended book and you make it about yourself, it changes everything. I hated school but I wished I would have learned this part about applying it to myself long ago."

If you love something, you will read about it. Or you will listen to audio-recordings and find articles and videos. People do this all the time. But when it comes to reflecting on your own growth and awareness, it feels like signing up for a root canal. The covenant with yourself means that you love yourself enough to learn about how to care for the self. So you become willing to read about various strategies for raising your awareness and you develop tools to improve your brain.

Some books are for information (examples are Daniel Goleman's *Focus* or Dan Siegel's *Mindsight*). Some are classics in recovery and mental health (examples are Scott Peck's *The Road Less Traveled* or Ernest Kurtz and Katherine Ketcham's classic *The Spirituality of Imperfection*). Some speak to you and your situations deeply (*The AA Big Book* or Melody Beattie's *The Language of Letting Go*). And some are so meaningful for you that you read and reread them, knowing that each time you pick them up you learn something new.

Some fiction series also have incredible depth about understanding the human condition (examples are J.R.R. Tolkein's *The Lord of the Rings* and *The Outlander* series by Diana Galbadon). You should always have books going at several levels. There are those who think they do not need to put that effort into reading and studying and can learn what they need to learn from their sponsors, groups, and therapist. This approach is sort of a "recovery by osmosis," and it misses the richness of the resources that are available, the importance of science, and the disciplined reflection that makes the brain grow. Remember, this is about neurostimulation (recall Norman Doidge's process of brain change in Chapter Two). With neurostimulation, your brain will be better and last longer.

The point is, you realize by now, that you have a brain problem. As a consumer of health information, you "take care of yourself" by learning about how to have a better brain. If you do these habits, including reading, there is substantial evidence that you boost your brain functions and not only to repair it but improve its capabilities beyond what you may have experienced thus far in your life. Siegel uses the term "transpirational," which means expanding the brain's abilities to integrate internally and externally. Decisions and intuitions improve and the deterioration of aging is postponed.

Expert System Habit Five – Reflection

There is no way around this. Every day, even if it is only a few minutes some days, you must have time to stop and center yourself. What works best is a habitual routine of reading, focusing, writing, and paying attention to your process. A morning routine for me is that I always have a book that I am working on. Some books I just read for content, but some I read for inspiration or real understanding. Then I begin to write in a journal to make a gratitude list. I follow that with jotting down what is going on with me and any vision work I may need to do. I also keep a list of what I need to do or who I need to reach that day. This process typically takes forty-five minutes to over an hour. The length of time depends on how long I read and the impact or utility it has for me.

Sometimes my writing is a version of Julia Cameron's morning pages process. In her book *The Artist's Way*, she describes a process in which she dumps all the stuff running through her head on paper, regardless of whether it makes sense or not. Out of that release and discharge, clarity emerges and ideas form. The morning pages are a perfect example of what the Inner Observer or "wise mind" discerns as what matters or is useful. It is a way of clearing out what Buddha called the "monkey business" of the chattering brain. Many mornings end up with that process, but I always start with gratitude as a baseline of what is true north so there is a yardstick as I unload my preoccupations. The goal is to keep my most important goals in front of me. Remember, rocks before sand.

Before I go to bed, I minimally complete what I call the Captain's Log. In *Star Trek*, Captain Kirk would log what happened on his starship, the Enterprise, that day. This actually is the way most ships (military and merchant) keep a record of what has happened. So, being a *Star Trek* fan, years ago I started to call it the Captain's log. In essence, it was my private joke. But there are nights that recording the facts of the day is all the energy I have. It takes just minutes. Yet over the years I have gone back to those logs and found that there is so much history that I would otherwise forget. Sometimes it documents my memory at critical moments, but, more importantly, reading my Captain's log years later provides me with amazing perspective. The idea is to be what the science fiction author Robert Heinlein called the "fair witness." In his early books, the character of the fair witness could only comment on what they actually saw. Therefore, they could also serve the state in resolving or making legal commitments such as marriages.

I have found it very useful during my Captain's log time to record notes about conversations that I want to remember, and also what I heard and saw. Especially when the conversations or events are difficult or significant. Having that reference has been critical at times. We all witness many things, and a few words can anchor our memories if we log them in at night.

I also use the Captain's log as a place to process the day and to think through my concerns. This does a few things. It clears my mind so sleep will be more restful. I can just leave my worries and concerns in my journal. Second, my Inner Observer helps to diffuse strong emotions and worry. Third, a strategy that has been documented in creativity research, neuroscience, and sleep medicine is to program problem-solving. Literally, you select a question or a problem you need to solve and you ask your brain to work on it while you sleep. Almost all of us have had the experience of suddenly awakening with clarity about a solution or idea. (The mistake is not to write it down. Unrecorded, it will be lost or muddled. The same is true for dreams, which are in reality connected to the same process. Your dreams can teach you a lot about your internal deliberations.) Being deliberate about asking the brain to work on these internal processes often can be more direct than daytime focus.

Whatever your routine is, you have to allocate space to integrate your meditation practice, therapy, and recovery work. Make it a habit that you know you can do and that those who live with you know you do. Set boundaries around these activities and agree on regular times that you allocate to it. You may have shorter practices during the work week and longer on the weekends. Do not be rigid, but do be pragmatic. Most importantly, carry into this the same spirit that Daniel Amen wrote about the shepherd dog becoming a guardian to your process. More than anything else, this will help you keep your promises and make the zone happen in your life.

Expert System Habit Six – Recovery Support

For myself, I hit a time when I was a single parent with four children, and I had a daunting set of choices in front of me. My experience in my own twelve step process prompted me to add some words to the serenity prayer. It seemed presumptuous and perhaps it was (and still is), but I put my version of the serenity prayer in one of my early publications. It fits this chapter, so I have included that piece of writing in **Figure 7.2**

Consciousness is marked by the trusting of the process we all share. If we start to trust ourselves, we trust others. The questions of larger purposes and what is a Higher Power are but waystations to living in your own call. You cannot do this alone. In war, fighting brings a closeness that become more important than the purpose of the war. Every commander knows his people fight first for their buddies. So it is in any adversity. It is the band of brothers and sisters who walk with you on the way that are the key habit.

Patrick Carnes' Serenity Prayer

God grant me the serenity...

Serenity meaning that I no longer recoil from the past, live in jeopardy because of my behavior now, or worry about the unknown future. I seek regular times to re-create myself and I avoid those times of depletion which make me vulnerable to despair and to old self-destructive patterns.

To accept the things I cannot change...

Accept change in that I not cause suffering for myself by clinging to that which no longer exists. All that I can count on it is that nothing will be stable except how I respond to the transforming cycles in my life of birth, growth, and death.

The courage to change the things I can...

Which means remembering that to give up my attempts to control outcome does not require I give up my boundaries or my best efforts. It does mean my most honest appraisal of the limits of what I can do.

And the wisdom to know the difference...

Wisdom becomes the never forgotten recognition of all those times when there was no way out and new paths opened up like miracles in my life.

Adaptation by Patrick Carnes
From *A Gentle Path though the Twelve Steps*

Figure 7.2

In watching people attending inpatient treatment, I have seen these people make lifelong friendships. As the technology has improved, that process is enhanced. The dynamic is as old as tribal clans. Shared common experience is the essential energy of intimacy and bonding—an energy that animates families, cultures, countries, and especially recovery groups. When specialists were trying to treat torture victims, they were very resistant to therapy until they were put into groups with other torture victims. When you share your experience and realize that everyone in the group has had identical or similar experiences, you experience safety. The brain only makes significant change when there is safety.

There are a variety of support groups that exist under the twelve step umbrella. It started when Dr. Bob and Bill Wilson met and both admitted to hiding bottles in the backyard doghouse.

There was an immediate connection. I remember the day I visited the home of Dr. Bob in Akron, Ohio. Workmen were there, making some renovations, and they found hidden in the wall one more forgotten bottle. For all of us, it was a reminder of Dr. Bob's original meeting with Bill Wilson and the common experience all addicts have of things hidden. I also remember my first meeting in an Adult Children's group when I read the 14 characteristics of being a child raised in a home of a dysfunctional family, and the immediate connection I felt with everyone present.

The twelve step format from a science point of view could not be better designed to start a process of change. There is safety, there is attention to the story, there are processes for connecting the dots, there is attachment with people who are kindred spirits, and there is the free mentoring. In this book, we have emphasized the importance of key relationships in your life and having a group that works for you and your unique issues. No other option exists. You must have a group that is not your family or friends who are in this process with you. That need never disappears. You may shift groups and even fellowships. Many of us do. But there has to be a gang or clan that you call your own and with whom you share a common history.

Expert System Habit Seven – Intuition

Intuition is your brain working behind your back. In other words, your brain works on things underneath your level of awareness. When a quarterback turns a failed play into an amazing play, how did he know what would work? Especially when his decision was made in a nanosecond? Intuition. The quarterback relied on the integration of many parts of the brain, including knowledge of his teammates as well as his opponents. His brain made nearly instant deductions about the strategies unfolding on the field on both sides, the game situation (time remaining, score, down and distance), his own abilities and limits, and the rules of the game. Among his many options were the deceptions, surprises, and existing fallback plans. And then he made his decision—all without conscious thought. In fact, his own awareness of how he pulled off this "miracle" play would be hard to explain, other than to say that he had an intuition about what would work.

The reality is that an expert system took over and coordinated exactly what was needed in the moment. Forged in focus, practice, and experience, an instant decision was made and action was taken.

We all have these expert systems, but they can be disrupted. Lou Cozolino writes extensively in *The Neuroscience of Psychotherapy* about the bridge-making in the brain that can be interfered with so that right decisions remain elusive. For instance, people with toxic stress and trauma compartmentalize their experiences, making it hard for the brain to connect the dots at critical moments. The anxiety of the stress interferes with the application of what they know. Shame can also paralyze the mind's ability to make decisions.

Sometimes the brain itself has damage that interferes with this integration of information. With Asperger's syndrome and autism, parts of the brain that affect emotions are impaired, so other people are perceived more like objects than holistic human beings. The same type of impairment is also found with psychopathic behavior—where people are again reduced to objects.

The capacity to build relationships is vital to brain change. Remember, whether it is trauma, shame, or brain dysfunction, the capacity to organize into a higher level of consciousness is a challenge. The result is that the brain copes with what it has to work with by creating default positions. Sadly, these default positions may be dysfunctional operating systems that become self-reinforcing and repetitive. These eventually become kamsaras—or trauma repetitions.

When kamsaras are deliberately disrupted by treatment and therapy, the brain starts to change. Compartmentalization starts to fail and new networks of understanding emerge. Earlier in this book, we used the term neurodifferentiation as integral to the brain's reorganizing process. Another way of describing this is "connecting the dots." The brain and emotions start to recognize that the rules of the operating systems were based on faulty assumptions. Usually, there is pain in this awareness, as there are most likely costs that have been incurred. However, the self is no longer keeping secrets from itself. In this way, therapy often becomes discovering what you already know. More significantly, what matters to you becomes clearer.

One breakthrough understanding will link with another realization, and you will have an "aha" moment. Soon there is a seemingly unending transformational cascade of awareness. The brain's capacity to reorganize itself expands exponentially. This is precisely the moment you start installing new expert operating systems to change your life. No longer do the default settings rule.

When I started treatment, my therapist at the Meadows asked how members of my family of origin would describe me as a child. My response was to say they probably would laugh and tell stories about how I was constantly in trouble. He asked what kind of trouble. I recited a list:

- When I was two, I found a bottle of turpentine and drank it. I was immediately in the hospital.
- When I was three, the ice melted out of the lakes in Minnesota and I waded into a lake in my snowsuit. An employee of my father spotted me and pulled me out of the freezing water.
- When I was four, I managed to get into the family station wagon, which was parked next to our home on top of a very large hill. I pulled it out of park and the car rolled

down the hill for a hundred yards and crashed into our milk house. My family would say I totaled my first car at the age of four.

- When I was five, I was riding with my father one morning when he had already been drinking. I fell out of the front seat window and he ran over me. He did not know where I was so he panicked and backed up—again running over me. In fact, he stopped while I was under the front right wheel. Fortunately, it was sandy and I survived.

As I continued the list of stories about how I was constantly in trouble, my caseworker stopped me. He asked if these incidents were considered to be my fault. I told him that was a strange question since, in each situation, I had clearly caused the problem. He responded: "Pat, none of these incidents were your fault. You were a small child and no one was watching you." It felt like a lightning bolt went through me. He went on to question how a child finds turpentine and no one notices, and how a child wanders into a freezing lake, and how a child gets into a car alone, or falls out a car window—all without an adult intervening or even noticing.

So many things flashed through my brain: the stress of post-World War II, the long hours of my parents, my father's alcoholism and violence, my many visits to the hospital, the laughter of my siblings and family when these stories were told. All these thoughts came together as my therapist explained how kids can be made into scapegoats. This insight flowed into me in amazing ways, and my understanding of my youth and family totally and irrevocably changed. Then the cascade of aha moments started.

When I came back from treatment, my family gathered at a resort in Northern Minnesota. I had that spring acquired a used boat. My children and I loved to water ski. At this gathering, we were launching this boat for the first time. There were some extra bindings with, which we were unfamiliar, holding the boat on the trailer. The result was the boat was not released from the trailer when placed in the water, creating a minor crisis. We pulled it out again, found the connections, and relaunched. I told my son and the resort owner I was glad my father did not see this. But then I looked up and there he was, standing at the end of the dock with his arms folded. He walked up and asked angrily how that had happened. I had some emotional tools to use post-treatment, so I did not react but simply related the facts.

The kids immediately wanted to ski, so I asked my father to be the observer keeping track of the skier (required by law) as I drove. As we got my son David up on skis, my father immediately bombarded me with questions about the boat, its cost, and its equipment. I looked in the rearview mirror and I could not see my son. I stopped and saw that he had fallen about 500 yards back. As we approached him, my father yelled to my son, "Your Dad was so busy trying to convince me this boat was a good buy, he did not even see that you fell." My therapist's voice echoed through my head. It was his role to watch the skier, but I was being blamed for it.

When David got into the boat, the ladder was loose so we went in and I tightened the screws. My father, of course, criticized how I was doing it. My nine-year-old niece, Sheila was standing next to him and she said, "Grandpa, he is doing the best he can." He actually turned to her and said that doing your best is not enough. He added that it would be like if she ever got less than A on her report card. Her response was, "Grandpa, that is not true. Doing your best is always good enough." Then she walked away.

In less than an hour, my cascade of understandings confirmed what I learned in treatment—including a good model of responding provided by a nine-year-old girl. This cascade of awareness changed my life forever.

It also changed my brain. I started processing the dynamics of my family differently. As my awareness was altered, my intuitions started to shift as well. I started to see and sense things very differently.

One way to look at intuition is to see that your internal systems make an immediate guess as to what is right or wrong about something, or if your perceptions fit or do not. You start to trust yourself more out of an expanded brain bandwidth, which adds information that can concretely be connected. However, with expanded awareness, you also start accessing the energies that surround you differently. You start to tune into and suspect what is about to happen on another level. Your awareness starts to plug in at a spiritual level.

Expert System Habit Eight – Spirituality

Dr. Larry Dossey, in his book *Healing Words: The Power of Prayer and the Practice of Medicine*, shared his research showing that when people who had cancer were prayed for, they healed faster and more completely than patients who had no prayer support. Dossey also showed that the power of prayer extends to all kinds of illnesses and situations. Further, it was clear that it did not matter what the religion or what the spiritual practice was of the person praying. Christian, Buddhist, or even First Nation shamanism—all had positive effect. A Buddhist aspiration (sending a wish for healing) worked as well as a Christian asking for divine intervention. The important part was the sending of some form of energy.

Physicians (and physicists) were very interested in Dossey's work, yet critical, even though elaborately controlled experiments verified his conclusions. In fact, the research is so conclusive that over a hundred medical schools now offer courses for training physicians in spiritual practices to improve outcomes. It has even been demonstrated that if the physicians pray for their patients, there is an improvement in outcomes. So the power of prayer is undeniable.

Lynne McTaggart, one of our best science writers, devotes a whole chapter in her book, *The Field*, to this phenomenon. The importance, from a healing standpoint, is the transfer of energy. Physics, of course, is about energy, and McTaggart documents how the role that energy plays in our modern understanding of addiction and mental health is critical.

Dossey's and McTaggart's work, taken together, is a breakthrough documenting the connections between spirituality, science, and our conscious intentionality.

What is being spiritual? Simply said, it is the connection to the energy of what matters. To know that is to pay attention to what is happening. An example should help. I was a rural Catholic boy with an Irish mother. Our country priest called my mother and asked if I would be available to be an altar boy to assist him in early Mass on Christmas morning. He had no one else available. When my mom told me about this, I protested that I had not been through the altar boy training program. She called Father Yanny, and his response was to ask her to bring me a few minutes early so he could teach me what I needed to know. He said he would say my Latin parts for me until I learned them.

My mother was excited because serving as an altar boy was the first step toward me becoming a priest. So, she called all of her family members to come to Mass on Christmas morning. Remember, though, that I was doing something publicly that I had no idea how to do— and now the whole family would be watching. I awoke with dread that I would make a mistake. We showed up early as requested. Father Yanny explained that on this morning there were only two things I would have to do. When he nodded at me, I was to come up to the altar and pick up the large book called the Missal on his right, genuflect in front of the altar, and place it on his right. I performed this function adequately but did wonder why he did not move it the 18 inches himself.

The other task was to ring the bells loudly when he gave me the signal. The signal was that he would place his right hand flat on the altar. With that, I was to ring the bells as hard as I could. In those times, since the service was all in Latin, the bells were also a signal to those attending that it was time to kneel, sit, or stand. There were actually little bell images to serve as signals in the missalettes used as prayer books so congregants could follow the order of the Mass.

Father Yanny at the time was in his mid-80s and not steady on his feet. He also had a reputation for taking a nip or two in the morning before Mass. Christmas morning must have been a significant holiday because that morning he was somewhat inebriated. The problem with that, from my perspective, was that he was unstable and periodically he needed to steady himself, and he did this by putting his right hand on the altar!

I immediately rang the bells. The service became chaotic because I had the congregation up and down way too many times and seldom in connection with what was happening during the mass. Everybody knew this, but they still moved. My mother was mortified. Father Yanny was actually amused, and my aunts told the story at all family events until they passed.

However, it is worth noting that everyone in the congregation obeyed the bells, even though their motions were not connected to the service. That is *not* spirituality. Spirituality is not going through the motions so people will see you as spiritual. Spirituality is responding to what matters. That said, rituals do matter and can help you find spiritual contact. If you are a member of a religious community, your connection can be incredibly rich and helpful to spiritual expression. All traditions are filled with metaphors, words, stories, and spiritual practices. Not to draw on their history and use their rituals would be to neglect a primary resource. Failure to learn from other traditions narrows the bandwidth of our own expressions of faith.

Spirituality is also personal. Spirituality emanates from the integration of the habits we have been describing. As you become more aware, you notice the unmistakable presence in the world of God, and you come to understand that you deserve a place on this planet. It happens:

- When you witness an aspect of nature that leaves you with no words.
- When a person appears or an event occurs at exactly the right time.
- When you intuitively know something is happening with a loved one, even though they are distant.
- When people pool around you and love you at a moment of great need.
- When you see the power and energy of prayer working.
- When you experience the death of your parents followed by others you love.
- When you make peace with dying yourself.
- When you did what you said you were going to do, and you experience the privilege of "I got to do this."
- When human events are at their worst and you see people rise above it.
- When you meet people with whom you immediately feel trust, and the conversation lasts a lifetime.
- When you participate meaningfully in the larger purposes of the universe, even though you only partially understand and have vision of those larger purposes.
- When you can tolerate uncertainty.
- When you use Yoda's words, "Train yourself to let go of everything you fear to lose."
- When you have to start over because you have to do this, and you know you will have to do it again.

For some people, spirituality can be a sudden set of realizations precipitated by some radical event. The term conversion has been used to describe the force of sudden insight of the importance of spirituality. For others, the connecting of the dots is more a matter of accretion. With time, spirituality finds rich soil in "the very ground of our being."

Lynne McTaggart followed her classic on modern physics to a larger vision of what all science is pointing us to in a book called *The Bond*. She builds a case that we are all connected to each other in ways we did not understand as little as 30 years ago. Our brains are actually transmitters and receivers of the larger energy of the universe. Furthermore, that collaboration always trumps competition, and empathy is critical especially in these times. She writes:

We have lost our sense of the Bond, but our loss is not irrevocable. We can recover wholeness in our lives and recapture our sense of the connection between things, but doing so requires a very different set of rules from the ones we currently live by. To live the Bond is to surrender to nature's drive for wholeness and to recognize the whole in every aspect of our daily lives. We have to ask ourselves some fundamental questions: How should we view the world as something other than a place for just ourselves? How should we relate to each other, if not competitively? How might we organize ourselves in our neighborhoods—the immediate tribe around us and our smallest group outside the family—to be mutually supportive rather than competitive? How do we move beyond I win, you lose?

Expert System Habit Nine – Perspective

Perspective means looking at choices with multiple lenses but especially at the larger picture. Keeping things in perspective means looking at a problem and taking into your awareness the many factors that are involved, including your goals. When DaVinci wrote about the process of using a "brain map," he was suggesting that we put everything on the table before proceeding.

When I started using this strategy, I had a family chess table that was exactly the size I needed—first for writing but now I use it for everything. It is the origin of the tables in *Recovery Zone* as a way to think about life. The "Why" underneath the "Why" makes the table ideal for drilling down through the layers of meaning. The Decision Table, Vision Table, and Legacy Table provide different ways to elaborate our purposes, processes, and the narratives of our lives.

In the Legacy Table, we asked you to take the perspective from 50,000 feet down to ground zero and the here and now. Using multiple perspectives provided insight into the totality of the issues in both your internal and external life. Most importantly, the exercise helped you put together the whole story. A way of looking at the Ultimate To Do List, for example, is when you are writing the end of the story.

Another Italian, Antonio Damasio, revolutionized at the beginning of this century our understanding of decision-making and brain function. He pieced together that the brain evolved because of its "autobiographical" nature. Every part of the brain is connected to the awareness of your story. That is how the brain evolved in human biological development, and it is still the anchor of how we currently grow in consciousness.

If the brain is to change in both functionality and awareness, you must alter your story. Telling or hearing a story is the most complex task that the brain does. You have the situations, the plot, the characters, the unexpected, the challenges and the meaning of a great story. Damasio's key insight was the fundamental role of integration of all parts of the brain in understanding your own story. Thus, we continuously ask you to look at your history from the point of view of your own "work to be done." For example, the role your Grievance Story played in your life. For this, we introduced you to the notion of kamsaras or repetitions of earlier scenes from your story.

We also underlined the role of story in change and the significance of Joseph Campbell's Hero's story and Nancy Duarte's map of Campbell's work. Norman Doidge's outline of brain-change and neurodifferentiation is essentially about gathering new perceptions about your story and connecting the dots. Additionally, we asked you to stand on Einstein's hill and look at the whole train. When your life is finished, what will it look like?

The core to recovery, renewal, and resilience is getting your own story straight. Twelve step programs are built on the stories and commonalities of the membership. One of the classic books on the recovery process is *The Spirituality of Imperfection: Storytelling and the Search for Meaning* by Ernest Kurtz and Katherine Ketcham. The authors underline the unending search and challenge of expanding your story.

Throughout this book, the two primary facts we have that brought to your awareness are that the brain changes when safety exists, and the story (the narrative) is altered.

Some of the best storytellers are standup comedians. Jay Sankey's book *Zen and the Art of Stand-Up Comedy* underlines that the most successful people in stand-up comedy are those who use material from their own lives. A good example would be Kevin Hart, who is one of the most successful comics in this century. He describes how he struggled with being funny in front of a crowd. It all changed for him when he decided to stop telling stories that he thought others would find funny and started to tell stories that he found funny. His stories came from family poverty, failure in high school, and a father who was in prison because of his problems with cocaine. His stories are hilarious but also moving, poignant, and meaningful. He has been an extraordinary success. Once he decided to be true to himself in his humor, the "blueprint" of his career and life unfolded before him. He talks of the blueprint as both a map and a call. The metaphor of the blueprint also works because blueprints rely on detail on several levels simultaneously, which is very analogous to our Ultimate To Do List.

What Hart describes fits Damasio's research on brain function. It is the same evolution of process. First, there is a realization about the "core self." This autobiographical awareness that you are in a story leads to a conscious life. Those who pursue that awareness reach "extended consciousness" or a higher level of brain function and awareness. Usually, this means using the struggle of your life as a source of meaning and a more profound awareness of the role of others. Perspective is a habit of preserving and understanding your story using different lenses such as humor. Sometimes, the struggle is just funny.

Expert System Habit Ten – Consciousness

Conscious awareness is essentially a brain upgrade in the interests of making your life different. It would be easy to assume after all this work that things will automatically be easier. Unfortunately, that is not the case. It is true that the problems that brought you to recovery become more remote. You make better decisions, the quality of your life improves, and you handle adversity much better. The problem is that you now feel things more deeply, and you now see the complexities of being human. So, you are rewarded for your hard work, but you know that challenge and growth are now a way of life. Therapy, learning new skill sets, and adding new dimensions and options raises more paradoxes, which adds difficulty to just being human. Plus, you will need a group, a mentor, and a clear path that is consistent with your core values and vision.

Honesty and accountability will continue to be difficult. They will also force you into a deeper sense of self that will test your courage. You will periodically have to reinvent yourself. The good news is that all of the habits described above deepen the experience of yourself and the world.

An oft repeated joke amongst seniors is that aging is not for sissies. You are constantly having to let things go and grieve the losses of your health and the deaths of your friends and family members. The same could be said for recovery. The hard choices, the discipline, and the courage to live in the world differently involve so much more than just stopping the behavior that was challenging you. Recovery firmly puts you into a path of losses acknowledged and departing from easy ways. You are not being a copy of yourself. To achieve that level of congruence is to face the reality of many adversities.

Buddha said suffering is clinging to that which changes. Recovery and being at your best, by definition, will call forth the wherewithal to face the next ordeal. This is the essence of the heroic journey.

When you look at a peaceful forest, with the harmony and tranquility it brings to you, remember that even in that forest an epic struggle exists. All plants compete for resources—air, soil, water, sunlight. Some win and grow. Some fail to thrive. Some die and become part of the other's process. All die eventually. Gaze at a beautiful lake and experience the calming rhythm of gentle waves. Underneath is a constant battle. Large predators lying in wait for smaller fish who are also searching for prey. A mother duck has her little ones close as she leads them along the shore. A swirl and a sucking sound, and part of her brood is gone forever. Not fair. Painful.

In the deep expanses of dark and empty space, physicists have found incredible amounts of energy. Among those expanses, energy surges, stars collapse, planets collide, and dark holes pull in anything in their path—never to be seen again. Within the universe of our bodies there is also unceasing war. White blood cells roam and attack invaders and threats. Our lives depend on these cells attacking and being deadly. In all situations, the cycle of life has rhythms with adversity at its core: birth, life, and death.

In *The Lord of the Rings*, the young hobbit Frodo, discouraged and overwhelmed, turns to Gandalf the wizard, who has been his guide, and admits his regret over making the commitment to returning the ring. "I wish I had never started this," he states. To which Gandalf replies, "All of us do in troubled times. Yet we have no choice—no choice about when we came into this life nor when we leave. It is what we do with the call we have been given that matters."

Ultimately, what matters is not the cards we have been dealt; it is how we play them that counts. People exist who have easy lives, but they still face the inevitable and they often lack the introspection, awareness, and inner-coherence that brings meaning to life. Thus, the matters of their own death they avoid. They are oblivious to an Ultimate To Do List. The ability to transform suffering into meaning is a life focused on what matters, and those who have an easy life lack this ability. The following phrase of Viktor Frankel's is one of the most famous expressions of spiritual teachings to come out of the horror of the concentration camps: "When we are successful in our congruency, we feel valued, happy, and real. And we survive."

Dietrich Bonhoeffer was a Lutheran pastor and theologian who challenged the German people to live up to their values. He was an outspoken critic of Hitler, and he lost his life for that. He used the term "the ground of our being," which meant living a purpose-filled, value-driven life. He felt the German people lost their courage to stand up for the deeply rooted values of Germany. His most famous book, *The Cost of Discipleship*, is regarded as a modern spiritual classic. His primary message, however, was that being coherent in your life, whatever challenges you face, comes with costs. This is why we have asked questions like "What are you willing to give up?" and "If nothing else I will...?" Once again, Master Yoda's comment on this issue is: "Train yourself to let go of everything you fear to lose."

Expert System Habit Eleven – Compassion

Central to our growing ability to define ourselves is the ability to get a fuller understanding of our own story or narrative. We have made the case that our brain grows as we look at our lives from all types of perspectives. In all stories, there are numerous characters who are a part of the story. When we read a story, whether fiction or history or even biology, we have to understand what drives the characters in ways that impact the scenario. We have used the example of "deconstructing" our abusers. We learned that placing ourselves in the shoes of those who hurt us gives us new pathways to grieving. Our hearts may break, but our emotional regulation now has perspective in letting go and living in mercy and forgiveness of others—and ourselves.

A classic and effective book on resolving conflict is *Difficult Conversations,* by Bruce Patton and Sheila Heen. Based on a famous study of problem-solving at Harvard University, the book shares a framework with one of the most common problems in life: how to have a difficult conversation with those we care about. As we noted as one of the core paradoxes in life, intimacy presents inevitable differences to both parties. One of Patton and Heen's most striking findings is that before even starting a difficult conversation, an indispensable strategy is to place yourself on the other side of the conversation. Patton and Heen say that once the conversation starts, the other side has "truths" that you likely did not know. Being open to that possibility at the start gives an openness to hearing what you did not know or appreciate.

During my marriage to my now deceased wife, Suzanne, we mostly were peaceful and happy. However, we had certain issues that kept reappearing. We did therapy, meetings, and compromises—but even so, they would come up. Sometime after she died, I sat down with her journals. As I read, there were some descriptions of me that were troubling—not because they were not accurate; they were—but because I suddenly had an unvarnished picture of myself through her eyes and I did not like what I saw.

The view of me presented in Suzanne's journals became a large part of my therapy and grief work. I learned from reading her journals that I had really missed what she was attempting to tell me, and it made our life harder as a result. I believe I am a much better person to live with today because of this understanding. I needed to inhabit her vision of the world (and our story together) without the heat of our disagreements. Seeing myself and our relationship from her perspective changed me profoundly.

Participating in ongoing support and therapy groups stimulates that kind of growth. Trauma and addiction both fundamentally alter the function of the "mirror neurons"—the neural network that allows us to care for others and place ourselves in their shoes. A support or therapy group that has no stake in the outcome can help us break through to the unconscious part of ourselves—that which we often term as denial. They become the mirrors that help us to have compassion for the other.

In twelve step research, the best predictor of success is not that you find a sponsor; rather, your success is more impacted when you become a sponsor. It is the long-term relationships in helping others that stimulates the mirror neurons and our abilities *to endure human differences and difficult conversations*. I find in teaching and therapy that, more often than not, the work is more helpful to me than my students or patients. This is why "passing it on" is the cornerstone of all twelve step fellowships.

Jung wrote about this fundamental human proposition, stating: "The self is made manifest in the opposites and in the conflict between them. [...] Hence the way to self begins with conflict."

St. John of the Cross aptly referred to this place of conflict and potential transformation as the dark night of the soul, where crisis must be endured and accepted until clarity is restored. The key is to tolerate the storm. That is why building a group of friends to walk with you, to provide perspective for you, to provide a mirror of vision of yourself, and to help you hold close what is happening for others in your life is so clarifying to whatever your intentions become.

Expert System Habit Twelve – Mindfulness

Spending regular time consciously directing awareness to present-moment experience can change the brain's capacities and structure. Many programs exist that teach meditation, and there are many varieties of meditation practice. There is also a wealth of good science about its benefits. Benefits of meditation include:

- Improved focus and attention.
- Lowered stress and higher resistance to the damaging effects of cortisol (the stress hormone).
- Emotional self-regulation is more effective.
- Reduced brain cell loss associated with aging.
- Reversed memory loss.
- Increased tolerance to pain.
- Many regions and parts of the brain become more dense and consequently more functional.
- Capacity for making good decisions improves dramatically and cognitive performance improves significantly.

Meditation is no longer regarded in medicine as a "fringe" or "experimental" intervention. It works in fundamental ways that extend life for women up to 15 percent and men 11 percent. Those that marginalize meditation as "counting your breathing" and not useful may need to reassess.

Jon Kabat-Zinn, mentioned earlier with our discussion of "zone" activities, built his systems in his work with pain patients (over 800 clinics nationwide). In a conversation with Oprah, he talked of his book, *Mindfulness for All*, as a "gentle glide" into meditation practice. At one point, he summarized in a fun way what the process of mindfulness is really about:

> *Mindfulness can be thought of simply as the awareness that comes from systematically paying attention on purpose in the present moment, and non-judgmentally, to what is closest to home in your experience: namely this very moment in which you are alive, however it is for you—pleasant, difficult, or not even on the radar screen—and to the body sensations, thoughts and feelings that you may be experiencing in any moment.*

In mindfulness, strange as it may sound, we are not trying to fix anything or to solve our problems. Curiously, holding them in awareness moment by moment without judging them sometimes leads over time to their dissolving on their own. You may come to see your situation in a new light that reveals new ways of relating to it creatively out of your own growing stability and clarity of mind, out of your own wisdom, and your caring for what is most important.

We are not trying to actively achieve a state of deep relaxation or any other state for that matter while practicing mindfulness. But interestingly, by opening to an awareness of how things actually are in the present moment, we often taste very deep states of relaxation and well-being, both of body and mind, even in the face of extraordinary difficulties.

I cannot tell you how many people have said to me recently, "I don't know what I would have done without this practice," referring to every conceivable difficulty and anguish we are apt to face as human beings at some point or other in our lives, usually when we least expect it and have the hardest time accepting it.

Mindfulness can reveal what is deepest and best in ourselves and bring it to life in very practical and imaginative ways just when we need it the most.

Ultimately, the effectiveness of these guided meditation programs depend on your willingness to practice with them regularly. I wish you all the best in this commitment you are making to yourself. It is nothing less than a radical act of love, an act of self-regard and of respect for your deep inner wisdom and capacity for healing.

May your mindfulness practice take root, grow, and continue to flower and nourish your life from moment to moment and from day to day.

Notice that mindfulness starts with a here and now focus. Several times, we have noted that people who have only a short time to live develop a capacity to value each precious moment. If that is true, why do we put off the things we really want to do? The answer is resistance.

If you have trouble determining some method of working on this, I recommend two movies. The first movie is based on the work of Stephen Pressfield, who wrote the book and produced the movie *The Legend of Bagger Vance*. The movie's storyline is about a golfer of great talent who was traumatized by World War I and, in response, avoided picking up his game and talent. The story is about overcoming his trauma and recovering his excellence. His caddy, Baggar Vance, was his mentor, telling him he had to "see" the field and then envision the stroke necessary.

The second movie is the *Way of the Peaceful Warrior*, the story of an Olympic athlete hampered by indulgent parents and a car accident. His mentor, a gas station attendant named Socrates, tells him that his performance in Olympic competition would be exponentially better if he was in the here and now. The turning point in the movie is when he realizes that there are no ordinary moments.

As mentioned earlier, another methodology for mindfulness is HeartMath. The creators of this practice have you breathe and synchronize the sinus rhythm with focus on what matters to you. You do this process with an app on a smartphone or a computer. During this process, a simple sensor attached to your ear lobe monitors your heart's activities. There is no doubt about the value of the practice when you can see on the app that your thinking and breathing, when harmonized, change the waves of your heartbeat. Doc Childre and his staff have two books, *HeartMath* and *Heart Intelligence*. Both are a gentle guide to being more conscious—and very worth the time.

There are many other great programs out there, and we have made a list of suggestions for you in this chapter's bibliography so you can look for one that is a good match for you. If you want to enhance therapy and recovery work, pick one, really practice it, and then start adding others. Over time, you will integrate strategies until you have the quarterback's ability to see immediately what you need to do next.

Your practice of the 12 habits plus your expert system builds a platform for your resilience.

Figure 7.3

Expert System Habits

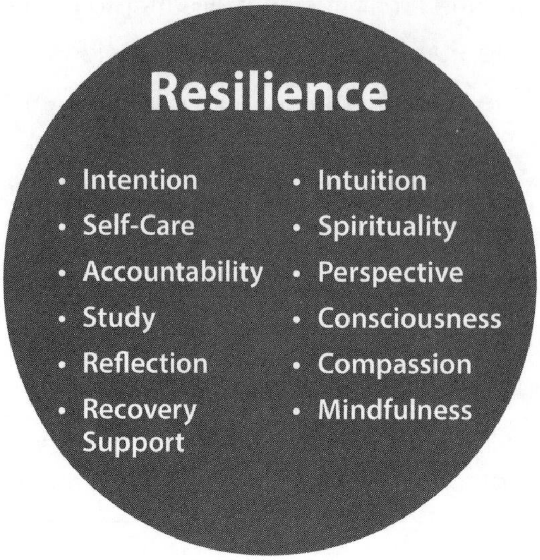

Resilience
• Intention
• Self-Care
• Accountability
• Study
• Reflection
• Recovery Support
• Intuition
• Spirituality
• Perspective
• Consciousness
• Compassion
• Mindfulness

Figure 7.4

At this point, all of these are familiar to you. Throughout both *Recovery Zone I* and *II*, these twelve skills have been embedded in both the internally and externally focused materials and the assignments you have completed. You have already been working on these skills! Identifying them as a unified skill set empowers you to focus on how you cope with chaos, setbacks, and disappointments.

Expert System Habits + Resilience Master Skills

Flow
Vision
Persistence
Acceptance
Knowledge
Emotional Regulations
Boundaries
Listen to Fear
Inner Observer
Flexibility
Inner Coherence
Empathy
Resilience
• Intention
• Self-Care
• Accountability
• Study
• Reflection
• Recovery Support
• Intuition
• Spirituality
• Perspective
• Consciousness
• Compassion
• Mindfulness

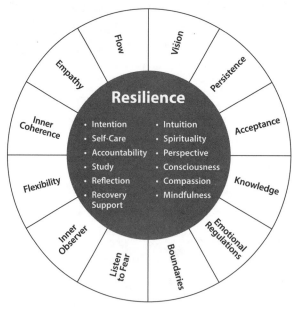

Figure 7.5

An Initial Assessment of Where You Are Now

On the following pages you will find a self-assessment which asks you to rate on a one to ten scale each of these habits that coalesce into an expert system that will support Resilience Skills and Strategies. A high rating in a dimension would indicate regular, intentional, and automatic use in your daily life. Another way of looking at it is to think that it is enough of a habit to contribute to being in the "zone" that supports your recovery. A low score would indicate that you recognize that you need to do more work to integrate that practice into a habit. After you have rated yourself, rank the habits you are most successful, and the ones in which you are least successful. You may wish to return to your Ultimate To Do List or the clipboard in the last chapter and integrate your perceptions into your planning process.

Rank the list of Habits from 1–10 with 10 being the BEST and 1 you need most improvement on.

Circle the number that best describes where you feel you stand on each Habit.

The 12 Habits		Needs Focus			Needs Improvement				Doing Well		
		1	2	3	4	5	6	7	8	9	10
Habit One – Intention		1	2	3	4	5	6	7	8	9	10
Habit Two – Self-Care		1	2	3	4	5	6	7	8	9	10
Habit Three – Accountability		1	2	3	4	5	6	7	8	9	10
Habit Four – Study		1	2	3	4	5	6	7	8	9	10
Habit Five – Reflection		1	2	3	4	5	6	7	8	9	10
Habit Six – Recovery Support		1	2	3	4	5	6	7	8	9	10
Habit Seven – Intuition		1	2	3	4	5	6	7	8	9	10
Habit Eight – Spirituality		1	2	3	4	5	6	7	8	9	10
Habit Nine – Perspective		1	2	3	4	5	6	7	8	9	10
Habit Ten – Consciousness		1	2	3	4	5	6	7	8	9	10
Habit Eleven – Compassion		1	2	3	4	5	6	7	8	9	10
Habit Twelve – Mindfulness		1	2	3	4	5	6	7	8	9	10

Exercise 7.2

Here is a list of programs or books that you may look into to get started in mindfulness:

- HeartMath at HearthMath.com
- Mindfulness 101
- *Mindfulness for Beginners* by Jon Kabat-Zinn and Sounds True Publishing House
- John Kabot-Zinn meditations at mindfulnesscds.com
- *Practicing Mindfulness: 75 Essential Meditations to Reduce Stress, Improve Mental Health, and Find Peace in the Everyday*
- *Mindfulness in Plain English* by Bhante Gunaratana

Chapter 8 **The Secret Logic of Resilience**

The thought manifests as the word. The word manifests as the deed. The deed develops into habit. And the habit hardens into character. So watch the thought and its ways with care. And let it spring from love, born out of concern for all beings.

Buddha (c.563–c. 483 BC)

"Your focus determines your future."

Qui-Gon Jinn to Young Anakin Skywalker *Star Wars—Episode One*

All your brain cells are replaced every two years. Your blood supply is renewed (or re-celled) every six months. It takes twelve years to renew your heart. The paradox is that your body is constantly regenerating itself even as it degenerates in the aging process. One of the great late 20th-century discoveries in neuroscience and brain research was the "neuroplasticity" of the brain, which is extraordinary and even astounding in terms or our development as human beings. Unfortunately, our educational, mental health, and physical health systems still assume that our abilities and character are fixed and, at most, can only be somewhat modified. This belief in effect rules out the basics of recovery and personal transformation.

In my early training, I heard it stated several times that alcohol destroys brain cells and they never come back. That was absolutely mythical but maybe useful in scaring alcoholics into sobriety. It is true that alcohol has the potential to do permanent damage to the liver, heart, and brain. But for most in recovery, brain repair and growth are very possible—with focus and care.

Similarly, there are those who argue for "set points" in the brain that the brain will return to automatically even if stretched for a bit. Weight would be an example. There are programs or diets that help people lose large amounts of weight, but people do not integrate what they have learned into their daily lives and as they start living "normally," they return to their old weight setting.

In family systems the set point may be certain patterns of dysfunction. Systems theory does say that systems are based on "homeostasis," a word that means a system returns to the same repetitive function. However, if the rules and roles of the dysfunctional family change, the system can be altered into "functional."

Throughout the *Recovery Zone* series we have presented some of the best thinking about how transformation happens in the brain: Daniel Amen's *The Brain Warrior's Way*, Daniel Siegel's "transpirational" brain, Norman Doidge's *The Brain that Changes Itself*, Daniel Goleman's top-down/bottom-up brain, and Lynne McTaggart's extensive documentation of our brains being energy beacons that interact with the larger forces of the universe. The essential premise of the zone and zone living is what Mihaly Csikszentmihalyi first identified as flow: by collecting and refocusing the existing "set points" into habits of living, a "zone" engages the brain in fulfilling and rewarding activities that ultimately represent meaning. Further, recovery is much more than sobriety, and it is impossible to preserve given the tugs of the old set points unless that zone (flow) is intentionally the focus. Finally, key to that intentionality is the role of story that Joseph Campbell documented and the essential autobiographical nature of the brain that Antonio Damasio demonstrated. The Ultimate To Do List becomes a perspective providing outline of one's story, which is only partially written—meaning the rest of it still is to be lived. Yet, without our story so far being deeply understood, our intentions remain random and zone living stays elusive.

In part, our biology is a mixed bag. When we are stressed or challenged, our body releases epinephrine, also known as adrenaline, which creates a cascade of short-term physiological changes that help us meet the challenges we face. Our blood flow speeds up and our digestive system slows down. Our immune system releases pro-inflammatory chemicals in case of potential injury or infection. We are geared up for battle. Our brain directs our energies into intense focus, but at the expense of memory and multi-tasking. Decision-making accelerates but critical thinking is sacrificed. Emotions take over, which feels right in the course of conflict or trouble, but can lead to negative thinking and decisions with long-term consequences.

Accompanying the release of adrenaline is the release of cortisol. Cortisol is called the "stress hormone" because it brings back normal body functioning. It manages body regulation (sleeping, regeneration, and appetites like sex and food) along with basic ongoing repair and maintenance. However, if toxic stress or trauma is prolonged, the body starts to take the presence of cortisol for granted. This can result in cortisol binding with and making changes to our DNA—to help us cope with excessive stress as a normal state. The results of this can be compulsive and addictive behavior, mental health disorders, and immune dysfunction. Stress itself can become addictive. Chris Hedges, for example, writes in his book *War Is a Force that Gives Us Meaning* about how war correspondents crave the danger and find that being in safe, peaceful conditions seems boring and unproductive. Living on the edge occupationally has been documented in many work situations, often leading to breakdowns.

Similarly, our relationship choices can be affected. Child development specialists have long documented the effects of stress on both the behavior and brain anatomy of children.

Abused children, when placed in normal, healthy families, actually try to precipitate abusive behavior in new caregivers. Adults who are attracted to people of high drama or high risk find nurturing, healthy, mature people boring. Toxic stress and trauma have a long research trail indicating a complex and intricate relationship with mental health problems, relationship issues, and addictive behaviors.

Yet, this series emphasizes the ordeal and challenge of a call as critical to achievement, life satisfaction, and happiness. Since this appears to be now (and in history) the core of the human story, how do we deal when life becomes difficult and dark? Resilience is the core expertise. The ability to live in a state of calm in spite of challenge, and, if derailed, to restore that calm are the ultimate skill sets for an expert system in resilience. This parallels what medicine describes as the sympathetic and parasympathetic nervous systems. Learning these habits and skills are core to brain change.

In the preceding chapter, we explored the essential habits for an expert system for living in a world of chaos and challenge. Like so many things, the sum of the parts is more significant than the whole. Together they "stick" and reinforce each other, creating a powerful, empowering force when the winds of life become adverse. A logic exists in their interaction that can be missed when considered individually. This logic appears to be a secret but it is really not, given what modern neuroscience and physics are making clear. Let us explore some of those interactive qualities.

Intentionality is the bedrock for a sense of purpose for the self. The unraveling story is constantly revealing one's purposes. The value put on the self demands that there be care for the self and acknowledgment of its importance. Part of that care and value of the self takes the form of focusing on what matters, as well as maintaining and protecting the body in which the self resides. It extends to living in integrity so the basis of the relationship with self and relationships with others is trust. This requires a commitment to learning all that is relevant to our intentions and purposes, including our own self-care.

Furthermore, we must surround ourselves with those who are on similar journeys and share similar purposes. All research on collective consciousness and problem-solving share one common agreement: We are smarter together than we are separately. We also stimulate our capacities for primary bonding, which reinforces all the dimensions of resilience—especially intention, acceptance, compassion, and flow.

Within the matrix of these dimensions, certain habits flourish. We become more intuitive and our wise mind is more attuned both situationally and to the long term. The spiritual skills of our wise-minded Inner Observer help access critical life strategies, which include letting go, forgiveness, and gratitude. These in turn become essential tools for navigating difficult moments. Our capacity to look at a situation from different perspectives is one of many ways to maintain our inner calm and to up our decision-making effectiveness.

The result is a level of consciousness in which we merge with the life around us with deeper awareness. We have used the words "showing up" to describe how such "here and now" presence in relationships appears in the real world. From this life position of "all in," compassion flows, which helps us to be connected with ourselves, our loved ones, and all that is the universe. Thus, no matter what happens or how grim the situation is, we stay in a mindfulness that keeps us in that channel of coherent function we call flow or the zone.

With our new habits in place, there is a coping platform—or, as I have termed it, a table—that is the playing field of life. Like the quarterback, my plan may have worked, but if in that particular play it went awry, I can still "see the field" because of the support base of my habits. Now I am able to bring forth my skills and strategies for the next right option. If I fail in my alternative attempt, I get to make more plays, and the game is not lost. Classically, I fall down seven times and then I get up for the eighth time.

Notice that the analogy of the quarterback adds two new dimensions: skills and strategies that go with the expert system. We determined some time ago that there are master skills for resilience. These skills rely on habits that can be cultivated; the skills and strategies also require practice.

In writing this series, we were inspired by the University of Hamburg's nine pillars of wisdom and Siegel's nine domains of brain development, and by many of the authors whose names have appeared in these pages. Importantly, the same skills kept appearing in every book and study we examined. Moreover, many of these have been known for a long time. Some were recommended by the stoics of ancient Rome as well as early Buddhist monks in ancient China. We did an extensive literature search and distilled twelve distinct practices as Resilience Master Skills:

- **Vision** — the capacity to picture your intentions.
- **Persistence** — the pure tenacity of picking yourself up eight times after seven falls.
- **Acceptance** — the capacity to cope with the realities in front of you.
- **Knowledge** — being a good consumer of information in all your needs and intents.
- **Emotional Regulation** — keeping yourself in a state of calm and maintaining the capacity to restore calm.
- **Boundaries** — having clear definitions of what works and what does not and insisting on what works for you.
- **Listening to Fear** — knowing danger and using your best intuitions.
- **Inner Observer** — the wise mind that rises above the turmoil of the brain, filtering out extraneous thoughts so we can focus on what really matters.
- **Flexibility** — the ability to explore and expand options.

- **Inner Coherence** — the integration of body rhythms with what means the most to us to achieve an inner stillness.
- **Empathy** — the ability to look at a problem from the other person's perspective and experience appropriate feelings.
- **Flow** — the capacity to stay in a range of behaviors that challenge you, matter to you, and generate happiness.

At this point, all of these are familiar to you. Throughout both *Recovery Zone I* and *II*, these twelve skills have been embedded in both the internally and externally focused materials and the assignments you have completed. You have already been working on these skills! Identifying them as a unified skill set empowers you to focus on how you cope with chaos, setbacks, and disappointments.

Now is the time to assess where you are with each skill, so you can reflect and see how the skills work together. In the following pages are master skill assessments. Each, at the top, lists the skill to be examined along with its definition. Beside that description are examples to illustrate how the skills might be used. Immediately below, you will be asked to write about a time or times you have used that skill and it worked for you. Then you are asked to think of times when matters did not go well and you now can see how that skill might have been useful to you. At the bottom of each sheet is a rating scale from 1 to 10. A low score means that you need improvement in the use of that skill. A high score would indicate high utilization and success with that skill.

After completing all twelve worksheets, you will find a sheet to collect your scores. You will then be asked to rank the master skills in terms of how well you use them. With this, you have a profile of habits and skills to work on. These are all summarized in what we call the Resilience Matrix, which follows at the end of the chapter

Resilience Master Skills

Vision — Having a vision of our future helps us to look at our dream and discover our purpose and intentions. Envisioning what our life would and could look like helps both our logical and creative mind to stay focused on the desires we hope to accomplish.

Persistence — Continued efforts to maintain a course of action in spite of difficulty or opposition.

Acceptance — Surrendering what is in front of you, starting with what is not what you wish you could be. Mental health is a commitment to seeing reality at all cost.

Knowledge — A familiarity, awareness, or understanding of something and/or ourself through education, research, self-evaluations, and many other fields. In the art of resilience, knowledge is vital to us as we continue to learn lessons from our adversities.

Emotional Regulation — Emotional regulation can be defined as a set of processes people go through to monitor and bring balance to emotions that are above or below the healthy range of feelings and the actions that are paired with them. It is essential when it comes to building a well-balanced life.

Boundaries — Personal boundaries are guidelines, rules, or limits that a person creates to identify reasonable, safe, and permissible ways for other people to behave towards them and how they will respond when someone passes those limits.

Listen to Fear — At the basic level, fear guides our fight, flight, or freeze responses and helps to keep us safe and alive. Fear heightens our senses and awareness; fear keeps us alert, it keeps us surviving and progressing, it is a thermometer that lets you know you are moving into a hot area and are doing something beyond the norm.

Inner Observer — Inner Observer is the part of our selves that monitors the traffic in our brain. It is sometimes called the higher self, the wise self, the functional adult. It is psychological detachment that Buddha describes as monitoring the "monkey business" of the brain.

Flexibility — Psychological, mental, or emotional flexibility is about being able to stay in the present moment, navigating the emotions, thoughts, or sensations that may arise and then being able to choose behaviors based on the situation at hand and core values.

Inner Coherence — The word "coherence" means to be connected with a logical bridge between different parts of a whole. Inner coherence means to be connected between our emotional, reasonable, and wise mind.

Empathy — Having the mental capacity to cooperate with others, build friendships, make moral decisions, and intervene when others are going through challenging and often sad times.

Flow — Flow is one of life's highly enjoyable states of being, wrapping us entirely in the present, and helping us be more creative, productive, and happy. Alternatively, this is also known as "being in the zone." Athletes, artists, song-writers, authors, plus many other creative people reference the art of flow as being at their core of their ability to be the best they can be in their field/careers.

RESILIENCE MASTER SKILL

Recovery Zone Strategies

VISION

- Seeking Options
- Seeking Alternative Perspective
- Long-Term Focus
- Goal-Setting

Record a time when you used this Resilience Master Skill and Recovery Zone Strategies and it worked for you.

Think of a time or situation when you could have used this master skill and strategies but didn't. How could this master skill have helped you?

Circle the number that best describes where you feel you stand on this Master Skill in terms of using it effectively when needed.

Master Skill	Needs Focus			Needs Improvement				Doing Well		
Vision	1	2	3	4	5	6	7	8	9	10

Exercise 8.1A

RESILIENCE MASTER SKILL   **Recovery Zone Strategies**

PERSISTENCE

- Focus
- Exercise
- Nutrition
- Rest

Record a time when you used this Resilience Master Skill and Recovery Zone Strategies and it worked for you.

Think of a time or situation when you could have used this master skill and strategies but didn't. How could this master skill have helped you?

Circle the number that best describes where you feel you stand on this Master Skill in terms of using it effectively when needed.

Master Skill	Needs Focus			Needs Improvement				Doing Well		
Persistence	1	2	3	4	5	6	7	8	9	10

Exercise 8.1B

RESILIENCE MASTER SKILL

Recovery Zone Strategies

ACCEPTANCE

- Problem-Solving
- Accepting Limits
- Congruency
- Reframing/Restructuring

Record a time when you used this Resilience Master Skill and Recovery Zone Strategies and it worked for you.

Think of a time or situation when you could have used this master skill and strategies but didn't. How could this master skill have helped you?

Circle the number that best describes where you feel you stand on this Master Skill in terms of using it effectively when needed.

Master Skill	Needs Focus			Needs Improvement				Doing Well		
Acceptance	1	2	3	4	5	6	7	8	9	10

Exercise 8.1C

RESILIENCE MASTER SKILL

Recovery Zone Strategies

KNOWLEDGE

- Seeking Facts
- Changing the Narrative
- Positive Self-Focus
- Brain Consciousness

Record a time when you used this Resilience Master Skill and Recovery Zone Strategies and it worked for you.

Think of a time or situation when you could have used this master skill and strategies but didn't. How could this master skill have helped you?

Circle the number that best describes where you feel you stand on this Master Skill in terms of using it effectively when needed.

Master Skill	Needs Focus			Needs Improvement				Doing Well		
Knowledge	1	2	3	4	5	6	7	8	9	10

Exercise 8.1D

RESILIENCE MASTER SKILL

Recovery Zone Strategies

EMOTIONAL REGULATION

- Managing Adversity
- Identifying Resistance
- Meditation
- Emotional Expression

Record a time when you used this Resilience Master Skill and Recovery Zone Strategies and it worked for you.

Think of a time or situation when you could have used this master skill and strategies but didn't. How could this master skill have helped you?

Circle the number that best describes where you feel you stand on this Master Skill in terms of using it effectively when needed.

Master Skill	Needs Focus			Needs Improvement				Doing Well		
Emotional Regulation	1	2	3	4	5	6	7	8	9	10

Exercise 8.1E

RESILIENCE MASTER SKILL

Recovery Zone Strategies

BOUNDARIES

- Showing Up – Vulnerability
- Service
- Accessing and Accepting Help
- Accepting Inconvenient Truths

Record a time when you used this Resilience Master Skill and Recovery Zone Strategies and it worked for you.

Think of a time or situation when you could have used this master skill and strategies but didn't. How could this master skill have helped you?

Circle the number that best describes where you feel you stand on this Master Skill in terms of using it effectively when needed.

Master Skill	Needs Focus			Needs Improvement				Doing Well		
Boundaries	1	2	3	4	5	6	7	8	9	10

Exercise 8.1F

RESILIENCE MASTER SKILL

Recovery Zone Strategies

LISTEN TO FEAR

- Embodiment
- Expansion of Awareness
- Reintegration of Memories
- Trust of Self

Record a time when you used this Resilience Master Skill and Recovery Zone Strategies and it worked for you.

Think of a time or situation when you could have used this master skill and strategies but didn't. How could this master skill have helped you?

Circle the number that best describes where you feel you stand on this Master Skill in terms of using it effectively when needed.

Master Skill	Needs Focus			Needs Improvement				Doing Well		
Listen to Fear	1	2	3	4	5	6	7	8	9	10

Exercise 8.1G

RESILIENCE MASTER SKILL

Recovery Zone Strategies

INNER OBSERVER

- Gratitude
- Letting Go
- Forgiveness
- Self-Compassion

Record a time when you used this Resilience Master Skill and Recovery Zone Strategies and it worked for you.

Think of a time or situation when you could have used this master skill and strategies but didn't. How could this master skill have helped you?

Circle the number that best describes where you feel you stand on this Master Skill in terms of using it effectively when needed.

Master Skill	Needs Focus			Needs Improvement				Doing Well		
Inner Observer	1	2	3	4	5	6	7	8	9	10

Exercise 8.1H

RESILIENCE MASTER SKILL

Recovery Zone Strategies

FLEXIBILITY

- Changing Perspective
- Adaptability
- Optimism
- Learning From The Past

Record a time when you used this Resilience Master Skill and Recovery Zone Strategies and it worked for you.

Think of a time or situation when you could have used this master skill and strategies but didn't. How could this master skill have helped you?

Circle the number that best describes where you feel you stand on this Master Skill in terms of using it effectively when needed.

Master Skill	Needs Focus			Needs Improvement				Doing Well		
Flexibility	1	2	3	4	5	6	7	8	9	10

Exercise 8.1I

RESILIENCE MASTER SKILL

Recovery Zone Strategies

INNER COHERENCE

- Affirmation
- Sinus Rhythm
- Integration
- Universal Connection

Record a time when you used this Resilience Master Skill and Recovery Zone Strategies and it worked for you.

Think of a time or situation when you could have used this master skill and strategies but didn't. How could this master skill have helped you?

Circle the number that best describes where you feel you stand on this Master Skill in terms of using it effectively when needed.

Master Skill	Needs Focus			Needs Improvement				Doing Well		
Inner Coherence	1	2	3	4	5	6	7	8	9	10

Exercise 8.1J

RESILIENCE MASTER SKILL

Recovery Zone Strategies

EMPATHY

- Attunement
- Connection/Relationship
- Validation/Witnessing
- Problem-Solving/Community

Record a time when you used this Resilience Master Skill and Recovery Zone Strategies and it worked for you.

Think of a time or situation when you could have used this master skill and strategies but didn't. How could this master skill have helped you?

Circle the number that best describes where you feel you stand on this Master Skill in terms of using it effectively when needed.

Master Skill	Needs Focus			Needs Improvement				Doing Well		
Empathy	1	2	3	4	5	6	7	8	9	10

Exercise 8.1K

RESILIENCE MASTER SKILL

Recovery Zone Strategies

FLOW

- Creativity
- Play
- Humor/Internal & External
- Challenging Activities

Record a time when you used this Resilience Master Skill and Recovery Zone Strategies and it worked for you.

Think of a time or situation when you could have used this master skill and strategies but didn't. How could this master skill have helped you?

Circle the number that best describes where you feel you stand on this Master Skill in terms of using it effectively when needed.

Master Skill	Needs Focus			Needs Improvement				Doing Well		
Flow	1	2	3	4	5	6	7	8	9	10

Exercise 8.1L

12 Resilience Master Skills Assessment

Using your Individual Master Skill Assessments, circle the number that corresponds to each Master Skill. Note that 8 to 10 puts your skill utilization in the zone!

Rank the list of Master Skills from 1–10 with 10 being the BEST and 1 you need most improvement on.

12 Resilience Master Skills Assessment

The 12 Master Skills	Circle the number that best describes where you feel you stand on each Habit.									
	Needs Focus			Needs Improvement				Doing Well		
Master Skill One – Vision	1	2	3	4	5	6	7	8	9	10
Master Skill Two – Persistence	1	2	3	4	5	6	7	8	9	10
Master Skill Three – Acceptance	1	2	3	4	5	6	7	8	9	10
Master Skill Four – Knowledge	1	2	3	4	5	6	7	8	9	10
Master Skill Five – Emotional Regulation	1	2	3	4	5	6	7	8	9	10
Master Skill Six – Boundaries	1	2	3	4	5	6	7	8	9	10
Master Skill Seven – Listen to Fear	1	2	3	4	5	6	7	8	9	10
Master Skill Eight – Inner Observer	1	2	3	4	5	6	7	8	9	10
Master Skill Nine – Flexibility	1	2	3	4	5	6	7	8	9	10
Master Skill Ten – Inner Coherence	1	2	3	4	5	6	7	8	9	10
Master Skill Eleven – Empathy	1	2	3	4	5	6	7	8	9	10
Master Twelve – Flow	1	2	3	4	5	6	7	8	9	10

Exercise 8.2

Recovery Zone Strategies

Within an expert system, there are strategies used to implement specific skills. There are many ways, for example, to track and utilize flow or being in the zone. Similarly, accessing your Inner Observer or having empathy for others can utilize a number of ways to achieve either. These basic strategies are very familiar to you but you have probably not thought of them as strategies or even as critical to your habits or skills you develop. We have identified them as they have frequently been woven throughout the *Recovery Zone* book series. We have synthesized 48 separate strategies that are used to maintain resilience as part of your habits and skills. **Figure 8.2** is a table of the 48 strategies with a working definition of each.

In any expert system, these strategies are essential to the "wax on, wax off" concept of building any complex response system. That is true of the quarterback, the surgeon, or the author. Integrating them requires naming them. Our purpose is also to show you how much you know already. As you look at the list, I am willing to bet that you know what each strategy is about already. You have been reading and studying for quite some time. Your resilience system is starting to emerge.

Yet notice how complex it can be and what a challenge it is to make the pieces work together. Gratitude is a great strategy. It sharpens intentionality by informing you about what matters. But also it is a critical component of spirituality, meditation, and emotional regulation. Or consider perspective, which helps empower your Inner Observer but also informs your sense of empathy. Here is a way of thinking about how it works:

48 Recovery Zone Operational Strategies

1. Seeking Options	13. Seeking Facts	25. Embodiment	37. Affirmation
2. Seeking Alternative Perspective	14. Changing the Narrative	26. Expansion of Awareness	38. Sinus Rhythm
3. Long-Term Perspective/ Focus	15. Positive Self-Focus	27. Reintegration of Memories	39. Integration
4. Goal-Setting	16. Brain Consciousness	28. Trust of Self	40. Universal Connection
5. Focus	17. Managing Adversity/ Uncertainties	29. Gratitude	41. Attunement
6. Exercise		30. Letting Go	42. Connection/ Relationship
7. Nutrition	18. Identifying Resistance	31. Forgiveness	43. Validation/ Witnessing
8. Rest	19. Meditation	32. Self-Compassion	44. Problem-solving-Community
9. Problem-Solving	20. Emotional Expression	33. Changing Perspective	45. Creativity
10. Accepting Limits	21. Showing Up— Vulnerability	34. Adaptability	46. Play
11. Congruency	22. Service	35. Optimism	47. Humor—Internal & External
12. Reframing/ Restructuring	23. Accessing and Accepting Help	36. Learning From the Past	48. Challenging Activities
	24. Accepting Inconvenient Truths		

Figure 8.1

Figure 8.2

Recovery Zone Strategies

Seeking Options — Searching for more than one way of achieving a goal; not being dependent on one specific role one occupies.

Seeking Alternative Perspective — Recognizing that in the long haul some things do not matter. Reacting in the short-term gains nothing. Consulting with others and accepting different viewpoints which may challenge our current vision.

Long Term Perspective/Focus — Being clear about current realities but never losing sight of your own vision.

Goal-Setting — The activity of achievement for desired accomplishments based in something specific, measurable, attainable, and in our reality, and in the timeliness of the events needed to fulfill the goal.

Focus — In an activity, being able to pay attention to something without emotional or sensory distractions. Concentrating and maintaining your own intent. Having a toolbox of mechanisms of attention.

Exercise — Having physical conditioning habits which stimulate the brain. Everything you do for your heart and lungs helps your brain

Nutrition — The organic process by which an organism assimilates food and water and uses it for growth and maintenance. Habits of choices that enable your body to heal, maintain, improve the immunological process, and support ideal weight.

Rest — Being still, relaxing your mind and body, allowing yourself to "just be" for a while.

Problem-Solving — Defining ownership of the problem, applying imagination, and examining multiple solutions, in the result of a plan of action motivated in creating a solution.

Accepting Limits — Having the peace of mind that there are certain limitations in your life that prohibit you from doing certain things in life

Congruency — Living a life that is in harmony and agreeance to your values, morals, and life philosophy

Reframing/Restructuring — Looking at a problem or challenge from another's perspective or in a new way can be more effective.

Seeking Facts — Finding out what you need to know in terms of information and procedures can reduce anxiety and apprehension.

Changing the Narrative — A shift in the perception of the public/person/or group concerned, regarding which version is right or closer to the truth of the story.

Positive Self-Esteem — Having a realistic awareness of ourselves as a confident and capable person.

Brain Consciousness — A commitment and focus on what is good in life for brain and body. Using resources to help integrate the brain and consciousness such as noticing body sensation in connection with feelings, efforts to use both sides of the brain hemispheres (left side – logic; right side – creative), and other brain improvement strategies to expand the synaptic growth.

Managing Adversity and Uncertainties — By first accepting that adversity is inevitable in life, then learning to build upon your inner resources which provide strength and courage and becoming intentional about the way you choose to live your life.

Identifying Resistance — Resistance is an invisible force shield that acts as a barrier from being productive in reaching of our goals, our dreams, our commitments in relationships, self-care, finances, etc. Being able to recognize your own patterns of procrastination, avoidance, and deferring on what you must do.

Meditation — Being open to the reality of the present moment, allowing all thoughts, emotions, and sensations to enter awareness without resistance or avoidance.

Emotional Expression — Emotional expressions are behaviors that communicate an emotional state or attitude. They can be verbal or non-verbal and can occur with or without self-awareness.

Showing Up – Vulnerability — Becoming courageous enough to open your inner self up to others without knowing the outcome; feeling cautious but sure it is the right thing to do.

Service — Demonstrating our servant-heartedness in specific recovery work, compassionate acts, and in our daily lives in general.

Accessing and Accepting Help — Using internal and external resources to combine information to act as a guide to solving problems. Seeking allies and recognizing them when they show up

Accepting Inconvenient Truths — An inconvenient truth is a fact or truth that people may or may not like because by accepting it there is a strong possibility that they must change behavior or beliefs in order to accommodate the fact.

Embodiment — An innate sense of everything we know and experience in a wordless, non-cognitive way, from the interior of our bodies. In a sense, it is being "at home" within ourselves, safe and secure.

Expansion of Awareness — Having the capability to achieve this expanded awareness increases our integration and our overall level of consciousness to ourselves and the world. It is expanded with every new opportunity, new relationship, new hobbies, new jobs, through interacting with a variety of people and cultures, etc.

Reintegration of Memories — Memory shapes the way we experience the present by reviewing the past and internalizing the "lessons" learned. Pursuing ongoing internal healing so that our life becomes an integrated narrative. As we heal, our brain heals, and our memoires become more fully integrated.

Trust in Self — When we begin to make decisions that are aligned with our core values and our life goals, we begin to establish a trust in ourselves. We learn that we can depend on our emotional states and that we think in a vulnerable and meaningful way.

Gratitude — Gratitude is the positive emotion we feel when overcome by actions of kindness and compassion, for events that happen, for good news we hear about our health, and other moments that support the euphoric feeling of peace and happiness.

Letting Go — The phrase "letting go" can connect to many cognitive experiences, both positive and negative. Mostly it means to allow our self to release control of the situation; not allowing the emotions that are paired with our negative memories, toxic relationships, trauma, and unhealthy situations that control our inability to experience happiness and joy.

Forgiveness — The act of letting go of resentment and moving into a level of consciousness that allows the mind to be free of hurtful memories. Forgiveness is a road which may require mobilizing your compassions and capacity several times on the same issue.

Self-Compassion — A practice in which we learn to be a good friend to ourselves when we need it the most—to become an inner ally rather than an inner enemy.

Changing Perspective — Looking at a problem or challenge from a different and more effective approach to an issue; combatting the tendency to have "tunnel vision" and releasing control and trusting the self to explore other options to meet your needs in the face of adversity.

Adaptability — Being able to see solutions to problems in more than one set of possibilities. Viewing from multiple concepts before settling on a course of action.

Optimism — The power of goodness that refreshes us with courage during difficult challenges; a general belief that this challenge or difficult time will pass and that you have what you need to navigate when things are dark, a belief that the light will show up.

Learning from the past — The willingness to look back at the past in both views of positive and negative experiences, then appreciating the lessons learned from each event.

Affirmation — Affirmations are positive statements that can help you challenge and overcome self-sabotaging and negative thoughts. These statements are a powerful tool to use because they release you from negativity, fear, worry, and anxiety.

Sinus Rhythm — A healthy sinus rhythm is formed when our brain and heart are connected through the unity and integration of mind, body, and spirit.

Integration — Integration in the brain means that separate areas become linked through synaptic connections and as these integrated linkages become more intricate, we grow our ability in unique areas such as insight, empathy, intuition, and resilience.

Universal Connection — Having a deeper sense of how you are connected to the world and others around you.

Attunement — Attunement is being aware of, and responsive to, another person. It is a state between two or more people where those people feel seen, heard, and emotionally connected with you.

Connection/Relationship — Feeling in touch with someone you care about; it means through an acquaintanceship, friendship, or someone you are romantically attracted to for more than the way they look but also the characteristic traits that come from inside them; you value their mind and spirit.

Validation/Witnessing — Validation is a meaningful connection with another person. It means you are acknowledging (not necessarily agreeing with) another person's emotions, thoughts, experiences, values, and beliefs.

Problem-Solving/Community — Learning to work as a team to problem-solve issues that impact the family system, community, and/or society as a whole; it is the ability to turn to others and collaborate in managing stress and overcoming adversities.

Creativity — Creativity is grounded in everyday capacities such as the association of ideas, reminding, perception, analogical thinking, searching a structured problem-space, and reflecting self-criticism. It helps you to find the bandwidth of mind space to have fun, be playful, and creative.

Play — Play involves a sense of imagination, creativity, and wonder. It is allowing yourself to open your mind, body, and spirit to the opportunities of having fun with self and others.

Humor — Internal/External—A quality of being able to see and express feelings of happiness with the outsource of laughter and joy. Having the capacity to see irony and to be playful even when under stress or challenge.

Challenging Activities — Challenging activities allow us to have perspective and not obsess on a work goal or course. Finding commonalities amongst our passions that lead us toward an end goal of projects, having a balance in all our life's activities. For example: A work/life balance: pursuing other activities that bring us joy and meaning in our life such as hobbies, relationships, work, play, and service.

Resilience at its core is the **Expert System Habits**, the habits are the platform for the **Resilience Master Skills**. Each Resilience Master Skill can utilize a toolbox of **Recovery Zone Strategies**.

Expert System Habits + Resilience Master Skills + 48 Recovery Zone Strategies

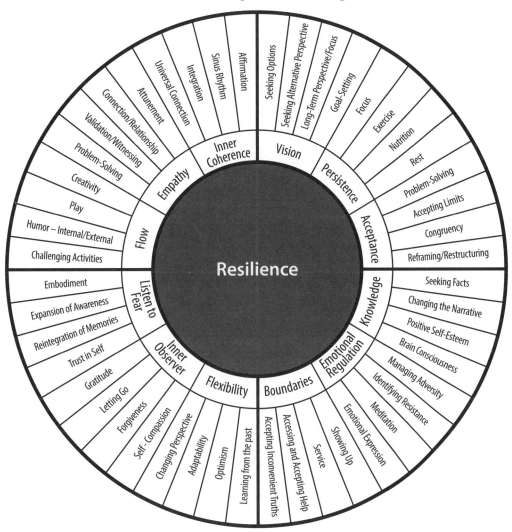

Figure 8.3

What happens is really a matrix of skills and strategies with which to pull your life into a more enlightened, functional, robust way of being. If you look at the graphic, imagine that each wheel can spin depending on what is called for by the challenge being faced. However, think about the number of combinations possible. To be really facile and nimble in your responses, it takes time to learn how and when to match what, for the right combination. The result is the ability to stay focused on a zone of being which is fulfilling.

It takes years to make a good pilot, speaker, or scientist. We started this book with the point that the transformation of recovery does not happen in a thirty-day inpatient stay or the fifty-minute hour. It takes dedicated focus for three to five years. And then focus on your growth becomes a way of life. Is it worth the time? How much are you worth? It is at least worth a year of focus to gain a level of mastery?

The Focus Year

Throughout the *Recovery Zone* process, we have periodically discussed the idea of taking a year to focus on your recovery. Actually, we encouraged you to take the year off and not work. As an alternative to not working, we suggested you reduce your current activities, except your family and work obligations, with a goal of making it a focus year for your recovery. Finally, at one point, we suggested that you might plan to take one year off every five years. All of these recommendations were made in the spirit of neurostimulation, as well as the neuro-relaxation of your brain.

By taking an occasional year off, you not only can reclaim your brain function but nourish and grow it to a level it never would achieve without intense focus. This progress in our original research occurred over a two-to-five-year period (roughly the "repair" stage in the model we distilled from actually following people in recovery). With focus, we believe you can do this in two years.

Immersing yourself in *Recovery Zone I* and *II* takes between twenty and twenty-five weeks—roughly half a year. Assuming you do the work in the chapters and process them in your therapy or in group (the better option), you will have made the transition from the chaos and challenge of recovering to a firm platform on which to work your recovery. What will remain is implementing your Ultimate To Do List. Hopefully, that includes the writing out of your legacy statement. Our experience is that translating your work from lists to a written statement is a declaration of purpose that deepens the commitment and understanding your story brings to your goals and your focus.

We have provided two lenses to view this process. All your planning was organized into four sections, each focused with themes. The hummingbird, turtle, dragonfly, and dolphin are the animals representing the nature of the work of each quadrant. It works best to take each quadrant and organize a quarter of the year around it. This suggested approach does not mean that you would not plan recovery practice (fourth quarter focus) in your first quarter. Similarly, the urgency of your will (second quarter focus) might be moved into your first quarter. Remember, flexibility is one of the key master skills.

Expert System Habits + Resilience Master Skills + 48 Recovery Zone Strategies + Legacy Table 4 Quarters of Focus

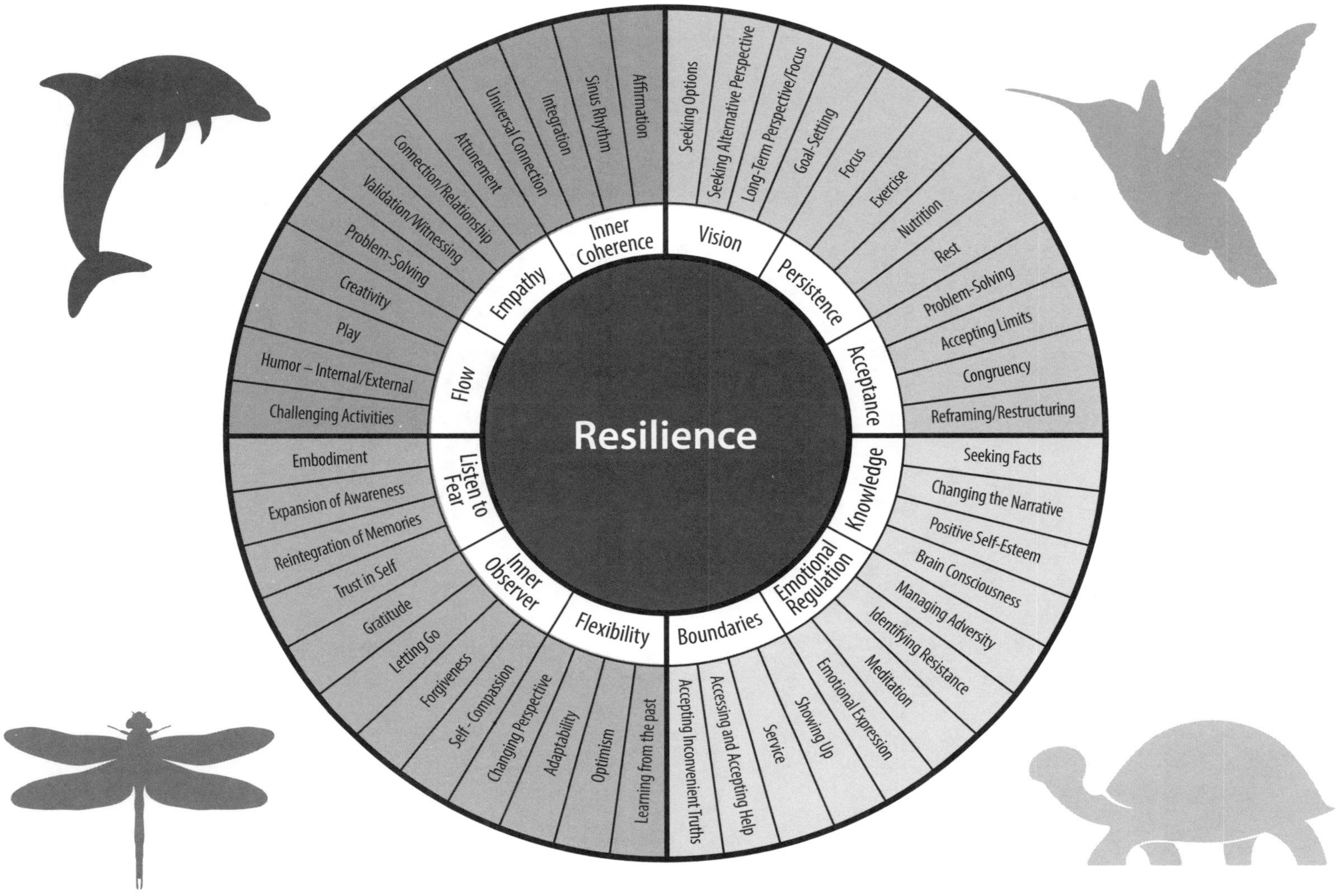

Resilience

Acceptance
- Reframing/Restructuring
- Congruency
- Accepting Limits
- Problem-Solving
- Rest
- Nutrition

Persistence

Vision
- Exercise
- Focus
- Goal-Setting
- Long-Term Perspective/Focus
- Seeking Alternative Perspective
- Seeking Options

Inner Coherence
- Affirmation
- Sinus Rhythm
- Integration
- Universal Connection
- Attunement
- Connection/Relationship

Empathy

Flow
- Validation/Witnessing
- Problem-Solving
- Creativity
- Play
- Humor – Internal/External
- Challenging Activities

Listen to Fear
- Embodiment
- Expansion of Awareness
- Reintegration of Memories
- Trust in Self
- Gratitude
- Letting Go

Inner Observer
- Forgiveness
- Self - Compassion
- Changing Perspective
- Adaptability
- Optimism
- Learning from the past

Flexibility

Boundaries
- Accepting Inconvenient Truths
- Accessing and Accepting Help
- Service
- Showing Up
- Emotional Expression
- Meditation

Emotional Regulation

Knowledge
- Identifying Resistance
- Managing Adversity
- Brain Consciousness
- Positive Self-Esteem
- Changing the Narrative
- Seeking Facts

Figure 8.4

Organizing your year this way also has an implicit logic to it built on how we know the brain changes.

First, there is the breaking down of "hardened categories." Option expansion and exploration to seek better alignment with your life's intent and the discarding of old beliefs and practices is the first order of brain change. Here, we use the metaphor of the hummingbird because of his ability to maneuver himself in any direction to make his options work to his best outcome. The inner spirit and mechanisms of this tiny bird makes him strong and resilient.

Second, there is the slower, thoughtful sifting of priorities and truths while diligently creating further alignment through bringing your life to the current. These are important skills to develop when working toward life goals and survival strategies. The metaphor we use for this section is the turtle. He is slow, diligent, and persistent with life. He does not let his limitations get in the way of where he is going—he just gets there.

The third quadrant is the quest for cohesive purpose and making meaning out of the work of the first two quadrants. The metaphor applied to this quadrant is the dragonfly. The symbolism of the dragonfly goes back many cultures' deep and is rich in history. For many years and through a variety of cultures, the dragonfly is referred to a messenger. It is told that when the dragonfly comes to visit, it is thought that he is passing along wisdom from our elders. For the Japanese—it symbolizes power, agility, and victory. The Chinese think of the dragonfly as representing prosperity, harmony, and good luck and many Native Americans believe it brings happiness, speed, and purity.

The fourth and final quadrant is integrating meaning into a long-term platform of recovery, thereby consolidating your intentions into a total reset of your brain and life. This takes learning how to be creative in your strategies, so the dolphin felt like the perfect fit for this quadrant's metaphor. When we think of the dolphin, we think of play, of rituals, and of activities. The dolphin is very intelligent, have excellent communication skills (have been known to communicate with people, therefore they display the ability to adjust to others outside their species).

The Resilience Matrix breaks down successful resilience into its component parts of habits, skills, and strategies. Mastering these and incorporating them into a regular practice are critical to moving from the special world of therapy, treatment, and recovery into the real, ordinary world.

If you look at the summary sheet at the end of the chapter, you will note that it too is organized in the quarterly format. On the far left is a schedule of weeks for four quarters. On the far right, the months and weeks are organized into our four-quadrant format. Thus, each week for a year can construct a skill-building focus for the week.

Notice that a modularity exists within the matrix. The categories are organized in the most likely combinations of habits, skills, and strategies. Remember that they are fluid and if it is working, they "stick together" as a whole. Gratitude, we have noted, is highly associated with Spirituality and the Inner Observer. However, it can be also powerful in shaping our Intent and Vision. The combinations and permutations of all parts of Resilience are exponential in terms of what you need. This is why we walked through each area of your "ordinary" life and introduced specific skills and strategies along the way.

To help illustrate how fluid and connected all the skills and habits are, we created the graphic with resilience habits at the core. Think of the skills and strategies as wheels that can move to make a combination for any and all setbacks we might face. Visioning, for example, can be used with any combination of habits, skills, or strategies. Our expert system is not a bunch of separate parts. Working together, the parts dramatically improve our coping and augment the utilization of our whole brain.

One of the "mechanisms of attention" many readers will be familiar with is the Personal Craziness Index (PCI) introduced in *Facing Addiction*, *Facing the Shadow*, and *A Gentle Path Through the Twelve Steps*. For those of you who are unfamiliar with the PCI, the process asks you to devise your own daily awareness scale focusing on what behaviors you need to integrate, and to chart your progress. After this chapter are PCI resilience worksheets in which you can tailor a PCI for every week of the year. Follow the instructions for these worksheets to help yourself focus and concentrate on what you need to change. (See the end of the chapter.)

Many of you use calendars and quarterly planners with their own goal-setting systems. You may wish to stick with familiar processes that work for you. If that is true, simply use those systems and integrate your work into them and track your goals that way. Keeping your focus is key and collaborating on your work each week is vital. In each chapter we have listed books, movies, and suggested activities you can use to enrich your year of focus. Many treatment centers and intensive outpatient programs have incorporated *Recovery Zone* into their own systems, which can also support your work. Many therapists and clinics also offer to their patients intensives, workshops, and ongoing groups. They "add in" to the materials additional reading and activities that can intensify the *Recovery Zone* work experience, as well as tailoring it to different populations.

Another option is the *Resilience: Living One Year in Focus and Meaning* program. Each quarter has a daily planner and calendar dedicated to each quarter. It is designed to implement your Ultimate To Do List and the Resilience Matrix for each quarter. In all, four planners exist—each about the size of a regular diary. In addition, it functions like a workbook that has exercises to support the Ultimate To Do List, along with a group discussion guide. The workbook adds research and science around the Resilience Matrix components, the recovery process, and brain support. It includes support information specific to each quarter's task, plus interesting and fun suggestions for the 52 weeks of the year. It is intended to be a deep dive into recovery and "resetting" your recovery platform.

Whatever process you select; one final consideration exists. The next chapter walks you through this consideration by asking a question which may shift your perspective: What would happen if your next year was your last?

Using the Personal Craziness Index to Monitor Resilience

Since 1988, many have used the Personal Craziness Index as a quick and easy way to track how they were doing in the course of their recovery of therapy. It first appeared in *a Gentle Path Through the Twelve Steps* and has appeared in several of our books since then. Other authors have used it as well because it is simple and it works.

The principle is that every day events occur in which you recognize you are not in balance with how you wish to live your life. The assumption is that these isolated behaviors or events when put together indicate that your life is becoming more unmanageable, that you are probably not handling stress well, and that you are not peaceful or in balance. You start by picking signs that are concrete and either happen or they do not. More importantly, they may indicate that you might be at risk for behavior that is dysfunctional, self-destructive, or even dangerous.

Identify things that you see as a sign that you are at risk. Examples might be:

- Behind in promised work
- Over two cups of coffee
- Running out of gas in your car
- Late for appointments throughout the day
- Usual recharge time used up for other purposes
- Failure to make your daily meditation or journal entries
- Skipping group or twelve-step recovery meetings
- Rescheduling therapy because of lack of time
- Failure to show up at children's events when promised

- Neglect of exercise
- Behind in financial self-maintenance (e.g., balancing checkbook)
- Weight increase over a pound
- Fast food that was about convenience and pressure

In other words, what would be signs that you are losing your resilience? List seven of the best indicators you can. Every day you record a score for the day. Each behavior is a point for a total of seven for each day. Zero would be best. At the end of the week, total the daily scores up. Zero to 9 would indicate balance and congruency with your goals. From 40 to 49 would mean you are doing what you intend and your margins of resilience would be low.

Below brain storm a list of 15 possible indicators. Select the best seven and start to track each week for a quarter (12 weeks). You will notice your awareness and purpose expanding!

Brain Storm List of Potential Problem signs	The Best Seven
1.	1.
2.	
3.	2.
4.	
5.	3.
6.	
7.	4.
8.	
9.	5.
10.	
11.	6.
12.	
13.	7.
14.	
15.	

Exercise 8.3

Personal Craziness Index for Resilience

DAY	Week	1	2	3	4	5	6	7	8	9	10	11	12
Sunday													
Monday													
Tuesday													
Wednesday													
Thursday													
Friday													
Saturday													
Weekly Total													

		Description
Optimum Health	0–9	Knows Limits: Has clear priorities; congruent with values rooted in diversity; supportive; has established a personal system; balanced, orderly; resolves crises quickly; capacity to sustain spontaneity; shows creative discipline.
Stable Solidarity	10–19	Recognized human limits; does not pretend to be more than he/she is; maintains most boundaries; well ordered; typically feels competent; feels supported, able to weather crises.
Medium Risk	20–29	Slipping; often rushed;- can't get it all in; no emotional margin for crisis; vulnerable to slip into old patterns; typically lives as it has inordinate influence over other and/or feels inadequate.
High Risk	30–39	Living in extremes (overactive or inactive); relationships abbreviated; feels irresponsible and constantly has reasons for not following through; lives one way, talks another; works hard to catch up.
Very High Risk	40–50	Usually pursuing self-destructive behavior, often totally into mission or cause or project; blames others for failures; seldom produces on time; controversial in community success; is achievement-oriented.

Scale:
- Very High Risk (50–42)
- High Risk (40–32)
- Medium Risk (30–22)
- Stable Solidarity (20–12)
- Optimum Health (10–0)

Exercise 8.4

Chapter 9 **One Year To Live: The Final Consideration**

Mental Health is a commitment to reality at all costs.

Scott Peck

My wife, Suzanne, came to me on a December Friday afternoon. She had been feeling ill and been through a plethora of tests that week. She had found some lumps in her breasts but they were extremely hard. (We later learned that they were solid lumps of a bone cancer.) She told me that the clinic had called to schedule a mammogram. Suzanne thought that might be painful and asked me to help her find out why they would want that test. I called our internal medicine doctor, who was a very seasoned woman physician. I put the question to her, and she said, "Let me look at the chart." There was a long silence and she said, "Well, we already know the answer. Pat, you are going to have to tell your wife she has cancer." There was something in her tone that told me this was not good news.

So I told Suzanne what our doctor said and the best we could do with that information was comfort each other. That day, her son was in town visiting us, and it was Christmastime, so we decided to go out to a nice restaurant and enjoy the holiday. It was very festive and a lovely meal. Yet, at the end, Suzie leaned back, sighed, and said, "Who knows? Next Christmas I might not even be here." I of course responded with all the reasons I thought she would be.

Over the next week, we learned how deadly Suzanne's type of cancer was. She was prophetic. The night of our dinner was December 19. She died of hyperplastic cancer on December 17 the following year. She indeed did not make it to the next Christmas.

Her struggle with cancer altered all of our priorities. A good example is how we spent Thanksgiving. We had all of our children and grandchildren together for the traditional meal. The next morning we gathered for a day-long set of activities to honor Suzanne—including making gratitude lists. She fought me on this and said it was "touchy feely." She feared our kids would not like doing it. Quite the contrary, they enjoyed it immensely. Suzie came to me the next day and thanked me for pulling it together and for the expressions by all generations of their appreciation of her. She made the comment that it was one of the best days of her life. I thought in my head how we could have done this many times before but did not. Writing this at the height of the COVID-19 pandemic and sharing with you some of my own "near misses," I am aware that this may seem a solemn note with which to conclude this volume. Yet the purpose is to get the most out of every moment—for there are no ordinary moments.

Early in my career, I wrote a guided imagery about experiencing the last year of life. I found it extremely helpful to both patients and professionals, so much so that I put it in *A Gentle Path through the Twelve Steps*. I have modified it for our purposes here.

Rumi (the famous 12th century mystic poet) has a poem in which he describes a Sufi mystic who said he lived his life as if a sharp sword was constantly dangling over his neck. The value of thinking about living with that was that it forced the treasuring of every moment. A bit dramatic we might think. But if we knew we had a limited time left, would we live our lives differently?

I remember about three months before Suzanne passed, we were talking on the deck of our little cabin on Woman Lake. She was reflective and "in her body," which was a state that would come and go. She said, "I think we made a mistake. We always thought we would have more time. The truth is, we don't." I believe that statement is always true. I would add for myself that I find that what little time I do have goes by so fast that it is easy to put things off.

One-Year-to-Live Fantasy

Reclaiming reality starts with a clear sense of our limitations as human beings. But we live in a culture that denies these limitations. We are constantly invited to overextend ourselves—for example, to spend more than we earn, work more than we need to, and eat more than we should. We live as if there were no end. We literally deny our own mortality.

A powerful exercise that can show you your own limitations is to picture your own death. Looking at death provides vital perspectives about what gives your life meaning, what priorities you are ignoring, and who your Higher Power is.

Make a voice-recording of the following fantasy, then set aside some uninterrupted time to listen to it and answer the questions provided at the end. Pause for ten to fifteen seconds where indicted before you continue. Make sure you are physically comfortable. If you do not have a recording device, you may read the fantasy or have your guide or a close friend read it to you. You may also visit PatrickCarnes.com and access an audio-recording I have done for you.

Fantasy

Imagine that you are in your physician's office. What does it look, smell, and feel like? Your doctor comes in and tells you that results from your recent test are in. You have a terminal illness. All the other doctors consulted agree. They think you will maintain your physical ability for about a year—but at the end of the year you will die. [pause]

Imagine your first reactions as you walk out of the office. What do you do? [pause] How do you spend those first few hours and days? [pause] Do you tell anyone? [pause]

As you start to adjust to your dying, do you change your life? Stop work? Do something different? [pause]

Maybe you want to do something different. Perhaps you wish to travel. Where would you go? Picture yourself traveling. Whom would you bring with you? [pause] Perhaps you might want to do things you have never done before. Activities like skydiving, scuba diving, and race car driving seemed too dangerous before, but now it doesn't make any difference. What have you always wanted to do but have been afraid to do? [pause] Picture yourself doing this. Who is with you? [pause]

Almost all of us have unfinished parts of our lives: a book we are writing, a family room to finish, a family project such as getting the family album in order for the kids. What unfinished projects would be important enough to finish before you die? [pause] Imagine yourself doing them. [pause]

For some of us, the unfinished parts include things not said to others—like "I'm sorry" or "I love you." Picture yourself saying the things you would need to say before you die. [pause]

It's now about three months before you die. You can start to feel your health fail. While you can still function, you decide to try one last thing. What would that be? [pause] What would be one of the last things you would want to do before you die? [pause] Who is with you? [pause]

It's now a matter of weeks before you die. Where do you go to die? [pause] Your home? A family farm? A lake? The mountains? The city? [pause] How do you spend those last days? [pause] Who is with you? [pause]

As you think over the events of this last year of your life, what were the most significant ones for you? [pause] In fact, think of these and all the events of your life. Which stand out now as the things that made life worthwhile? [pause]

As you reflect on these events, be aware that you are working on this workbook. And you are very much alive. Be aware of your current surroundings. Wiggle your fingers and toes to bring yourself all the way back to the present, and become ready to move on to your next activity.

About the Fantasy

Often, this fantasy helps people touch their own grief about losses in their lives. If you feel sad, do not avoid the feelings. Rather, use them and let them support you in coming to terms with your losses. Sharing the fantasy and your feelings with your guides can deepen your understanding of the issues the fantasy raises. First, record the details of your fantasy in the space provided. Then answer the questions that follow.

One Year to Live Fantasy

Describe your first reactions.

List the changes you would make in your life.

Exercise 9.1A

One Year to Live Fantasy

List the new things you would try.

Explain the unfinished things you would want to complete.

Exercise 9.1B

One Year to Live Fantasy

State the things you would need to say before you die.

Describe what your last adventure would be.

Exercise 9.1C

One Year to Live Fantasy

Explain the spiritual preparation you would take.

Describe where and how you would spend your last days.

Exercise 9.1D

One Year to Live Fantasy

Throughout the fantasy, there were key moments involving significant persons in your life. Name those you would involve and what you might learn about your relationship priorities.

During the fantasy, you may have found yourself doing things significantly differently from how you live now. Why would this be so? What prevents you from doing those things now?

Exercise 9.1E

One Year to Live Fantasy

How do you feel about your own death?

Thinking about death provides a way to look at what is real and what is important in our lives. How have your ideas of what is important and real to you changed after experiencing this death fantasy? What can you change in your life now to reflect these new priorities?

Exercise 9.1F

If you found that there are things that were important and you are not doing them now, revise your Ultimate To Do List accordingly. And for this, solemnity is not the note we end on; perspective is. We return to Einstein's Hill and see what our story is about. At the same time, we live each day with a determination of doing what we intend. Those who live in that paradox see that their stories are but one of many, and their epics will end. Thus, they have little wasted motion and live in the certainty that their intention matters.

Chapter 10 **Hearing or Listening?**

If God is an author and the universe is the biggest novel ever written, I may feel as if I'm the lead character in the story, but like every man and woman on Earth, I am a supporting player in one of billions of subplots. You know what happens to supporting players. Too often they are killed off in Chapter 3, Chapter 10, or in Chapter 35. A supporting player has always to be looking over his shoulder.

Dean Koontz—*Life Expectancy*

The last chapter was a look over your shoulder. The exercise of facing your own death quickly raises awareness of opportunities missed, clarifies priorities, and sharpens your attention to the moment. In many ways, that is what *Recovery Zone* is as a series. It is an introduction to the process. Most mental health issues involve the loss of awareness. Addiction is a mindless quest that hijacks the brain and you lose control of your choices. It is identity theft. Domestic abuse as the largest unreported crime in America means staying with someone who hurts you. Identity theft. Depression dampens all awareness and abilities to function. Trauma requires the suppression of extraordinary hurts, damage, and realities. Identity theft. So it is with almost all mental health issues.

One of the great classics of mental health issues and their origin is Ernst Becker's *The Denial of Death*. An instant Pulitzer Prize winning book, he opened a whole different perspective on why human beings distract themselves in various forms: denial of their own mortality. He uses the term "the vital lie" which means that people seek vitality by the illusion they will not die. If you ask most of us what the worst is that can happen to us, we would answer our death. If you, in your core self, are accepting and are comfortable with the inevitable, the usual drivers of mental health problems will not plague you. If you are okay with the worst, there is nothing else to be anxious about. There is no need to escape in addictions, obsessions, or dramatic distractions. However, Becker was one of the pioneers to say, embracing life differently (showing up for what you have) becomes a life well lived. There are no "ordinary" moments in a conscious life.

As always, a paradox exists. The less consciousness that exists about the self within, the more likely a person will be influenced by it. Yet they remain unconscious of that. Usually something happens that forces a person to a deeper level of self-knowledge. Ginger Grant describes this process starting with Carl Jung who was a master at identifying paradoxes and their spiritual nature:

As Jung notes: the self is made manifest in the opposites and in the conflict between them.... Hence the way to self begins with conflict." St. John of the Cross referred to this place of conflict and potential transformation as the dark night of the soul, where crisis must be endured and accepted until clarity is restored.

This deep process of development continues throughout life and becomes one in which the state of transformation and a deeper level of consciousness and awareness are the goals pursued. No one wants to start therapy, treatment or recovery—and often they do not know that they need it until the house of cards falls. Being a more conscious person means the expansion of your awareness bandwidth. And they discard the vital lie which is you always "think you have more time."

For example, in training foster parents, there is a careful explanation of the difference between hearing and listening. Foster children who have been traumatized will hear what you say, but more than likely are not listening. The research shows that their anxieties, distrust, and hypervigilance work as a filter to what is being said. They may not take in and appreciate the meaning or significance of the words they hear. This problem of not being able to hear the other accompanies many who have been traumatized including both young and old—and for some that condition persists their whole lifetime. Listening as opposed to hearing means:

- Acknowledge what was said.
- Make meaning out of what was said by understanding the statement, request, or question.
- Identify the feelings and intentions behind the statement, request, or question.
- Remember what was said and the implications for them you took personally.
- Take action if necessary.
- Relate to the content or how it fits their story or understanding at the moment.
- Respond to the meaning of what they heard.
- Hear the message both explicit and "in between the lines."
- Suspend your responses, objections, critiques, or challenges.
- Notice nuances including sounds, appearances, and distraction.

The true listener is noticing the nuances, the interactions, the context, and motivations of the other. Most importantly, when clearly significant, they place themselves in the "shoes" of the person in order to fully grasp the perspective of the other.

Foster parents learn this because they might misinterpret the foster child tuning the parents out. Recovery requires also learning how to listen as opposed to evaluating, ignoring and not responding. Hearing is translating the sounds into words. Listening is a form of awareness about what is being said. Many of us have tuned out family, friends, work, and even the whole world. If you do not listen, your anxieties are less. In the supercharged, often dramatic world of addiction and dysfunctional relationships, it is easier to mimic listening.

This is an easy metaphor which can be expanded to help us understand the many ways to ignore your awareness of what is going on around you. Starting with hearing and listening, let us add examples to the list. You could:

- Hear but not listen.
- See but not notice—colors, textures, movements, energy in motion.
- Fail to notice all the senses, including smell, touch, and movement.
- Ignore how nature is happening around you.
- Be physically present but not aware.
- Spend time with children but not show up personally for them during that time.
- See threats you explained away in your head but did not protect yourself.
- Repeat dysfunctional behaviors but not change them.
- Recycle harmful relationships but not disrupt the pattern.
- Recognize there were attachments of which you needed to let go but just adjusted or increased your grip.
- Start things (books, projects, hobbies, education, writing, pursuing a dream, step work, therapy, mental health practices) but did not pursue to the end or master them.
- Have many passions but never allowed yourself to follow where they led.

Other people would:

- Repeatedly tell you things but you would "forget."
- Provide observations which were virtually the same as others had pointed out about your behavior and you would dismiss their relevance and ignore that evidence was growing about your behavior.
- Try to engage you in relationships but you did not have "time" to respond.
- Stop counting on you to follow through but you failed to notice they no longer trusted your follow-through or promises.
- Challenge you but you would not step up to the plate to bring things to resolution.
  - Remember:
    You are the owner of the image in your mirror.
    Your future belongs to you.
    Your awareness of all that transpires around you is critical.
    Your sense of what matters is all you need and guides what you do.
    Jump.

We receive countless messages every day which are too many to respond to individually. Yet they are like the music of many instruments and voices, and collectively there are movements to the concert of your life they emerge from. Their performance is your life, your story. As the sole audience, that can be moved by its beauty, meaning or message, you are the only one who can make the next chorus and rhythms different. You have to ask on what note does this performance end

Automaticity and focus change the bandwidth to hear the message. All the above are about awareness of self and others. The necessary skills in healthy recovery become automatic but require systematic focus to change. The acquisition of the skills often is an immersion. In the previous chapter, you realized that you had to scramble to integrate the most meaningful parts of your life as part of your passing. Awareness of death sharply amps up your awareness and probably some sadness about what you have missed.

Surgeons may start their careers by wanting to help people and have the respect, money, and prominence that an MD confers. They spend endless hours mastering medicine and specialties. Residency is an immersion process to speed up the physician's ability to integrate the many skills and strategies needed for healing. The physicians that are most successful, heads and shoulders above their peers, have some unique features about being in the zone. Sure, helping people is meaningful work, but the great surgeon actually sets that aside and every day he challenges him or herself, "Can I do this surgery better than I did yesterday?" His work was amazing to others the day before but can he improve upon it today. And he gets so good in his expert system, he ends up doing things beyond his own awareness. He is in the zone and immerses himself in the challenge. The problem becomes that he has difficulty explaining to his peers how he does it. This is a common issue in medical education.

Or the quarterback we have referenced so often. Let us say he is 40 plus years old and wants to play one more season. He may have to change teams to do it. He knows that his potential for injury is at its height. He has all the money he could want. Why do this? We keep witnessing this scenario over and over. He does it for one more chance to make the play no one else can. Afterwards he becomes a coach and finds it challenging to explain to younger athletes what they need to know.

The author of Romance novels who has over 200 titles many of which have been bestsellers for years, has carefully noted the balance of detail, adventure, and plot lines so that the books by her hand always do well. When her team of ghostwriters work on books based on her work using her name independently for her in the same genre, it is with mixed results. She can see what needs to be done with a manuscript but has a challenge in articulating the formula that has constantly worked and improved her work.

In psychiatry and psychology, written tests can reveal specify diagnoses. However, even in working with experienced therapists, the remarkable interpretations done by master clinicians look like magic during case conferences. When the experienced interpretation by a seasoned master clinician is presented, how did the clinician, who has never met the client, know this piece of the client's history? She describes it with certitude and the therapist who sees the patient confirms, yes, that happened. The psychotherapists present ask themselves; how did she know that? The clinical assessment tool speaks to her in ways that appear very remarkable. Yet, she has trouble explaining how that came to her awareness.

Expert systems can be found in many contexts, ranging from the mechanic who only has to listen to the engine and maybe touch it while it is running to decode what the malfunctions are, to the literary agent who picks the ten potential great books out of 1,500 submitted that month. How does this happen? Immersion and focus. Automaticity means the effortless integration of thousands of subtle and obvious bits of awareness into an accurate assessment, the next right decision, or most important action to take. Talent and abilities flourish in this zone of focus. To accomplish this, usually there is an initial phase of deep immersion. Physicians, for example, go through a deep trial of total focus called residency. They have to cease everything but the task before them: becoming a healer. Their brain constantly integrates and grows below their conscious awareness. This immersion accelerates learning and initiates a constant pattern of learning and skill building. Thus, as they move forward, their progress accelerates and constantly aggregates the depth of their understanding. Yet, if asked to explain how they do this, they fumble for words and describe large concepts and summarize steps. Newcomers listen and wonder if they ever will get it—whatever it is.

Take people in recovery. In your early recovery, you meet people who have put many years into their recovery. Immersion experiences are the constant. Treatment, therapy, intensive workshops, reading, and deep investment in their support communities. You hear phrases like 90 and 90 (meaning ninety meetings in ninety days). When they speak, it is with great insight or pointed in an obvious direction. Listeners wonder why they did not see this. Yet, these "practitioners" do not rush in to give advice. They speak shorthand with words like "amends," "dark side," and "second step issues." They appear to be peaceful—even about very real challenges in their own lives. When asked by the newcomer how to change something, a smile appears and he is told to "keep coming back." Your therapist almost speaks a foreign language but stays focused on the immediate challenges. The new patient/group member shouts inside: "Will somebody give me some answers other than trust the process." The truth is like any expert system, recovery is difficult to explain at first. *Recovery Zone* is designed to bridge that gap and help start personal transformation.

Addiction and mental health issues involve the whole brain. Years of intense concentration went into their development. Supportive dysfunctional environments and even sometimes the well-intentioned efforts simply were catalysts for addicts to be masters at serving the insanity of it all. The phrase that is often used is "your best thinking got you here" rings true. When people object to the costs of intense treatment, the question is raised, "What did your behavior cost you?" How much time, money, and energy went into your insanity? Your practice was built on bargains with and trading your future for shortcuts, bypasses, and an "easier, softer way."

Remember, when you started, it was with a crisis. Your first tasks were to problem-solve the immediate issues and clear out bad, dysfunctional or addictive behavior. The goal was to set the chaos aside with enough focus to start traction with treatment or therapy. *Recovery Zone* started with stimulating your brain and putting order in the chaos using the decision table. Also, by understanding the zone, you started with establishing the beginnings of what life can be like for you. In that sense, when you completed those exercises you also started developing the levels of focus of survival and resilience that Admiral Stocksdale defined as critical. You started to tackle the here and now and have developed a vision of where you wanted to be. Then you looked at the landscape of addiction and dysfunction through the lens of interaction, brain function, and different ways of losing yourself. The next step was to initiate the descent into the dark night of the soul by starting to understand emotional intelligence and discern those that were affecting you, whether you were aware of it or not. Anger, shame, grief, fear and traumas made seamless grievance stories driving the insanity. Finally, we asked you to take the step of making yourself a priority to you. The stories through out this volume use the examples of Viktor Frankl, Randy Pausch, Admiral Stocksdale, and Ernest Becker have a theme, it is often crisis that pushes you into the realms of reality. As my wife Suzanne in her last days said, you "think you have more time" but really you don't. The previous chapter's purpose was to create a sense of the importance of that delusion.

With all this awareness, *Recovery Zone II* asked you how you want to implement the "self" in the real world to complete the movement of what did not work to what does and will. Work, money, relationships, purpose, and life satisfaction translated into action through an achievable zone of living. We have used the heroic journey as a basic way to conceptualize this examination and transformation of self. Ginger Grant describes this as a "developmental tool .... serving as a container for this process of raising the level of consciousness awareness." One of the world's most recognized neural biologist, Antonio Damasio, pioneered the concept of the autobiographical brain. He underlined the critical aspects of developing consciousness in the role of feelings, the amount of extremely complex integration that goes on behind the scenes (translate: out of your awareness), and the importance of storytelling. Put in another way, transformation of the brain is incredibly complex, but the evolution of one's story is of significant importance even in the big picture of culture and species. Dean Koontz commented on this phenomenon in his book *Life Expectancy*:

> Maybe it's our free will misdirected or just a shameful pride, but we live our lives with the conviction that we stand at the center of the drama. Moments rarely come that put

us outside of ourselves, that divorce us from our egos and force us to see the larger picture, to recognize that the drama is in fact a tapestry and that each of us but a thread in the vivid weave, yet each thread is essential to the integrity of the cloth.

In recovery, one hears comments about how they dislike the twelve steps and spiritual quest of recovery. What they want is the Damascus-like experience of St. Paul, or Bill W's fateful wind, or the tornado of the Alchemist: an event that transforms us all at once. In each case, crisis started the transformation and precipitated the journey. When you started recovery, it was because of some eventful storm in your life that forced you to step out and reexamine all of it. That is part of your story. You recognize you are part of a larger picture, but how your story ends is important to all. In short, it is the story that helps the brain mobilize behind the scenes the platforms needed for new skills and perspectives. The uniting perspective is that we are all in this together—including all other living things.

So many who write about this process end up with that conclusion. Larry Dossey started out on the role of energy generated by prayer but most recently writes of how we participate in One Mind. Lynne McTaggert's book on *The Bond* is about how science teaches how we are connected to all of life. Eckhart Tolle speaks the "indestructible essence of our being... beyond the myriad of life forms that are subject to life and death." Ultimately, some things we all have in common.

We as humans are part of a much larger drama but each has a significant "thread in the weave." Moral behavior is not based on rules but the impact of our behavior on all. Plus, now you realize that really there are no secrets. All of it matters. Further, it is difficult. Many speak of being spiritual but really spirituality can be what has been termed a "spiritual bypass." It is an effort to avoid critical feelings, the destructive forces within us, and leave all the ugly truths about ourselves behind. We cannot do that since these difficult and sometimes excruciating facts of our lives are vital to our stories and our spirituality. You cannot pray it away. Christian pastor, Dietrich Bonhoeffer described that spirituality needed to be found in the "ground of our being." But he also said there is a cost to discipleship, for true spirituality involves speaking your truth no matter the cost. In his case, his speaking out against Hitler meant his execution in a concentration camp. Ordering Bonhaffer's execution was one of the last orders Hitler gave before he suicided. To pass over the truth, the horror, the intolerable feelings is really what Bonhoeffer called cheap (kostloss) grace.

But there is also the listening versus hearing. The recovering person who steadily resists the "suffering into meaning" concept and claims spirituality does not help him. In the same report he speaks of his spouse's complaints about how he does not listen to her. He hears but is not listening. Resilience requires listening at a very advanced level no matter how inconvenient the truth. And so it is on many levels. Carol Clark observes in her book *Addict America: The Lost Connection.*

> Addiction is about filling that hole in our souls that is the emptiness caused by the loss of Connection. It is about running away from the pain of Dis-Connection. It is about distracting ourselves from the hopelessness we feel when we don't believe we will ever be Connected. It is about not being present, or not being in the moment and it is about allowing fear to dominate us.

Two conditions need to exist for brain change. One is safety. Thus, the relationships with trusted peers and dedicated therapists and sponsors/mentors are very healing. But, safety starts with taking care of your own self even when you are most vulnerable. The phrase "inner child" translates into that inner self that did not have the security that a child needs for healthy attachment. We can make up the deficits, but not erase the experience. Trusting yourself and consistently coming to your own assistance allows for secure attachment. Without that anxiety, even the most difficult challenges can be faced—including contemplating your own final days.

The other condition is working with your own story. Telling of the way "I used to be" and the way "I am now" is not sufficient. The truth is in between those two pictures. A powerful exercise used in the treatment of childhood trauma was to write the story as if it was a children's story or a fairy tale. The patient starts with "Once there was a little girl (boy) .... Then the assignment calls the patient or participant to write out what happens to that child in simple, sparse prose in no more than one page. The limiting to one page creates an economy of truth. There is no room to embellish, or explain, or to soften your responsibility or your portrayal of those who were to take care of you. All that there is, is the reality of what happened. Reading that out loud made the assignment a powerful experience.

We have expanded that experience in the following exercise. It starts with one page that says Once there was a (boy, girl, man woman) who was __ years old named _____. Anyone can start the story at the time they wish to begin it. At the end of the page is the word NOW and space is provided to record the date of writing. A second page starts with NOW and the date. This page carries the story into the rest of life. Again simple, clear sentences with no explanations, rationales, or expressions of hope. It is just the story from this point on. The page ends with END OF LIFE. You can do this in this book or you can take larger sheets to write it. Limit yourself, however, to the two sheets: life to this point, and your version of life to its end. Please remember this is for you. No one needs to see this. It may be that you wish to eventually share with those trusted members of your circles of intimacy. However, do not write for them. This is your opportunity to express with great clarity the whole picture and answer the question what life looks like in the end.

Once There Was.... An exercise In Storytelling – Part 1

Once there was a (boy, girl, man woman) who was ____ years old named _____

| NOW | Date of Writing: _____ |

Exercise 10.1A

Once There Was.... An exercise In Storytelling– Part 2

This page carries the story into the rest of life. Again simple, clear sentences with no explanations, rationales, or expressions of hope. It is just the story from this point on.

NOW

END OF LIFE	Date of Writing: _____

Exercise 10.1B

To make that story happen you too will need some sort of intensive program, and we recommend a year dedicated to really immersing yourself in your recovery epic. Consider it a recovery residency. Yes, it may be costly, inconvenient, and hard on those who love you. The level of functional awareness will more than make good the investment of money and energy. Plus, you will have the connections and skillsets to work with in building a reservoir of resilience. Remember the concept of putting distance between you and the ditch.

You have to think about what tools you have for a one-year immersion. What Buddha described as the "work to be done" is not done by reading a couple of books and the fifty-minute hour of your therapist. You will need an immersion into the recovery process to accelerate your process and aggregate your skills. Your brain is willing to help you but you have to do the work. You now have surveyed the scope of the work to be done. You have twelve habits to cultivate in your training. Twelve special skills exist which you master in your training. There are forty-eight strategies you utilize in daily practice. Twelve habits times 12 skills times 48 operational strategies—the combinations possible could be intimidating. (See Appendix G.) Plus one has to think of the permutations and combinations of all the above. The answer is found in breaking it down into daily skill building. Focus well and your brain will integrate many connections for you.

Consider the example of learning to drive a car. Reflect on all the things you had to learn: accelerator, brakes, turn signals, transmission, traffic signs, rules of the road, wipers, gas, oil,—a myriad of things that today you do not even think about. Or consider the language(s) you speak: vocabulary, nouns verbs, spelling, conjugation, colloquial usage, pronunciation—so much to learn, but you did. People who learn a new language do best in immersion. That is also true of recovery. Below, we summarize what we have collected on the next pages, the graphics which integrate from "wash on, wash off" to a recovery system. A lot to do? Yes. But people do it all the time with focus. Worth it? Unqualified yes! Just look at your original decision table!

As mentioned earlier, your therapist may already have a program in place. Or you may have a system you are already working. As described, in Appendix G is a fifty-two week schedule with skills and strategies laid out for each day. You can integrate this in numbers of ways. The seductive part is that once sobriety and change have started, the temptation is to settle for getting well enough to get by. To complete the story you wrote, what will you have to do in order to make that happen? Knowing what you want your part of this story to look like gives you a measure so you do not settle for less or sell yourself out. Many ways exist to lose your identity. You have lots of experience with that process. Now you have a path. This should be integrated into your long-term treatment plan. Remember when we started, the process was outlined as a three-to-five-year process. Also, by now it is clear that continuous progress is what keeps the brain growing. It truly is the journey, not the destination.

In Chapter Eight, we also mentioned Resilience: Living One Year in Focus and Meaning which continues what you started in *Recovery Zone*. It is a weekly diary/planner designed to utilize and immerse you in the habits, skills and strategies. There is a book divided into the four sections of your Ultimate To Do List so you can focus on your goals and legacy quarter by quarter. You can organize writing out your legacy statement using the principles practiced in each quarter. It is broken down into weeks and days so it deepens the habits you will need for a sustainable recovery. In Appendix H, is a portion of the introduction to that program to give you a sense of how that program is organized.

No matter how you do it, the task now is to put order in all the work you have done. My colleague and friend Claudia Black in her book *Changing Course*, writes about going forward but you will have to also get about finishing your past. There will be times that going forward with completing the story will be the occasion forcing the finishing of the past. There is in this an implicit paradox in what you must let go of as you change how your story ends. The work in *Recovery Zone I* requires a change in how you live out the rest of the story.

In order to help you we have created a way to collect out of all your "purposes" and clarify your most important. Entitled "Organizing Your Ultimate To Do List," it provides a way to consolidate your work so you can focus on the "Now to the End" part of your work. In other words, you have the outline in one page. You know the pieces but the narrative of how that all works together is best written and it takes time. This is why we have organized it into four parts so that within a year, you will have a thoughtful narrative which will influence how that story ends. Breaking into quarters will help you focus. Simultaneously, you will, as Claudia Black suggests, get to a level of currency so the momentum of the story is not hindered.

Organizing your Ultimate To Do List

You have identified things you wish to be on your Ultimate To Do List (UTD).

☐ List those items yet to be done in each of these respective categories (Achievement, Exit, Legacy, Recovery).

☐ When finished, return to Chapter Four and your vision table work. Are there any items on you vision table that you want in your life that you overlooked on your UTD List?

☐ Also review your early work in Chapter Six going back to the beginning of *Recovery Zone I*. Do not forget your Forget Me Not Clipboard exercise.

☐ When you have the most complete list possible, you will note columns marked with an "X" or a checkmark.

☐ Place an X next to all items which match your goals and values.

☐ Place a checkmark next to all items that fit the category of "if nothing else I must do."

☐ Hint Review your work in Chapter Nine to think about those categories what merit a checkmark.

☐ When complete think about the first step to take for each task.

Organizing your Ultimate To Do List

Place an X next to all items which match your goals and values. Place a checkmark next to all items that fit the category of "if nothing else I must do."

Achievements	✘	✓
1		
2		
3		
4		
5		
6		
7		
8		
9		
10		

Exercise 10.2A

Organizing your Ultimate To Do List

Achievements – First Steps To Take
1
2
3
4
5
6
7
8
9
10

Exercise 10.2B

Organizing your Ultimate To Do List

Exit and Planning Strategies	✗	✓
1		
2		
3		
4		
5		
6		
7		
8		
9		
10		

Exercise 10.2C

Organizing your Ultimate To Do List

Exit and Planning Strategies – First Steps To Take
1
2
3
4
5
6
7
8
9
10

Exercise 10.2D

Organizing your Ultimate To Do List

Lessons	✘	✔
1		
2		
3		
4		
5		
6		
7		
8		
9		
10		

Exercise 10.2E

Organizing your Ultimate To Do List

Lessons – First Steps To Take
1
2
3
4
5
6
7
8
9
10

Exercise 10.2F

Organizing your Ultimate To Do List

Recovery Legacy	✗	✓
1		
2		
3		
4		
5		
6		
7		
8		
9		
10		

Exercise 10.2G

Organizing your Ultimate To Do List

Recovery Legacy – First Steps To Take
1
2
3
4
5
6
7
8
9
10

Exercise 10.2H

Endnote: Listening to Trees

The *Recovery Zone* series has been long in the making. It has been all the things of the zone that we talk about as the journey of all of us: a great challenge, an adventure beyond my expectations, and certainly more to it than I knew. I had moments of despair and I knew moments of joy. In many ways it was a gift because of how it forced me into more than I was reaching for. I have gratitude for all the help I had which I acknowledge in the acknowledgements at the end of the book. Yet, the book is in many ways my story and the flaws in it are mine. But in the end if you are reading this, I have the gift that you are one of the listeners.

For many years, I asked people to think in pictures about their recoveries. In writing this volume I reviewed many of those drawings. One of the most common depictions of starting recovery was being lost in a forest and often in the distance was a doorway or sometimes a gate with the title "recovery." The challenge implicit in these first drawings was that there was a secret doorway which if they could get to, they have the answers of how to really do "recovery." Yet, the irony is that really is not the task to find the "secret" doorway. The challenge is to learn how to live in the forest. Everything is there that you need.

Outside my window is an old maple. It has scars where limbs have been pruned and evidence of many storms over time. The tree is aging. In its center I know there is a record of every year encoded in every cell—some years difficult and some filled with growth. Yet, at the end of many branches you can see the new growth. Around the old maple are three young maples, much smaller, filled-out trees which show little battering yet during the years. They too are reaching out. If the temperature gets into the mid-forties, the buds on the trees turn green. And if you look closely and the timing is right, all the buds of all the species of trees around them also turn green. It is possible to watch all the buds unfurl into leaves on each of them in a single day. I know that is true since I have watched this happen. The power of photosynthesis is employed in the renewal of the world around me and I am awed by its energy and purpose. If you tune in, you can hear it! The trees are like recovery. Renewal is possible throughout and over the cycle of life. This book is part of my thread in the tapestry of that life. And my desire is that you have the gift of adding your thread. For we both are making each of our threads be the best we can. And if we focus, we can hear it .... if we listen.

1. The whole point of Clark's book is that the endpoint is we have this extraordinary larger connection, and addiction and dysfunction is the doorway.
2. Claudia Black's *Changing Course: Healing From Loss, Abandonment, and Fear* reflects her deep influence in the recovering community on what we have termed as identity theft. She pioneered these concepts first with adult children of alcoholic's but has placed these learnings at the service of all of us in the recovering community.

The Story Behind the Resiliency Matrix
.... Acknowledgements

If you were told that simple changes in your life would add to your longevity by 14%, you most likely would make the effort. However, it is hard to translate that concept in isolation or without a structure. In the last two decades, a wealth of information has flowed towards that conclusion using words like mindfulness, focus, meditation, intentionality and resiliency. These are common to bestselling books, media platforms, workshops and seminars. The Super Soul Sunday series by Oprah is an enlightened example of bringing these ideas to the public. She and her production staff have done a wonderful service over the years of creating awareness about the importance of this new emerging consciousness.

At the same time, there was a burst of research demonstrating that these skills are teachable. Trauma researchers like Michael Linden, Dan Siegel, and Allan Schore have described the importance of teaching resilience to those who have experienced profound toxic stress. The University of Hamburg "wisdom" team showed the impact of what they termed the nine elements of wisdom when taught. The Palix Foundation working with Harvard's early childhood project clearly demonstrated the practicality and vital importance of teaching basic resilience to children. Lubyskya and colleagues brought sophistication to what they termed the "the architecture of wisdom" and how to teach it. Perhaps one of the most public and well thought out summaries about the challenge of such learning was Dan Goleman's book *Focus*. He described how the "Top Down" mind could systematically alter the automatic power of the "Bottom Up" brain. He clearly showed the importance of an intentional "expert system" which made the next right decisions automatically. He also was most clear that it had to be intentional, diligent practice or the skills would not "take hold."

To achieve that level of focus Goleman adds a daily, intensive effort of focus until each skill or strategy is automatic. To that we would add that this daily effort needs a platform built on the best consensus of what resilience skills are and how to practice them. Recognizing that, the group most in need of a transformational focus process were those suffering from addiction, trauma, and mental health issues. So, we as a team set out to summarize all the research commonalities about strategies for resilience. What emerged is that there existed overarching "master skills" which were core to building resilience. Under this umbrella were specific strategies also critical for maintaining resilience. This resulted in the Resiliency Matrix.

Then we broke down those defined skills and strategies into teachable daily practices of integration. We put it within a One Year to Live context to help put in perspective about what mattered in life. The prioritization we learned helped in the motivation and the actual decision-making embedded in the process. Then we tested the process out on groups of alumni emerging from rehab centers and intensive outpatient centers.

Over a decade ago, *Recovery Zone I* appeared to introduce people to the process. *Recovery Zone I* focuses on what had not worked in life as well as starts the introduction to what was necessary to change one's life internally. Strategically placed however, were very critical elements out of the Resilience Matrix. The second volume used that work as a backdrop to what you really wanted or felt called to do. It is the classic conundrum, if you define what no is, then you need to understand what yes means. With that clarity, one can take the *Recovery Zone* Books and its companion Resilience Planner series and start to operationalize "yes." Our whole effort was to get people to living and inhabiting what yes was to them.

A project of this magnitude involved the efforts of many people:

First, there is an abbreviated bibliography at the end of this book. An extended bibliography can be found on PatrickCarnes.com. We stand on the shoulders of all the researchers who have been fighting upstream to help understand trauma, addiction, recovery and resilience. We also are profoundly grateful to the patients, graduate students and staff on the Meadows Behavioral Health campuses. Particularly Aleah Johnson and the alumni groups were patient, enthusiastic, and clear about what worked and what did not. Managing multiple groups, weekends, and virtual meetings was a challenge to keep track of. The executive director of the Gentle Path program as well as Willow House, Dr. Jerry Law, was steadily at my side teaching and processing. The Meadows senior fellows who have pioneered in trauma work have influenced this work including Pia Mellody, Claudia Black, John Bradshaw, Peter Levine, Bessel van der Kolk, and Richard Schwarz. My daughter, Stefanie Carnes, is also a Meadows Senior Fellow but has been a patient and persistent special source of support for all of us. The whole CSAT (Certified Sex Addiction Therapists) and CMAT (Certified Multiple Addiction Therapists) have had tremendous patience waiting for the series to be completed. This series now adds another platform for the task-centered approach of International Institute for Addiction and Trauma Professionals. They all mobilized around this project including a substantial number of their graduate students who spent weekends helping with bibliographic issues.

The Palix Foundation in Canada continues to be prime movers to help professionals understand the role of toxic stress and the brain (AlbertaFamilyWellness.com). In my own learning heritage, Howard Williams and Norman Sprinthall, taught me the critical role of community and psychological education in therapeutic change. I believe it still is the most underserved topic in the training of mental health professionals of all varieties including psychiatry, psychology, and addiction medicine.

Finally, there are no words that can adequately recognize the contribution of our executive coordinator, Kelly Reece, whose heart was really in getting these manuscripts coordinated, and ready for production. In the same category is Bonnie Phillips who as a writing partner, researcher, and coauthor of the Resilience: Living One Year in Focus and Meaning series in addition to all her responsibilities as an Assistant Professor has been indispensable. My wife, Pennie Carnes, whose collaboration with Bonnie as a coauthor,was critical both professionally and personally. She added insight and an ability to see how things match up—or did not—that was beyond invaluable. On an even more personal note, her love and belief in me helped me to find things within me of which I did not know. To my dear family of all generations, your stories are part of the weave of all my writing, and, in that, priceless.

As for the errors, inconsistencies, and opinions ... Well, they are all mine.

Patrick J. Carnes

The Twelve Steps of Alcoholics Anonymous[1]

1. We admitted we were powerless over alcohol—that our lives had become unmanageable.

2. Came to believe that a Power greater than ourselves could restore us to sanity.

3. Made a decision to turn our will and our lives over to the care of God as we understood Him.

4. Made a searching and fearless moral inventory of ourselves.

5. Admitted to God, to ourselves, and to another human being the exact nature of our wrongs.

6. Were entirely ready to have God remove all these defects of character.

7. Humbly asked Him to remove our shortcomings.

8. Made a list of all persons we had harmed, and became willing to make amends to them all.

9. Made direct amends to such people wherever possible, except when to do so would injure them or others.

10. Continued to take personal inventory and when we were wrong promptly admitted it.

11. Sought through prayer and meditation to improve our conscious contact with God as *we understood Him*, praying only for knowledge of His will for us and the power to carry that out.

12. Having had a spiritual awakening as the result of these steps, we tried to carry this message to alcoholics, and to practice these principles in all our affairs.

---

1 The Twelve Steps of AA are taken from Alcoholics Anonymous, 3d ed., published by AA World Services, Inc., New York, N.Y., 59–60.

The Twelve Steps of Alcoholics Anonymous Adapted for Sexual Addicts[2]

1. We admitted we were powerless over our sexual addiction—that our lives had become unmanageable.

2. Came to believe a Power greater than ourselves could restore us to sanity.

3. Made a decision to turn our will and our lives over to the care of God, as *we understood Him*.

4. Made a searching and fearless moral inventory of ourselves.

5. Admitted to God, to ourselves, and to another human being the exact nature of our wrongs.

6. Were entirely ready to have God remove all these defects of character.

7. Humbly asked Him to remove our shortcomings.

8. Made a list of all persons we had harmed, and became willing to make amends to them all.

9. Made direct amends to such people wherever possible, except when to do so would injure them or others.

10. Continued to take personal inventory and when we were wrong promptly admitted it.

11. Sought through prayer and meditation to improve our conscious contact with God as *we understood Him*, praying only for knowledge of His will for us and the power to carry that out.

12. Having had a spiritual awakening as the result of these steps, we tried to carry this message to others and to practice these principles in all our affairs.

2   Adapted from the Twelve Steps of Alcoholics Anonymous.

Introduction

[1] Paulo Coehlo's introduction to the Alchemist contains one of the most elegant, cogent descriptions of how identity theft works. Unfortunately, a new introduction, not by Coehlo in the newest edition has replaced the original which is a loss. This particular quote comes from the last edition it appeared in: *Paulo Coelho (1998). "The Alchemist—10th Anniversary Edition", HarperSanFrancisco*

[2] The first major large study of this phenomenon appeared in the medical journal of Pediatrics. Wolak, J., Mitchell, K., & Finkelhor, D. (2007). Unwanted and Wanted Exposure to Online Pornography in a National Sample of Youth Internet Users. *PEDIATRICS*, *119*(2), 247–257. https://doi.org/10.1542/peds.2006-1891

[3] This particular version was presented by Ginger Grant in her book, *Re-Visioning The Way We Work: A Heroic Journey*

[4] We again thank her for allowing us to use this version in our graphic.

Chapter One

[1] For a description of this process of aggregate crises, see Patrick Carnes, *Don't Call It Love*, Bantam, 1991.

[2] We adapted this from Duarte's classic work on presentations: Nancy Duarte, Resonate.

Chapter Two

[1] Bessel van der Kolk's 1988 paper is my nominee for one of the top trauma papers of the twentieth century. He was one of the first to integrate advances in modern neuroscience, medicine, trauma, and addiction. Critical was his observation about being able to create interventions in reactivity associated with PTSD. Van der Kolk citation: Cox, A. D. (1987). Psychological Trauma. By Bessel A. van der Kolk. Washington: American Psychiatric Press. 1987. 237 pp. $25.00. *British Journal of Psychiatry*, *151*(5), 716. https://doi.org/10.1192/s0007125000284560

2 The "window of tolerance" is a phrase first used by Dan Siegel in his book *Mindsight*. The choice of words aptly described the challenge of reactivity to toxic stress and has been use by many in the trauma field including this author. We built a framework around this theme in an exercise called the Window of Tolerance which appears in this chapter as another version of this exercise.

3 PSY 5 Reference. Harkness AR, Finn JA, McNulty JL, Shields SM. The Personality Psychopathology-Five (PSY-5): recent constructive replication and assessment literature review. Psychol Assess. 2012 Jun;24(2):432–43. doi: 10.1037/a0025830. Epub 2011 Oct 10. PMID: 21988184.

4 This appeared in volume four of the Outlander, The Drums of Autumn Gabaldon, D. (1997). *The Drums of Autumn* (Reissue ed.). Dell.

Chapter Three

1 Pressfield has had an amazing career. His fiction and non-fiction books are simply some of the best writings on resistance. He has amazing clarity about how addiction, compulsivity, traumatic bonding, and dysfunctional relationships combine to keep a person stuck. *Bagger Vance* (movie and book) is a masterpiece about addiction and trauma and how they sustain resistance. It is a great metaphor around the power of positive visualization.

Chapter Four

1 Writing this out I feel compelled to point out that this is not an invitation for further suggestions. I already have plenty of people who wish to direct my choices in my life including 42 children and grandchildren—some of who have strong opinions about these matters.

Chapter Five

1 Joel Osteen, The Power of I Am. Osteen, J. (2016). *The Power of I Am: Two Words That Will Change Your Life Today*. FaithWords.

2 Rokelle Lerner, The Object of My Affection is in my Reflection. Another good book on the struggle of narcissism is Gayle Bohlman's Mirror, Mirror: Transforming Narcissism to Self-Realization. It not only reflects this chapter but the larger cultural issues implicit.

Chapter Six

1 A challenging book full of ideas of thinking about is Jack Canfield's book, *Chicken Soup for the Soul*. For openers, he is writing from the perspective of having had a huge impact and knows the value of focus and diligence in making the most out of life. Canfield, J., & Switzer,

J. (2015). *The Success Principles(TM)—10th Anniversary Edition: How to Get from Where You Are to Where You Want to Be* (10th Anniversary ed.). William Morrow Paperbacks.

Chapter Seven

[1] The creating of habits as part of building an expert system has appeared in many forms. For example, *The Seven Habits of Successful People* by Stephen Covey has been a successful best seller for decades. While his focus is different, some of the same principles apply. The early adopters of vision work including Napolean Hill and Charles Haanel clearly understood the habituation of ways to access the best of life. Steven Pressfield's works in many ways come from the opposite side of the resistance to a change in habits. An interesting introduction to the creation of habits in a consumer economy is Nir Eiyal's *Hooked: How to Build Habit Forming Products* echoes the *Recovery Zone's* message of the importance of taking charge of your choices or someone or something else will.

Appendix C **Bibliography**

Introduction:

Miller, A. (1997). *The Drama of the Gifted Child: The Search for the True Self, Revised Edition* (Third edition). Basic Books.

Carnes, P. J. (2009). *Recovery Zone, Vol. 1: Making Changes that Last—The Internal Tasks* (First edition). Gentle Path Press.

Pausch, R. (2008). *The Last Lecture* (First edition). Hyperion.

Coelho, P. (2006). *The Alchemist[THE ALCHEMIST] By Coelho, Paulo (Author) Apr-25-2006 Paperback*. HarperTorch.

A. (2002). *Alcoholics Anonymous: The Big Book* (Fourth edition). Alcoholics Anonymous World Services, Inc.

Ghaemi, N. (2012). *A First-Rate Madness: Uncovering the Links Between Leadership and Mental Illness* (Reprint ed.). Penguin Books.

Tolkien, J. R. R., & Lee, A. (1988). *The Lord of the Rings* (First edition). Houghton Mifflin.

Chapter 1:

Carnes, P. J. (2009). *Recovery Zone, Vol. 1: Making Changes that Last—The Internal Tasks* (First edition). Gentle Path Press.

Peck, S. M. (1985). *The Road Less Traveled—A New Psychology Of Love, Traditional Values And Spiritual Growth—Deluxe Trade Paperback Edition* (Flex-bind ed.). Touchstone/ Simon & Schuster.

A. (2002). *Alcoholics Anonymous: The Big Book* (Fourth edition). Alcoholics Anonymous World Services, Inc.

Duarte, N. (2010). *Resonate: Present Visual Stories that Transform Audiences* (First edition). John Wiley and Sons.

Doidge, N. (2016). *The Brain's Way of Healing: Remarkable Discoveries and Recoveries from the Frontiers of Neuroplasticity* (Updated ed.). Penguin Books.

Goleman, D. (2006). *Emotional intelligence*. New York: Bantam Books.

Lesser, E. (2017). *Marrow: Love, Loss, and What Matters Most* (Reprint ed.). Harper Wave.

Chapter 2

Carnes, P. J. (2009). *Recovery Zone, Vol. 1: Making Changes that Last—The Internal Tasks* (First edition). Gentle Path Press.

Zukav, G. (1989). *By Gary Zukav—The Seat of the Soul* (Reprinted edition). Prentice Hall & IBD.

Goleman, D. (2015). *Focus: The Hidden Driver of Excellence* (Illustrated ed.). Harper Paperbacks.

Childre, D. L., Martin, H., & Beech, D. (2000). *The HeartMath Solution: The Institute of HeartMath's Revolutionary Program for Engaging the Power of the Heart's Intelligence* (Reprint ed.). HarperOne.

Childre, D., Martin, H., Rozman, D., & McCraty, R. (2016). *Heart Intelligence: Connecting with the Intuitive Guidance of the Heart*. Waterfront Digital Press.

Kabat-Zinn, J. (2016). *Mindfulness for Beginners: Reclaiming the Present Moment and Your Life* (Book & CD) (First edition). Sounds True, Inc.

Siegel, D. J. (2010). *Mindsight: The New Science of Personal Transformation* (Reprint ed.). Bantam.

Byrne, R. (2012). *The Magic (Secret (Rhonda Byrne)* (Illustrated ed.). Atria Books.

Carnes, P. J. (2019). *The Betrayal Bond: Breaking Free of Exploitive Relationships* (Revised ed.). Health Communications Inc.

Singer, M. A. (2007). *The Untethered Soul: The Journey Beyond Yourself* (First edition). New Harbinger Publications/ Noetic Books.

Peck, S. M. (1985). *The Road Less Traveled—A New Psychology Of Love, Traditional Values And Spiritual Growth—Deluxe Trade Paperback Edition* (Flex-bind ed.). Touchstone/ Simon & Schuster.

Tolkien, J. R. R., & Lee, A. (1988). *The Lord of the Rings* (First edition). Houghton Mifflin.

Hannah, K. (2015). *The Nightingale: A Novel* (First edition). St. Martin's Press.

Gabaldon, D. (1992). *Outlander*. Delta.

Kushner, H. S. (2004). *When Bad Things Happen to Good People* (Reprint ed.). Anchor.

Chapter 3

Haanel, C. F. (2008). *The Master Key System*. Manor Thrift.

Carnes, P. J. (2009). *Recovery Zone, Vol. 1: Making Changes that Last—The Internal Tasks* (First edition). Gentle Path Press.

Tsabary, T. S. (2017). *The Awakened Family: How to Raise Empowered, Resilient, and Conscious Children* (Reprint ed.). Penguin Books.

Pressfield, Steven. (1996). *The Legend of Bagger Vance: A Novel of Golf and the Game of Life* (Reissue ed.). Avon Books.

Pressfield, Steven, & Coyne, S. (2012). *The War of Art: Break Through the Blocks and Win Your Inner Creative Battles*. Black Irish Entertainment LLC.

Carnes, P. J. (2001). *Out of the Shadows: Understanding Sexual Addiction* (Third edition). Hazelden Publishing.

Pausch, R. (2008). *The Last Lecture* (First edition). Hyperion.

Canfield, J., Hansen, M. V., & Newmark, A. (2013). *Chicken Soup for the Soul 20th Anniversary Edition: All Your Favorite Original Stories Plus 20 Bonus Stories for the Next 20 Years* (20th Anniversary ed.). Chicken Soup for the Soul. Health Communications, Inc.

Chapter 4

Needleman, J. (1994). *Money and the Meaning of Life* (New edition). Doubleday.

Carnes, P. J. (1992). *Don't Call It Love: Recovery From Sexual Addiction* (Reprint ed.). Bantam.

Muller, W. (2000). *Sabbath: Finding Rest, Renewal, and Delight in Our Busy Lives* (First edition). Bantam.

Komisar, R. (2001). *The Monk and the Riddle: The Art of Creating a Life While Making a Living* (First Printing edition). Harvard Business Review Press.

Carnes, P. J. (2009). *Recovery Zone, Vol. 1: Making Changes that Last—The Internal Tasks* (First edition). Gentle Path Press.

Singer, M. A. (2007b). *The Untethered Soul: The Journey Beyond Yourself* (First edition). New Harbinger Publications/ Noetic Books.

Sanderson, B. (2021). *Stormlight Archive Series Brandon Sanderson Collection 4 Books Bundles Set*. Gollancz.

Tolkien, J. R. R., & Lee, A. (1988). *The Lord of the Rings* (First edition). Houghton Mifflin.

Pausch, R. (2008). *The Last Lecture* (First edition). Hyperion.

Tsabary, S. (2017). *The Awakened Family: How to Raise Empowered, Resilient, and Conscious Children* (Reprint ed.). Penguin Books.

Childre, D., Martin, H., Rozman, D., & McCraty, R. (2016). *Heart Intelligence: Connecting with the Intuitive Guidance of the Heart*. Waterfront Digital Press.

Siegel, D. J. (2010). *Mindsight: The New Science of Personal Transformation* (Reprint ed.). Bantam.

Pausch, R. (2008). *The Last Lecture* (First edition). Hyperion.

Goleman, D. (2015). *Focus: The Hidden Driver of Excellence* (Illustrated ed.). Harper Paperbacks.

Chapter 5

Carnes, P. J. (2009). *Recovery Zone, Vol. 1: Making Changes that Last—The Internal Tasks* (First edition). Gentle Path Press.

A. (2002). *Alcoholics Anonymous: The Big Book* (Fourth edition). Alcoholics Anonymous World Services, Inc.

Lerner, R. (2008). *The Object of My Affection Is in My Reflection: Coping with Narcissists* (Illustrated ed.). Health Communications Inc.

Keller, T. (2011). *The Prodigal God: Recovering the Heart of the Christian Faith* (Reprint ed.). Penguin Books.

Ruiz, D. M. (2018). *The Four Agreements: A Practical Guide to Personal Freedom (A Toltec Wisdom Book)*. Amber-Allen Publishing, Incorporated.

Levine, S., Levine, O., & Starr, M. (2019). *Unattended Sorrow: Recovering from Loss and Reviving the Heart* (Second edition). Monkfish Book Publishing.

Pausch, R. (2008). *The Last Lecture* (First edition). Hyperion.

Gilbert, E. (2007). *Eat, Pray, Love: One Woman's Search for Everything Across Italy, India and Indonesia*. Riverhead Books.

Chapter 6

Dyer, D. W. W. (2018). *You Are What You Think: 365 Meditations for Purposeful Living*. Hay House Inc.

Carnes, P. J. (2009). *Recovery Zone, Vol. 1: Making Changes that Last—The Internal Tasks* (First edition). Gentle Path Press.

Lynne McTaggart the Intention Experiment (Reprint ed.). (2007). Atria Books.

Campbell, J. (1973). *The Hero With A Thousand Faces* (21st edition). Princeton University Press.

Cloud, H., Townsend, J., & Arnold, H. O. (2018). *Boundaries, Updated and Expanded Edition: When to Say Yes, How to Say No to Take Control of Your Life* (Library ed.). Zondervan on Brilliance Audio.

Chapter 7

Carnes, P. J. (2009). *Recovery Zone, Vol. 1: Making Changes that Last—The Internal Tasks* (First edition). Gentle Path Press.

Pausch, R. (2008). *The Last Lecture* (First edition). Hyperion.

Coelho, P. (2006). *The Alchemist[THE ALCHEMIST] By Coelho, Paulo* (Author) *Apr-25-2006 Paperback*. HarperTorch.

Hannah, K. (2015). *The Nightingale: A Novel* (First edition). St. Martin's Press.

Goleman, D. (2015). *Focus: The Hidden Driver of Excellence* (Illustrated ed.). Harper Paperbacks.

Siegel, D. J. (2010). *Mindsight: The New Science of Personal Transformation* (Reprint ed.). Bantam.

Ruiz, D. M. (2018). *The Four Agreements: A Practical Guide to Personal Freedom (A Toltec Wisdom Book)*. Amber-Allen Publishing, Incorporated.

Kurtz, E., & Ketcham, K. (1993). *The Spirituality of Imperfection: Storytelling and the Search for Meaning* (Revised ed.). Bantam.

Amen, D. A. G., & Bsn Rn, A. T. (2017). *The Brain Warrior's Way: Ignite Your Energy and Focus, Attack Illness and Aging, Transform Pain into Purpose* (Illustrated ed.). Berkley.

Covey, S. R. (2013). *The 7 Habits of Highly Effective People: Powerful Lessons in Personal Change* (Anniversary ed.). Simon & Schuster.

Pressfield, Steven, & Coyne, S. (2012). *The War of Art: Break Through the Blocks and Win Your Inner Creative Battles* (47716th edition.). Black Irish Entertainment LLC.

A. (2002). *Alcoholics Anonymous: The Big Book* (Fourth edition). Alcoholics Anonymous World Services, Inc.

Beattie, M. (2005). *The Language of Letting Go*. Hay House Inc.

Tolkien, J. R. R., & Lee, A. (1988). *The Lord of the Rings* (First edition). Houghton Mifflin.

Gabaldon, D. (1992). *Outlander*. Delta.

Cameron, J. (1992). *The Artist's Way* (First edition). Tarcher.

Cozolino, L. (2010). *The Neuroscience of Psychotherapy: Healing the Social Brain* (Second edition). *(The Norton Series on Interpersonal Neurobiology)* (Second edition). W. W. Norton & Company.

Dossey, L. (1995). *Healing Words: The Power of Prayer and the Practice of Medicine* (First edition). HarperOne.

McTaggart, L. (2008). *The Field: The Quest for the Secret Force of the Universe* (Updated ed.). Harper Perennial.

McTaggart, L. (2012). *The Bond: How to Fix Your Falling-Down World* (Reprint ed.). Atria Books.

Sankey, J. (2012). *Zen and the Art of Stand-Up Comedy*. Taylor & Francis.

Bonhoeffer, D., & Metaxas, E. (1995). *The Cost of Discipleship* (First edition). Touchstone.

Stone, D., Patton, B., Heen, S., & Fisher, R. (2010). *Difficult Conversations: How to Discuss What Matters Most* (Illustrated ed.). Penguin Books.

Kabat-Zinn, J. (2019). *Mindfulness for All* (Illustrated ed.). Hachette Books.

Pressfield, Steven. (1996b). *The Legend of Bagger Vance: A Novel of Golf and the Game of Life* (Reissue ed.). Avon Books.

Millman, D. (2006). *Way of the Peaceful Warrior: A Book That Changes Lives* (Revised ed.). HJ Kramer.

Childre, D. L., Martin, H., & Beech, D. (2000). *The HeartMath Solution: The Institute of HeartMath's Revolutionary Program for Engaging the Power of the Heart's Intelligence* (Reprint ed.). HarperOne.

Childre, D., Martin, H., Rozman, D., & McCraty, R. (2016). *Heart Intelligence: Connecting with the Intuitive Guidance of the Heart*. Waterfront Digital Press.

Sockolov, M. (2018). *Practicing Mindfulness: 75 Essential Meditations to Reduce Stress, Improve Mental Health, and Find Peace in the Everyday*. Althea Press.

Gunaratana, B. (2011). *Mindfulness in Plain English* (First edition). Wisdom Publications.

Matthews, Z. (2017). *Mindfulness 101—Concepts, Misconceptions & Practices: Easy and Powerful Meditation Techniques Proven to Reduce Stress, Sleep Better, Lower Blood Pressure & Improve Memory*. CreateSpace Independent Publishing Platform.

Chapter 8

Amen, D. A. G., & Bsn Rn, A. T. (2017b). *The Brain Warrior's Way: Ignite Your Energy and Focus, Attack Illness and Aging, Transform Pain into Purpose* (Illustrated ed.). Berkley.

Doidge, N. (2007). *The Brain That Changes Itself: Stories of Personal Triumph from the Frontiers of Brain Science* (Reprint ed.). Penguin Books.

Hedges, C. (2014). *War Is a Force that Gives Us Meaning* (Reprint ed.). PublicAffairs.

Carnes, P. J. (2009). *Recovery Zone, Vol. 1: Making Changes that Last—The Internal Tasks* (First edition). Gentle Path Press.

Carnes, P., Carnes, S., & Bailey, J. (2011). *Facing Addiction: Starting Recovery from Alcohol and Drugs* (0 ed.). Gentle Path Press.

Carnes, P. (2015). *Facing the Shadow* (Third edition)*: Starting Sexual and Relationship Recovery* (Third edition). Gentle Path Press.

Carnes, P. C. J. (2012b). *A Gentle Path through the Twelve Steps: The Classic Guide for All People in the Process of Recovery* (Third edition). Hazelden Publishing.

Chapter 9

Carnes, P. C. J. (2012b). *A Gentle Path through the Twelve Steps: The Classic Guide for All People in the Process of Recovery* (Third edition). Hazelden Publishing.

Chapter 10

Koontz, D. (2012). *Life Expectancy: A Novel* (Reprint ed.). Bantam.

Becker, E. (1973). *Ernest Becker / The Denial of Death First Edition 1973*. Generic.

Clark, C. (2011). *Addict America: The Lost Connection*. CreateSpace Independent Publishing Platform.

Black, C. (2019). *Changing Course: Healing from Loss, Abandonment, and Fear* (Reissue ed.). Central Recovery Press.

Appendix D **Contact information**

Two recovery-supporting websites can be accessed at sexhelp.com and recoveryzone.com.

For general or purchasing information regarding our publications, please visit sexhelp.com or gentlepath.com.

For information on both inpatient and outpatient treatment services you may contact:

Gentle Path
1-866-811-8265
gentlepathmeadows.com

Willow House
1-877-860-3893
willowhouseforwomen.com

For information on finding therapists in your area along with additional treatment services and additional online tools contact:

Sex Help
sexhelp.com

For more information about Dr. Patrick Carnes, his speaking engagements, and videos access his website at patrickcarnes.com. There are many other videos available of Patrick Carnes' lectures and interviews on YouTube.

patrickcarnes.com

For information on training for counselors and other helping professionals, call the International Institute for Trauma and Addiction Professionals (IITAP) at 1866-575-6853 (US Toll-Free) or access them via the internet at iitap.com.

Appendix E **Resource Guide**

The following is a list of recovery fellowships that may be helpful to you in your particular situation.

Adult Children of Alcoholics
310-534-1815
www.adultchildren.org

Alateen (ages 12–17)
800-356-9996
www.al-anon-alateen.org

Al-Anon
800-344-2666
www.al-anon.org

Alcoholics Anonymous
212-870-3400
www.alcoholics-anonymous.org

Co-Dependents Anonymous
602-277-7991
www.codependents.org

Co-Dependents of Sex Addicts
763-537-6904
www.cosa-recovery.org

Cocaine Anonymous
800-347-8998
www.ca.org

CoAnon
520-513-5028
www.co-anon.org

Debtors Anonymous
781-453-2743
www.debtorsanonymous.org

Emotions Anonymous
651-647-9712
www.mtn.org/EA

Families Anonymous
310-815-8010
www.familiesanonymous.org

Gamblers Anonymous
213-386-8789
www.gamblersanonymous.org

Marijuana Anonymous
212-459-4423
www.marijuana-anonymous.org

Narcotics Anonymous
818-773-9999
www.na.org

Nicotine Anonymous
415-750-0328
www.nicotine-anonymous.org

Overeaters Anonymous
505-891-2664
www.oa.org

Recovering Couples Anonymous
781-794-1456
www.recovering-couples.org

Runaway and Suicide Hotline
800-RUN-AWAY
www.1800runaway.org

S-Anon
615-833-3152
www.sanon.org

Sex and Love Addicts Anonymous
www.slaafws.org

Sex Addicts Anonymous
713-869-4902
www.sexaa.org

Sexaholics Anonymous
866-424-8777
www.sa.org

Sexual Addiction Resources/
Dr. Patrick Carnes
www.sexhelp.com

Sexual Compulsives Anonymous
310-859-5585
www.sca-recovery.org

Society for the Advancement of
Sexual Heath
706-356-7031
www.sash.net

Survivors of Incest Anonymous
410-282-3400
www.siawso.org

Adult Children of Alcoholics

Adult Children of Alcoholics/Dysfunctional Families, Anonymous

It Will Never Happen to Me: Growing Up with Addiction as Youngsters, Adolescents, Adults, Claudia Black

My Dad Loves Me, My Dad Has a Disease: A Child's View: Living with Addiction, Claudia Black

Grandchildren of Alcoholics: Another Generation of Codependency, Ann W. Smith

Adult Children of Alcoholics, Janet G. Woititz

Marriage On The Rocks: Learning to Live with Yourself and an Alcoholic, Janet G. Woititz

Healthy Parenting: How Your Upbringing Influences the Way You Raise Your Children, and What You Can Do to Make It Better for Them, Janet G. Woititz

Codependency

Codependent No More: How to Stop Controlling Others and Start Caring for Yourself, Melody Beattie

Mending a Shattered Heart: A Guide for Partners of Sex Addicts, (Second edition) Stefanie Carnes

Boundaries: Where You End and I Begin, Anne Katherine

Living in the Comfort Zone: The Gift of Boundaries in Relationships, Rokelle Lerner

Facing Codependence: What It Is, Where It Comes from, How It Sabotages Our Lives, Pia Melody & Andrea Miller

The Drama of the Gifted Child: The Search for the True Self, Alice Miller

Is It Love or Is It Addiction?, Brenda Schaeffer

Codependency continued

Choicemaking: For Spirituality Seekers, Co-Dependents and Adult Children,
Sharon Wegscheider-Cruse

Learning To Say No: Establishing Healthy Boundaries, Carle Wills-Brandon

Co-Sex Addiction

Open Hearts: Renewing Relationships with Recovery, Romance & Reality, Patrick Carnes, Mark
Laaser, Deborah Laaser

Healing Together: A Guide to Intimacy and Recovery for Co-Dependent Couples, Wayne Kritsberg

Relationships in Recovery: Healing Strategies for Couples and Families, Emily Marlin

Facing Codependence: What It Is, Where It Comes from, How It Sabotages Our Lives, Pia Mellody

Back from Betrayal, Jennifer Schneider

Rebuilding Trust: For Couples Committed to Recovery, Jennifer Schneider & Burt Schneider

Sex, Lies and Forgiveness, Jennifer Schneider & Burt Schneider

*Women Who Love Sex Addicts: Help for Healing from the Effects of a Relationship With a
Sex Addict,* Douglas Weiss & Donna DeBusk

Family of Origin

It Will Never Happen to Me: Growing Up With Addiction As Youngsters, Adolescents, Adults,
Claudia Black

Changing Course: Healing from Loss, Abandonment and Fear, Claudia Black

Healing the Shame that Binds You, John Bradshaw

Family Secrets: The Path to Self-Acceptance and Reunion, John Bradshaw

The Emotional Incest Syndrome: What to do When a Parent's Love Rules Your Life, Patricia Love

Healing The Child Within: Discovery and Recovery for Adult Children of Dysfunctional Families,
Charles L. Whitfield, M.D.

Men's Issues

When He's Married to Mom: How to Help Mother-Enmeshed Men Open Their Hearts to True Love and Commitment, Kenneth Adams

Longing for Dad: Father Loss and Its Impact, Beth Erickson

The Knight in Rusty Armor, Robert Fisher

Fire in the Belly: On Being a Man, Sam Keen

If Only He Knew: What No Woman Can Resist, Gary Smalley & Norma Smalley

Mission Development

The Artist's Way, Julia Cameron

First Things First, Stephen R. Covey

Money Issues

Money Drunk, Money Sober; 90 Days to Financial Freedom, Mark Bryan & Julia Cameron A

Currency of Hope, Debtors Anonymous

Deadly Odds: Recovery from Compulsive Gambling, Ken Estes & Mike Brubaker

The Financial Wisdom of Ebenezer Scrooge: Five Principles to Transform Your Relationship with Money, Ted Klontz, Rick Kahler, & Brad Klontz

Money and the Meaning of Life, Jacob Needleman

Recovery and Twelve Step

Adult Children of Alcoholics/Dysfunctional Families, Anonymous

Alcoholics Anonymous, Anonymous

Al-Anon Faces Alcoholism, Anonymous

Al-Anon's Twelve Steps and Twelve Traditions, Anonymous

Alateen—A Day at a Time, Anonymous

Alateen—Hope for Children of Alcoholics, Anonymous

Recovery and Twelve Step continued

Codependents Anonymous, Anonymous

Having Had a Spiritual Awakening, Anonymous

Hope for Today, Anonymous

One Day at a Time in Al-Anon, Anonymous

Sex Addicts Anonymous, Anonymous

Sex and Love Addicts Anonymous, Anonymous

The Courage to Change, Anonymous

The Dilemma of the Alcoholic Marriage, Anonymous

Twelve Steps for Overeaters, Anonymous

Twelve-Step Prayer Book, Anonymous

A Gentle Path Through the Twelve Steps: The Classic Guide for All People in the Process of Recovery, Patrick Carnes

A Woman's Way Through the Twelve Steps, Stephanie Covington

Twelve Steps for Adult Children, Veronica Ray

Trust the Process: An Artist's Guide to Letting Go, Shaun McNiff

The Addictive Personality: Understanding the Addictive Process and Compulsive Behavior, Craig Nakken

Sex Addiction

When He's Married to Mom: How to Help Mother-Enmeshed Men Open Their Hearts to True Love and Commitment, Kenneth Adams

A Gentle Path Through the Twelve Steps: The Classic Guide for All People in the Process of Recovery, Patrick Carnes

Contrary to Love: Helping the Sexual Addict, Patrick Carnes

Don't Call It Love: Recovery From Sexual Addiction, Patrick Carnes

Facing the Shadow: Starting Sexual and Relationship Recovery, Patrick Carnes

Out of the Shadows: Understanding Sexual Addiction, Patrick Carnes

Sexual Anorexia: Overcoming Sexual Self-Hatred, Patrick Carnes

The Betrayal Bond: Breaking Free of Exploitive Relationships, Patrick Carnes

Clinical Management of Sex Addiction, Patrick Carnes & Kenneth Adams

In The Shadows of The Net: Breaking Free from Compulsive Online Sexual Behavior,
Patrick Carnes, David Delmonico & Elizabeth Griffin

Disclosing Secrets: When, to Whom, and How Much to Reveal, Deborah Corley &
Jennifer Schneider

*Lonely All The Time: Recognizing, Understanding, and Overcoming Sex Addiction, for Addicts
and Co-dependents,* Ralph Earle & Gregory Crowe

Women, Sex and Addiction, Charlotte Kasl

Ten Smart Things Gay Men Can Do to Improve Their Lives, Joe Kort

Ready to Heal, Kelly McDaniel

Cybersex Exposed: Simple Fantasy or Obsession?, Jennifer Schneider & Rob Weiss

Cruise Control: Understanding Sex Addiction in Gay Men, Rob Weiss

Untangling the Web: Sex, Porn, and Fantasy Obsession in the Internet Age,
Rob Weiss & Jennifer Schneider

Shadows of the Cross: A Christian Companion to Facing the Shadow by Craig Cashwell,
Pennie Johnson, and Patrick Carnes

Sexual Abuse

Silently Seduced: When Parents Make their Children Partners—Understanding Covert Incest,
Kenneth Adams

The Courage to Heal: A Guide for Women Survivors of Child Sexual Abuse, Ellen Bass &
Laura Davis

Against Our Will: Men, Women, and Rape, Susan Brownmiller

Abused Boys: The Neglected Victims of Sexual Abuse, Mic Hunter

Victims No Longer: The Classic Guide for Men Recovering from Sexual Child Abuse, Mike Lew

Spirituality and Meditation

Answers in the Heart: Daily Meditations For Men And Women Recovering From Sex Addiction, Anonymous

Days of Healing, Days of Joy, Anonymous

Spirituality and Meditation continued

Food for Thought: Daily Meditations for Dieters and Overeaters, Anonymous

The Courage to Change, Anonymous

Journey to the Heart: Daily Meditations on the Path to Freeing Your Soul, Melody Beattie

The Language of Letting Go, Melody Beattie

Spiritual Skill Set: Pt 1 —Discernment, Patrick Carnes & the Voices From Afar (CD)

Spiritual Skill Set: Pt 2—Resilience, Patrick Carnes & the Voices From Afar (CD)

Each Day a New Beginning: Daily Meditations for Women, Karen Casey

Yesterday's Tomorrow: Recovery Meditations for Hard Cases, Barry B. Longyear

The Spirituality of Imperfection: Storytelling and the Search for Meaning, Ernest Kurtz & Katherine Ketcham

Addiction and Grace: Love and Spirituality in the Healing of Addictions, Gerald G. May

The Four Agreements: A Practical Guide to Personal Freedom, A Toltec Wisdom Book, Don Miguel Ruiz

Serenity Through Meditation (CD), Sue Neufeld-Ellis

Trauma

The Betrayal Bond: Breaking Free of Exploitive Relationships, Patrick Carnes

Heartwounds: The Impact of Unresolved Trauma and Grief on Relationships, Tian Dayton

Trauma and Addiction: Ending the Cycle of Pain Through Emotional Literacy, Tian Dayton

Waking the Tiger: Healing Trauma : The Innate Capacity to Transform Overwhelming Experiences, Peter Levine & Ann Frederick

Women's Issues

Perfect Daughters, Robert Ackerman

Motherless Daughters: The Legacy of Loss, Hope Edelman

Women, Anger & Depression: Strategies for Self Empowerment, Lois Frankel

My Mother/My Self: The Daughter's Search for Identity, Nancy Friday

The Princess Who Believed in Fairy Tales: A Story for Modern Times, Marcia Grad

Women, Sex, and Addiction: A Search for Love and Power, Charlotte Kasl

Father Hunger: Fathers, Daughters, and the Pursuit of Thinness, Margo Maine

Women Who Hurt Themselves: A Book of Hope and Understanding, Dusty Miller

Ready to Heal, Kelly McDaniel

She Has a Secret: Understanding Female Sexual Addiction, Douglas Weiss

Women Who Love Sex Addicts: Help for Healing from the Effects of a Relationship With a Sex Addict, Douglas Weiss & Diane DeBusk

Additional Recommended Reading from Recovery Zone II

The Drama of the Gifted Child: The Search for the True Self, Alice Miller

The Last Lecture, Randy Pausch

The Alchemist, Paulo Coelho

Alcoholics Anonymous: The Big Book

A First-Rate Madness: Uncovering the Links Between Leadership and Mental Illness, Nassir Ghaemi

The Lord of the Rings, J. R. R. Tolkien

The Road Less Traveled—A New Psychology Of Love, Traditional Values And Spiritual Growth, M. Scott Peck

Resonate: Present Visual Stories that Transform Audiences, Nancy Duarte

The Brain's Way of Healing: Remarkable Discoveries and Recoveries from the Frontiers of Neuroplasticity, Norman Doidge

Emotional Intelligence: Why It Can Matter More Than IQ, Daniel Goleman

Marrow: Love, Loss, and What Matters Most, Elizabeth Lesser

The Seat of the Soul, Gary Zukav

Focus: The Hidden Driver of Excellence, Daniel Goleman

The HeartMath Solution: The Institute of HeartMath's Revolutionary Program for Engaging the Power of the Heart's Intelligence, Doc Lew Childre

Heart Intelligence: Connecting with the Intuitive Guidance of the Heart, Doc Lew Childre

Mindfulness for Beginners: Reclaiming the Present Moment and Your Life, Jon Kabat-Zinn

Mindsight: The New Science of Personal Transformation, Daniel Siegel

The Magic, Rhonda Byrne

The Betrayal Bond: Breaking Free of Exploitive Relationships, Patrick Carnes

The Untethered Soul: The Journey Beyond Yourself, Michael A. Singer

The Nightingale: A Novel, Kristin Hannah

Outlander, Diana Gabaldon

When Bad Things Happen to Good People, Harold S. Kushner

The Master Key System, Charles F. Haanel

The Awakened Family: How to Raise Empowered, Resilient, and Conscious Children, Shefali Tsabary

The Legend of Bagger Vance: A Novel of Golf and the Game of Life, Steven Pressfield

The War of Art: Break Through the Blocks and Win Your Inner Creative Battles, Steven Pressfield

Out of the Shadows: Understanding Sexual Addiction, Patrick Carnes

Chicken Soup for the Soul, Jack Canfield, Mark Hansen, & Amy Newmark. First book of the series.

Money and the Meaning of Life, Jacob Needleman

Don't Call It Love: Recovery From Sexual Addiction, Patrick Carnes

Sabbath: Finding Rest, Renewal, and Delight in Our Busy Lives, Wayne Muller

The Monk and the Riddle: The Art of Creating a Life While Making a Living, Randy Komisar

Stormlight Archive Series, Brandon Sanderson

The Prodigal God: Recovering the Heart of the Christian Faith, Timothy Keller

The Four Agreements: A Practical Guide to Personal Freedom, Don Miguel Ruiz

Unattended Sorrow: Recovering from Loss and Reviving the Heart, Stephen Levine

Eat, Pray, Love: One Woman's Search for Everything Across Italy, India and Indonesia. Elizabeth Gilbert

You Are What You Think: 365 Meditations for Purposeful Living, Wayne Dyer

The Intention Experiment, Lynne McTaggart

The Hero With A Thousand Faces, Joseph Campbell

The Spirituality of Imperfection: Storytelling and the Search for Meaning, Ernest Kurtz and Katherine Ketcham

The Brain Warrior's Way: Ignite Your Energy and Focus, Attack Illness and Aging, Transform Pain into Purpose, Daniel G. Amen

The 7 Habits of Highly Effective People: Powerful Lessons in Personal Change, Stephen Covey

The Language of Letting Go, Melody Beattie

The Artist's Way, Julia Cameron

The Neuroscience of Psychotherapy: Healing the Social Brain, Louis Cozolino

Healing Words: The Power of Prayer and the Practice of Medicine, Larry Dossey

The Field: The Quest for the Secret Force of the Universe, Lynn McTaggart

The Bond: How to Fix Your Falling-Down World, Lynn McTaggart

Zen and the Art of Stand-Up Comedy, Jay Sankey

The Cost of Discipleship, Dietrich Bonhoeffer

Difficult Conversations: How to Discuss What Matters Most Douglas Stone

Way of the Peaceful Warrior: A Book That Changes Lives, Dan Millman

Mindfulness in Plain English, Bhante Gunaratana

Mindfulness 101—Concepts, Misconceptions & Practices: Easy and Powerful Meditation Techniques Proven to Reduce Stress, Sleep Better, Lower Blood Pressure & Improve Memory, Matthew Sockolov

The Brain That Changes Itself: Stories of Personal Triumph from the Frontiers of Brain Science, Norman Doidge

War Is a Force that Gives Us Meaning, Chris Hedges

Facing Addiction: Starting Recovery from Alcohol and Drugs, Patrick Carnes

Facing the Shadow Starting Sexual and Relationship Patrick Carnes

A Gentle Path through the Twelve Steps: The Classic Guide for All People in the Process of Recovery, Patrick Carnes

The Denial of Death, Ernest Becker

Addict America: The Lost Connection, Carol Clark

Changing Course: Healing from Loss, Abandonment, and Fear, Claudia Black

Resilience: Living One Year in Focus and Meaning, Bonnie Phillips and Pennie Carnes

The How of Happiness: A New Approach to Getting the Life You Want (2008) by Sonja Lyubomirsky

	12 Habits	Master Skills	Operational Strategies	Animal
Q1M1W1	Intention	Vision	Seeking Options	Hummingbird
Q1M1W2			Seeking Alternative Perspective	
Q1M1W3			Long-Term Perspective/Focus	
Q1M1W4			Goal-Setting	
Q1M2W1	Self Care	Persistence	Focus	Hummingbird
Q1M2W2			Exercise	
Q1M2W3			Nutrition	
Q1M2W4			Rest	
Q1M3W1	Accountability	Acceptance	Problem-solving	Hummingbird
Q1M3W2			Accepting Limits	
Q1M3W3			Congruency	
Q1M3W4			Reframing/Restructuring	
Q2M1W1	Study	Knowledge	Seeking Facts	Turtle
Q2M1W2			Changing the Narrative	
Q2M1W3			Positive Self-Focus	
Q2M1W4			Brain Consciousness	
Q2M2W1	Reflection	Emotional Regulation	Managing Adversity	Turtle
Q2M2W2			Identifying Resistance	
Q2M2W3			Meditation	
Q2M2W4			Emotional Expression	
Q2M3W1	Recovery Support	Boundaries	Showing Up—Vulnerability	Turtle
Q2M3W2			Service	
Q2M3W3			Accessing and Accepting Help	
Q2M3W4			Accepting Inconvenient Truths	
Q3M1W1	Intuition	Listen to Fear	Embodiment	Dragonfly
Q3M1W2			Expansion of Awareness	
Q3M1W3			Reintegration of Memories	
Q3M1W4			Trust of Self	
Q3M2W1	Spirituality	Inner Observer	Gratitude	Dragonfly
Q3M2W2			Letting Go	
Q3M2W3			Forgiveness	
Q3M2W4			Self-Compassion	
Q3M3W1	Perspective	Flexibility	Changing Perspective	Dragonfly
Q3M3W2			Adaptability	
Q3M3W3			Optimism	
Q3M3W4			Learning From the Past	
Q4M1W1	Consciousness	Inner Coherence	Affirmation	Dolphin
Q4M1W2			Sinus Rhythm	
Q4M1W3			Integration	
Q4M1W4			Universal Connection	
Q4M2W1	Compassion	Empathy	Attunement	Dolphin
Q4M2W2			Connection/Relationship	
Q4M2W3			Validation/Witnessing	
Q4M2W4			Problem-solving/Community	
Q4M3W1	Mindfulness	Flow	Creativity	Dolphin
Q4M3W2			Play	
Q4M3W3			Humor—Internal & External	
Q4M3W4			Challenging Activities	

Appendix H Resilience: **Living One Year in Focus and Meaning**

Bonnie Phillips, PhD,
Pennie Carnes, LPC,
Patrick Carnes , PhD

This is the sequel to the Recovery Zone II series and is forth coming in the Fall of 2021

Welcome to the *Resilience: Living One Year in Focus and Meaning* planner. We are grateful for your journey and your desire to start this process.

Often as we begin a new journey, we find ourselves feeling a wide range of emotions: excitement, eagerness, anxiety, hope, and perhaps a bit of fear. We know we want to start but we do not know what lies ahead. The adventure of Bilbo Baggins comes to mind as he embarks on his unique life adventure in J.R.R. Tolkien's, *The Hobbit*. There is something that is pulling him toward the adventure and a drastic life change, yet there remains the comforts of home and all that is known. In fact, Bilbo states, "Sorry! I don't want any adventures, thank you. Not Today. Good morning! But please come to tea—any time you like! Why not tomorrow? Good bye!"

It is possible you feel the same as Bilbo did. Yet, the pull for change and adventure lingers, and if you have read *The Hobbit* or seen the movies, you know that Bilbo eventually chooses adventure, even though he has no idea what is in store for him. He steps out of his cozy hobbit hole in the Shire and heads out for the unknown.

The early scenes from *The Hobbit* depict what Joseph Campbell referred to as the Hero's Journey, which is a common structure to many stories, myths, movies, etc. The character starts out in what Campbell called the Ordinary World and then feels the Call to Adventure. The character, like Bilbo, initially refuses the Call to Adventure, deciding that the Ordinary World is where he or she would like to remain. At this point, the character meets the mentor (enter the wizard Gandalf) and, at some point, the character crosses the threshold and moves into action.

This decision-making process is wonderfully depicted in the early scenes of *The Hobbit*. Bilbo, enjoying a peaceful evening reading a book by the fire in his hobbit hole, is interrupted by a knock at his door. He does not know it yet, but this is the beginning of his Call to Adventure. When he answers the door, he is surprised to find a dwarf, who enters, inquiring if any of the others have arrived. This goes on for several more minutes—a knock at the door and then the entry of another dwarf. As it turns out, they are all hungry and chaos ensues. Eventually, the wizard Gandalf arrives (the mentor). Bilbo was unfamiliar with the dwarves, but he does know Gandalf. The final knock comes from Thorin, King of the Dwarves Under the Mountain.

Thorin tells Bilbo that the dwarves are forming a company to return to their home and take it back from the dragon Smaug, who has been residing there for years. More importantly, Gandalf has volunteered Bilbo to join the company as their burglar because they need someone to enter the mountain unknown to the dragon. As all of this is unfolding and Bilbo tries to keep up and manage the sudden chaos in his cozy home, his peaceful life is upended by a new possibility—a Call to Adventure. What lies outside the boundaries of the Shire? What could Bilbo experience if he was willing to venture out and take a risk? This is the beginning of Bilbo's Hero's Journey.

This book can be the beginning of your Hero's Journey. In fact, we hope the process of this planner is a Call to Adventure that significantly changes your life.

All of us, when we are faced with a decision to change, go through a process similar to the one Bilbo encountered. We must decide if we want to stay where it is comfortable or if we will follow our personal equivalent of Gandalf, Thorin, and the other dwarves to lands unknown. At times, we feel the pull of something more, and at times we are thrown into change through something unexpected or even through a life crisis. Navigating each of these Calls to Adventure requires resilience. It is our hope that as you start this process, you will arrive at a deeper state of resilience and connection to yourself, others, and the world around you.

As the name of this planner suggests, this process is about building your resilience. Resilience is often defined as the ability to bounce back from difficulties or challenging life circumstances. In fact, the origin of the word derives from the Latin *resilines*, which means to recoil or rebound.

Resilience may come easier to some than others. That said, it is a skill that can be learned and built upon. As you navigate challenging life circumstances, you can always rely on past experiences to manage and overcome current and future difficult times. As you do this, you begin to trust your capacity for resilience, and you are able to pursue life goals and dreams in a more meaningful way. As you do so, you will assuredly change in meaningful ways.

As you can imagine, when Bilbo Baggins returns to his home in the Shire after his adventures and perils in *The Hobbit*, he is a very different hobbit. He has changed. He has gone through challenges, loss, pain, and battles, and has experienced new depths of friendship and belonging. All of which change him. He returns with a greater sense of confidence and resilience. He has a deeper awareness of the world and his place in it. He has experienced the depths of friendship and the pain of loss. He has had to be vulnerable and he has had to be brave, despite his fear.

This is true for all of us. As we are tested and come through, we change and our capacity to navigate life expands. When we connect deeply with others and work through challenges together, we change.

Along with resilience comes flexibility and adaptability. The more possibilities we envision, especially during difficult times and challenges, the more we allow ourselves to overcome and expand as individuals.

This planner is built around the concept of transformational change. Its purpose is to offer a year to focus on and build a deeper recovery—to help you dig into the realities of your life in order to facilitate shifts in relationships, priorities, and in your brain. The design of this planner takes you through four quarters, with each quarter having a different focus, including issues related to meaning and mortality.

In Kristin Hannah's book *The Nightingale*, the core teaching is that love tells you what you want but war tells you who you are. The Hero's Journey is much the same, focusing on overcoming difficulty and overwhelming circumstances as a way of refining the truth about oneself. Abraham Lincoln fought a war that cost more lives than any other war that the United States has experienced. He was also bipolar, so he had internal demons to face. He said, "Every man is born an original, but sadly most men die copies." The purpose of recovery is to no longer be a copy of someone else's vision. So, the question remains: Once you start this thing called recovery, how do you weave what you learn on your journey into a meaningful recovery that lasts?

And the answer is you intentionally create an expert system. If you have read and worked through *Recovery Zone II* by Dr. Patrick Carnes, you have learned various aspects of how to recover the self that has been separated, and how to implement the original facets of you into how you live. "Wax on, wax off," Mister Miyagi said to young Daniel in the movie *Karate Kid*. But how does it come together? Concentration, focus, danger, conflict, success, but, above all, weaving what you learned into habits and new neuronal algorithms that govern your life when there is no time to think about it. The bottom-up brain incorporates new habits—the habits of recovery.

The system presented in the *Resilience: Living One Year in Focus and Meaning* workbook and planner is exactly that. It is an expert system designed to create a system of recovery built on resilience. This resilience matrix is built on resilience master skills and recovery zone strategies.

There are twelve core resilience master skills. We have arrived at these twelve out of the research and literature about resilience and recovery. Each month over the course of the year, you will focus on one skill. These skills, when practiced, will help to build your resilience overall, increasing your capacity to respond to trauma and stress moving forward.

In addition to the resilience skills, you will be introduced to four recovery zone strategies. These strategies, when practiced, help to support and enhance the development of each master resilience skill. You will focus on one strategy per week.

The goals of this planner reflect the intense process that happens for many people when they learn that they have a limited amount of time left to live. If confronted with our own mortality, would we change the way we live? Would we prioritize life in a different way? Studies have shown that this type of death reflection can enhance gratitude and intrinsic motivation compared to people who do not think about or reflect on their own mortality. This is similar to what can occur for people when they navigate a crisis or heal from trauma. Often, there is a deeper gratitude for life, a deeper sense of meaning, and a clarity about priorities.

How would you live over the next year if you knew you only had one year to live? It can be scary to face questions related to our own mortality, and these are issues that many strive to avoid at all costs. It can also be inspiring and focusing if you are willing to ask yourself such questions. That is what this planner does. For the next year, these will be the difficult issues and questions you will be encouraged to face and work through. It will be a time of growth, depth, and meaning. You will have the opportunity to reflect daily, monthly, and quarterly to assess your progress. It is a year dedicated to change and to resilience.

The process is designed to help you create your core values as well as your life goals and then translate those into a daily reality. The journey will be supported by readings and tips to help you in the process. There will also be a companion workbook with several activities to help you focus. This process is about making decisions, visualizing how to make your decisions a reality, and then committing to working towards your decisions each and every day. Intention is central to the work. Focusing your intention for your day, week, month, quarter, and life will move you toward who you want to be and how you want to be in the world.

We want to highlight that whenever you make this type of decision to improve your life, you will face adversity and challenge. In his book, *The War of Art,* Steven Pressfield states, "Remember our rule of thumb: The more scared we are of a work or calling, the surer we can be that we have to do it. ... Resistance is experienced as fear; the degree of fear equates to the strength of Resistance. Therefore, the more fear we feel about a specific enterprise, the more certain we can be that enterprise is important to us and to the growth of our soul. That's why we feel so much Resistance. If it meant nothing to us, there'd be no Resistance."

The planner is designed to help you work through the resistance that shows itself as you strive to grow. At each stage of growth, you have faced this. It happened as you made the decision to embark on a journey of recovery. It happens as you make any major life change. As you work through the areas of focus in this planner, it will show itself again. The process is designed to help you navigate that resistance and build your resilience.

Using what we have learned from research in recovery, resilience, trauma, healing, and neuroscience, the planner helps to consolidate the best strategies to continue to grow, heal, and thrive in our lives. Dr. Daniel Siegel, a leading researcher, speaker, and writer in the area of neuroscience, states in his book, *Mindsight*, "One of the key practical lessons of modern neuroscience is that the power to direct our attention has within it the power to shape our brain's firing patterns, as well as the power to shape the architecture of the brain itself."

Over the course of this year, you will be directing your attention to different areas of focus while continuing to build resilience, which can change your life, your relationships, and even the architecture of your brain.

In her book, *Wild,* Cheryl Strayed details her journey along the Pacific Crest Trail at a time in her life when she was desperate for change, healing, and to discover a depth within herself. The book describes her journey, setbacks, challenges, and joys. It was a journey that she was completely unprepared for but took anyway. And that is often the case. We take the journey not because we are prepared to or because we know what the outcome will be; we set out on the journey because we have to. We are desperate for change in our lives. We crave something more, something bigger and deeper.

In her book, Cheryl Strayed states, "I'd finally come to understand what it had been: a yearning for a way out, when actually what I had wanted to find was a way in." This is our hope for your journey over the next year, that you will find a way in to living life in a completely different way, full of hope and meaning, while learning to navigate the challenges with resilience and perseverance. It will not be easy, but it is our hope that it is truly life-changing.

Working at Your Pace and Self-Compassion

We want to take a few minutes and discuss entering into this process with compassion for yourself. You are starting something new. Developing new habits is difficult. There will be days when you do better than other days. You may be someone who struggles with perfectionism. Be gentle with yourself.

As we mentioned earlier, resilience is on a continuum. Work to increase your overall resilience but know that you won't do this perfectly. Brené Brown writes beautifully about the difference between perfectionism and healthy striving in her book, *The Gifts of Imperfection*. "Perfectionism is not the same thing as striving to be your best. Perfectionism is the belief that if we live perfect, look perfect, and act perfect, we can minimize or avoid the pain of blame, judgment, and shame. It's a shield. It's a twenty-ton shield that we lug around thinking it will protect us when, in fact, it's the thing that's really preventing us from flight."

The aim is for healthy striving. Strive each day to do your work, to move toward your life goals, and to live within your core values. Strive to do your readings and write out your reflections at the end of the day. Strive, but do so with grace and patience for yourself. This is a process. We also hope it will be fun and not a burden.

We love the book *The Four Agreements: A Practical Guide to Personal Freedom* by Don Miguel Ruiz. In this treasure of a book, Ruiz talks about the transformational power of four specific agreements we can make with ourselves. One of these agreements is "always do your best." At any moment, always do your best. At times, your best will be deeply connected with your flow. You are living in your optimal recovery zone. Other times, your best may be to simply get out of bed that day. There will be days when you are sick or are traversing a personal crisis. You may have a work project that has an intense deadline. In these times, our best can look very different than other times. If you commit to this agreement, there is no judgment for yourself. We hope that as you rest each night you can reflect on your day and say, "I did my best."

We are inviting you into a process that will help you live within your core values, move toward your life goals, and become more resilient. It will be challenging, but we also hope you enjoy the process. We are thankful that you are here. You have planned to begin. What a beautiful gift you are giving yourself. Trust the process and enjoy the ride.

Maya Angelou said, "If you must look back, do so forgivingly. If you must look forward, do so prayerfully. However, the wisest thing you can do is to be present in the present, gratefully."